Fundamentalism & Freemasonry

Fundamentalism & Freemasonry

The Southern Baptist Investigation of the Fraternal Order

GARY LEAZER, Ph.D.

M. Evans and Company, Inc.
New York

All Scripture quotations are from the New Revised Standard Version of the Holy Bible (Nashville: Holman Bible Publishers, 1989), Division of Christian Education of the National Council of Churches of Christ in the United States of America, unless noted.

M. Evans and Company, Inc.
216 East 49th Street
New York, New York 10017

Library of Congress Cataloging-in-Publication Data

Leazer, Gary H.
Fundamentalism and Freemasonry : the Southern Baptist investigation of the fraternal order / Gary Leazer. – 1st ed.
p. cm.
Includes bibliographical references (p.) and index.
ISBN 0-87131-775-3 (cloth) : $19.95
1. Southern Baptist Convention–History–20th century. 2. Southern Baptist Convention–Membership. 3. Fundamentalism–History 4. Freemasonry–Religious aspects–Southern Baptist Convention–History–20th century. 5. Freemasonry–United States–History–20th century. 6. Baptists–United States–History–20th century. 7. Baptists–Membership I. Title.
BX6462.3.L43 1995
286.'132'09045–dc20 94-49038
CIP

Book design by Charles A. de Kay

Typeset by AeroType, Inc.

Manufactured in the United States of America

9 8 7 6 5 4 3 2

Contents

Foreword

THIS IS THE MOST COMPREHENSIVE DOCUMENT ON THE BACKGROUND, METHods, and results of the modern day anti-Masonic movement to have crossed my desk. This volume has a place in every Seminary, Bible College, Masonic, and Public Library. Every Grand Lodge should buy this book and present it to the clergy in their jurisdiction. It will remain the single most important study on the topic of anti-Masonry from this century. It is mandatory reading for every Southern Baptist but it is more than that. It is a thorough study of the rise of religious radical fundamentalism in Christianity and its attack on freedom of thought and liberty. The book is complex because it brings together the various strands of thought, action, and patterns of fundamentalism, exposing the inner workings and methods used to gain their ends and exercise control. *Fundamentalism & Freemasonry* is valuable because of the author.

Gary Leazer, Ph.D., is a dedicated and conservative Christian scholar, minister, and author. He is not a Freemason and as far as I know belongs to no fraternal organization. He was ordained to his ministry of the Interfaith Witness Department of the Home Missions Board of the Southern Baptist Convention. As Department Head he was appointed the task of conducting research and writing a report on the study of Freemasonry. This study would be brought to the Convention when it voted on a proposal, by anti-Masons, that would not allow membership in the Masonic Fraternity to Southern Baptists. The Convention had been embroiled in an attack on Freemasonry since 1985.

Dr. Leazer did a thorough study investigating each charge brought by various groups and individuals who were anti-Masonic. His study was received by the Board and immediately came under attack by the anti-Masonic forces who ordered significant changes made in the report. He refused to sacrifice his integrity and would not sign the revised report. He was fired from his position. This book is the full report on the events leading up to that moment and includes full disclosure as well as the original report. It is not a pro-Masonic report. It is a factual account of the investigation and reveals some amazing and documented facts that every Mason and every other adherent of liberty and truth need to know.

The book blends in an amazing way the multiple strands of thought, actions, and events that lead up to the climax of the refusal of the Board to accept a non-biased report on the study of anti-Masonry. It is also a very personal and moving documentary of the personal courage of a man who stood alone against deceit, bigotry, and malpractive of a group who would destroy the truth. For those of us who believe in liberty and freedom this book reveals, in vivid detail, the workings of those who, under the guise of religious faith, would destroy us.

–Forrest D. Haggard
President of the Philalethes Society (Freemasonry's oldest and largest international research society)
Past Grand Master of Masons in Kansas
Past President of the World Convention of Churches of Christ, Christian Churches and Disciples of Christ

INTRODUCTION

RELIGION IS EASILY DISTORTED. WE SAW THIS DISTORTION IN THE FIERY END TO the siege of the Branch Davidian compound near Waco, Texas. We see this distortion in Lebanon between Orthodox Christians and Muslims, and between Israeli Jews and their Muslim neighbors. We see this distortion in the terrorist attacks between Protestants and Catholics in Northern Ireland. We see this distortion in the civil war between Serbian Orthodox, Croat Catholics, and Bosnian Muslims in the former Yugoslavia.

We are seeing that religion is easily distorted in the struggle that has divided churches, friends, and family since 1979 in the Southern Baptist Convention.

Religion becomes distorted, or toxic, when individuals misuse their faith for power, prestige, revenge, or control. Few individuals intend to distort religion. They distort religion as a reaction to events over which they have no control. They distort religion when one aspect of theirs is emphasized so much that another, equally important aspect of their faith, usually unintentionally, is deemphasized. Truth and love are both essential aspects of a healthy, valid faith.

The subject of this book is fundamentalism and Freemasonry. I am not implying that all fundamentalists are opposed to Freemasonry. Many fundamentalists are Masons and convincingly argue that membership in the fraternity is not incompatible with their faith. Others, who call themselves fundamentalists, are actually conservatives who, like me, hold to the historical fundamentals of the faith. While I hold to certain beliefs about God, I do not require that everyone else believe exactly as I do before I will fellowship with him or her as a child of God. The fundamentalism that I write about is that mindset that demands everyone believe and act as they do. Christians failing to measure up to these fundamentalist kinds of narrow definitions of orthodoxy are cast out as unbelievers and infidels.

The date was March 1967. The setting was the Café du Monde, a popular eatery in the French Quarter of New Orleans. The scene was of two men, with their wives, eating beignets and drinking café au lait. One of the men was Paul Pressler, a Texas Appeals Court judge from Houston. The other man was Paige Patterson, a graduate student at the New Orleans Baptist Theological Seminary. This midnight meeting at the Café du Monde would change the history of the largest Protestant denomination in America and launch what would become known as the Pressler–Patterson coalition.[1]

Concerned about an alleged "liberal drift" within the Southern Baptist Convention, Pressler proposed a political takeover by electing a string of like-minded presidents who would nominate only like-minded people to the Convention's committee on committees. This committee would, in turn, nominate like-minded people to the committee on boards. This second committee would nominate like-minded trustees and directors to Southern Baptist agencies and institutions that would hire only like-minded staff in those agencies and institutions. The trustees and directors were said to be "the jugular," or lifeblood, of the agencies and institutions. "Go for the jugular" was the rallying cry.

While Pressler's secular politics would develop the political strategy, Patterson's fundamentalism would provide the theological foundation. The plan was put into motion in 1979 with the election of Adrian Rogers, pastor of the Bellevue Baptist Church of Memphis, Tennessee. The strategy worked like the best-oiled political machine. In less than twelve years, every Southern Baptist agency and institution was controlled by a mindset, alien to Baptist life, called fundamentalism.

The date was June 1990. The setting was the Café du Monde, a popular eatery in the French Quarter of New Orleans. The scene this time, also late at night, was of a larger group of men, about two dozen, eating beignets and drinking café au lait. One of the men climbed upon a table and announced to the customers that the group wanted to sing the hymn "Victory in Jesus" to celebrate twelve years of victory over the moderates in the Southern Baptist Convention. Customers sat with their mouths open as the group heartedly sang the hymn.

As fundamentalist trustees and directors were elected to Southern Baptist agencies and institutions, the orthodoxy and faith of staff, who did not share their narrow view of "truth," was questioned. Individuals who were not believed to be like-minded were rejected for employment or appointment. Others didn't even bother to apply.

Restructuring and eliminating agency positions and programs removed a number of staff. A few staff saw the "handwriting on the wall" and found other positions. Other staff took early retirement, either voluntarily or involuntarily. A number of staff resigned, often involuntarily. A few staff were fired outright.

To the victor belongs the spoils. Staff vacancies were filled by individuals who had been active in, or at least supportive of, the takeover by the fundamentalists. The office of president of the various agencies and institutions was given to the most faithful leaders.

Baptists have been known historically as strong proponents of religious tolerance and liberty, freedom of conscience and association, missions, evangelism, and the autonomy of the local congregation even as they cooperated with larger denominational entities. Today, those historic Baptists ideals are threatened, not from outside the Church, but from within Baptist life itself.

It has been said that those who do not know history are condemned to repeat it. We will examine the changes that have been occurring in life of the Southern Baptist Convention. These changes have been seen and felt most since 1979, but the undercurrent of change was there long before the election of Adrian Rogers as president of the Southern Baptist Convention in June 1979.

In addition to changes in leadership and direction of the Southern Baptist Convention, a number of individuals, with their personal agendas, began attempts to enlist approval and support of the Convention. Some were worthy issues that needed discussion. Others were on personal vendettas. One such personal vendetta is the Freemasonry issue brought to the attention of the Convention in 1985 and 1991, and continually since then. This book attempts to examine the Freemasonry issue that has consumed the lives of too many Southern Baptists for too many years.

1 Baptists and Religious Liberty

Said King James I, "I will make them conform, or I will harry them out of the land."[1]

Baptists are a freedom-loving people. We were born of men and women who believed every person had the God-given right to worship God as he or she felt led by God. We were harassed; bounties were put on our heads. We were imprisoned and put to death; all this only made our resolve stronger.

THE FIGHT FOR RELIGIOUS LIBERTY

Baptists have made a remarkable contribution to the Christian faith since the founding of the first Baptist church. Baptists can trace their ancestry to early seventeenth-century England during the reign of King James I (1566–1625), after whom the King James Version of the Bible is named. James I, a strong supporter of the Church of England, or Anglican Church, believed in the divine right of kings. This belief held that kings received the authority to rule from God, rather than from the people. Those opposed to this belief were harassed or imprisoned, or they fled to countries such as Holland or America.

Among these dissenters were the first Pilgrims who came to America seeking religious liberty. Prior to the settlement of Plymouth Colony in 1620, dissenters found in Holland they were able to worship God as they understood and interpreted the Bible. Three dissenters forced to flee to Holland in 1606 were John Smyth, Thomas Helwys,[2] and John Murton. They rejected the government of the Church of England and its practice of infant baptism. As a result, they became known as Separatists because of their call for separation from the Church of England.

Smyth died in Holland, but Helwys and Murton returned to England to found the first Baptist church on English soil in 1611 or 1612. Facing certain persecution, Helwys wrote *A Short Declaration of the Mystery of Iniquity*, asserting a belief in full religious liberty, the first such book published in England. Helwys asserted that only God, not the king, had authority over the souls of people. For this, Helwys was imprisoned, where he died about 1616. Baptists today honor Helwys for laying the foundation of Baptist insistence on separation of church and state, and an individual's freedom to worship God as he or she feels led by the Spirit of God.

William Kiffin (1616–1701), who became a Baptist at 22, was born the year Helwys died. Kiffin became pastor of a new Baptist church in Devonshire Square, London, at 24, where he remained for sixty-one years. Within a year of becoming pastor of the Baptist church, Kiffin was imprisoned for six months after being charged with the crime of holding a public service without approval of civil authorities. During his life, Kiffin was arrested and tried in court at least eight times. His critics brought false charges against him, all of which were found to be without merit.

Benjamin Keach (1640–1704), pastor of a Baptist church in the Horsleydown section of London, was pilloried twice, once for writing a book, *The Child's Instructor*, to teach children about the Christian faith. The book was publicly burned in front of the pilloried Keach. Upon his release, Keach promptly rewrote the book, one of forty-three books credited to him. One book of three hundred hymns, called *Spiritual Melody*, was the first hymnbook published by any church group. Because he encouraged singing in his worship services, he was criticized because he allowed women to sing when they were supposed to be silent in church and because some people sang "out of tune." Keach, like other early Baptists, fought for the freedom of every person to worship God in his or her own way.

In England, Baptist John James was charged with treason because he called Jesus Christ the King of England, Scotland, and Ireland. For this crime, James was convicted, hung, and drawn and quartered in 1661. His church members who refused to renounce James were imprisoned.

Two thousand "nonconforming" clergy in England lost their livelihood on St. Bartholomew's Day in 1662, among them Baptists, Quakers, Congregationalists, and Catholics.

John Bunyan (1628–1688) became a Baptist in 1653 and was baptized in the River Ouse. Within two years of his conversion, his wife died, leaving him with four small children, one of whom was blind. Bunyan began preaching at 27 in Bedford, England. He was soon imprisoned for preaching without a license in a dissenting church in England. After spending most of the next twelve years in prison, Bunyan was released but returned to preaching. This led to a second imprisonment, this time for six years.

Bunyan wrote eleven religious books during his several imprisonments. He wrote the religious allegory *The Pilgrim's Progress*, which has made him known around the world, during his third imprisonment, a six-month sentence in solitary confinement. In *The Pilgrim's Progress*, Christian, the hero, sets out on a journey from the City of Destruction to heaven or the Celestial City. Along the way, he meets people who try to prevent him from reaching his goal, such as Apollyon and Giant Despair. He also finds those who help him, including Interpreter and Faithful, and he reaches the Celestial City.

The belief in religious liberty extended even to the most basic of Baptist beliefs, that of the baptism of persons only after they had made a personal commitment to Jesus Christ as Savior and Lord. In spite of the first Baptists' rejection of pedobaptism, or infant baptism, they generally tolerated those who held to pedobaptism. In some Baptist churches, persons holding to believers' baptism could be found worshiping next to those who held to pedobaptism. While the sentiment was for the position that the church should be composed only of baptized believers, churches with mixed memberships were the practice.[3]

Baptists continued to suffer persecution because of their intense belief in religious liberty. In America, Roger Williams (1599–1683), who had fled from Salem, Massachusetts, in 1636, is credited with forming the first Baptist church in America at Providence, Rhode Island, in 1639. Rhode Island was unique among all the colonies for guaranteeing religious liberty.

Freedom-loving radicals of all kinds, Baptists, Quakers, and other independent thinkers found in Rhode Island a sanctuary to worship God as they felt He led them. Williams published his *Bloudy Tenet of Persecution for the Cause of Conscience Discussed* in 1644, in which he pleaded for religious liberty. He wrote a sequel, *The Bloudy Tenet Yet More Bloudy*, in 1651.

In the same year, Baptist John Clarke wrote *Ill Newes from New England* to tell how he and two other Baptists had been fined, whipped, and imprisoned in Massachusetts for preaching Baptist doctrines there. Clarke, who spoke of himself as "a prisoner of Iesus [*sic*] Christ at Boston in the behalf of my Lord, and of his people," argued that "no servant of Christ hath such authority from his Lord to smite his fellows."[4] He started the second Baptist church in America at Newport, Rhode Island, around 1644 and remained as pastor of this church for most of his life. Clarke secured a royal charter for Rhode Island in 1663. The charter reiterated that "no person within the said Colony, at any time hereafter, shall be in any wise molested, punished, disquieted or called in question, for any differences in opinions in matters of religion."[5] Securing the charter guaranteeing freedom of worship was perhaps his greatest service.

William Screven (1629–1713) of Kittery, Maine, was arrested in 1675 because he stopped attending public meetings of the state church in his hometown. He was also charged with conducting Bible studies in his home. Later, he was arrested and imprisoned on the charge of "a blasphemous teaching about baptism," a charge stemming from his teaching about baptism after a personal commitment to Jesus Christ as Lord and Savior. Upon his release, a group of believers formed the Baptist Church of Kittery and called Screven as pastor in 1682. Screven and twenty-nine of his forty church members moved from Kittery to Charleston, South Carolina, in 1696 for reasons other than persecution.[6] Although First Baptist Church, Charleston, had been organized fourteen years earlier, the arrival of the Kittery Baptists is often seen as the beginning of Baptists in the American South.

Isaac Backus (1724–1806) fought against a law taxing individuals to support the state church. Because only ministers preparing to serve in the established state church could attend New England universities, Backus helped form Rhode Island College, later named Brown University, in 1776 to provide training for young Baptist ministers.

As late as 1769, Baptist James Ireland was convicted and imprisoned for five months for preaching "vile, pernicious, abhorrible, detestable, abominable, diabolical doctrines."[7] There were others. John Waller went to prison on four occasions rather than agree to stop preaching. In an August 17, 1771, letter from Urbanna Prison in Middlesex County, Virginia, Waller wrote about his imprisonment.

> The magistrate, and another, took hold of brother Webber, and dragging him from the stage, delivered him, with brethren Wafford, Robert Ware, Richard Falkner, James Greewood and myself, into custody and commanded that we should be brought before him for trial. . . . we were asked if we had license to preach in that county; and learning we had not, it was required of us to give bond and security not to preach any more in the county, which we modestly refused to do. . . . We find the Lord gracious and kind to us beyond expression in our afflictions. We cannot tell how long we shall be kept in bonds. . . ."[8]

It is said Waller preached through the windows of his cell to passersby. John Pickett was jailed for three months. John Weatherford and Jeremiah

Walker were jailed; Patrick Henry paid the jail fees for Weatherford. Joseph Spencer was imprisoned in 1773 for "teaching and preaching the Gospel as a Baptist, not having license."[9] Upon hearing of Spencer's imprisonment, James Madison urged a friend in Philadelphia to "pray for liberty of conscience to all."[10]

> *That religion, or the duty which we owe to our Creator, and the manner of discharging it, can be directed only by reason and conviction, not by force or violence, and therefore all men are equally entitled to the free exercise of religion according to the dictates of conscience; and that it is the mutual duty of all to practice Christian forbearance, love and charity towards each other.*[11]

South Carolina Baptist Richard Furman avoided unnecessary involvement in political concerns, but felt compelled to fight for the cause of religious and political liberty. So much so, that Lord Cornwallis placed a bounty of £1000 on his head "to make an example of so notorious rebel."[12] Furman served as president of the Charleston South Carolina Baptist Association from 1776 until his death in 1825. During his presidency, the association voted in 1798 that the matter of Baptist membership in Freemasonry should "be left with the judgment of the individual."[13] He served as pastor of the Charleston Baptist Church from 1790 until his death. Basil Manly said of Furman, "He took charge of a small flock a good deal weakened and discouraged. He left it a large, vigorous, united church, ready for every good work, and 'adorning the doctrine of God their Savior in all things.' "[14]

The Southern Baptist Convention was formed after the General Convention for Foreign Missions told Alabama Baptists that no missionary candidate who owned slaves could be appointed. Upon hearing of this prohibition, the Virginia Baptist Foreign Mission Society issued a call for a meeting of Baptists in the South "to confer on the best means of promoting the Foreign Mission cause, and other interests of the Baptist denomination in the South."[15] The call led to the formation of the Southern Baptist Convention in May 1845 emphasizing local church autonomy over a denominational hierarchy. Southern Baptists and Southern Baptist churches have been fiercely independent since that meeting in Augusta, Georgia. We are a freedom-loving people.

Free to own slaves, anyway.

R. B. C. Howell, who was elected president of the Southern Baptist Convention five times between 1851 and 1859, contributed to early Southern Baptist church polity by calling for local church independence and autonomy, limited denominational controls, ministry as a partnership of pastor and congregation, and full and free communication with church members through a free press.[16]

These and dozens of other unnamed and unknown Baptists helped develop a historic Baptist identity: a rejection of traditionalism and ritualism; emphasis on the priesthood of all believers; autonomy of the local congregation; freedom of conscience and speech; separation of church and state; and opposition to intolerance.

Today, however, Southern Baptists appear to be suffering from an identity crisis. This historic Baptist identity has come under attack by an alien, non-Baptist mindset intent on changing the direction of the denomination. Using a secular political strategy, a small number of fundamentalists, beginning in 1979, have succeeded in securing a majority of votes at annual meetings of the Southern Baptist Convention and electing agency trustees and directors who, in turn, elected agency presidents who would follow their plan to change radically the direction of the denomination. Agency employees who resisted the change or who refused to support wholeheartedly the new leaders were regularly, and continue to be, fired or forced to take early retirement. As a result, the Southern Baptist Convention of a quarter century ago is gone forever.

PRIESTHOOD OF ALL BELIEVERS

The Baptist emphasis on the priesthood of all believers is a major contribution to Christianity. This teaching says each believer is a priest before God. Each believer is said to have free and equal access at all times to God through Christ. Baptists have traditionally opposed any distinction between ordained clergy and laity. Baptists have traditionally held that each believer has the right and responsibility to interpret the Bible as he or she is led by the Holy Spirit. While still at the heart of Baptist teachings, a growing number of Southern Baptist laypersons are relying more and more on pastors of mega-churches, churches with memberships of several thousands, to interpret the Bible for them.

At the 1988 convention in San Antonio, Texas, messengers approved a controversial resolution, "On the Priesthood of the Believer." It affirmed a call for uniformity of doctrine. The resolution cautioned that the priesthood of the believer did not mean that a person could believe anything he or she wished and remain a loyal Southern Baptist. Furthermore, the resolution stated that the priesthood of the believer "in no way contradicts" the "role, responsibility, and authority of the pastor."[17]

Few Southern Baptists have argued that the priesthood of believers allows a person to believe anything he or she wished. Southern Baptists are conservative in theology, even those who have been given the name "moderates," and take the Bible seriously. They contend they interpret the Bible under the leadership of the Holy Spirit. Southern Baptist liberals are so rare that when asked to name liberals in the convention, fundamentalists are hard-pressed to do so. We are a conservative people.

Many Southern Baptists interpret the 1988 resolution "On the Priesthood of the Believer" as an attempt to take away the freedom to worship God as the believer is led by the Holy Spirit and to replace it with authority resting in the pastor of the church, much like the Catholic dogma of the infallibility of the pope affirmed by Vatican Council I in 1870 in the face of growing Italian nationalism.

Respected Associated Press religion writer George W. Cornell observed that the principle of the priesthood of the believer and the autonomy of local Baptist churches "had been somewhat muted" in recent years since the new leadership of the Southern Baptist Convention "began excluding some local churches deemed out of line."[18] Cornell has put his finger on the major changes in the Southern Baptist Convention. The historic Baptist position allowing a diversity of theological uniformity as dictated by a select few.

AUTONOMY OF THE LOCAL CONGREGATION

The Baptist Faith and Message, a statement of faith adopted by the Southern Baptist Convention in 1963, speaks of the local church as an autonomous body that operates through a democratic process where each member has equal responsibility in the decision-making process of the church. This has always been the hallmark of Baptist polity.

William C. Boone, in *What We Believe*, said no authority can dictate to a local congregation what it must or must not do. He reminded Baptists that no authority, whether governing board, association, convention, or individual, has authority over the local congregation. No authority can force a local congregation to abide by its recommendations or carry out its plans, nor can any authority censure a local congregation if it decides not to work with the authority or accept its decisions. The local congregation, Boone reminds us, is subject to Christ alone.[19] This historic Baptist distinctive, has also come under attack since 1979.

Michael J. Clingenpeel, editor of Virginia Baptist's *Religious Herald*, charged that the Southern Baptist Convention's executive committee, headquartered in Nashville, and its officials

> are control freaks who give verbal assent to local church autonomy, but practice a polity that gives power to a denominational hierarchy centralized in a [*sic*] Nashville. Their preferred direction of decision-making flows downward from Nashville rather than upward from the churches to Nashville.[20]

FREEDOM OF CONSCIENCE AND SPEECH

Related to the principle of the priesthood of all believers is the Baptist principle that no individual Baptist speaks for all Baptists. Masons have much in common with Baptists at this point. Anti-Masons repeatedly argue that Albert Pike, Albert G. Mackey, Walter L. Wilmshurst, and other Masonic writers are "embraced by Masons" as authorities. Masons insist that statements by Masons and books by Masons reflect the personal opinions of the individuals and the authors.[21] Some Masons agree with these well-known Masons, but not all do, and there is no requirement that any do. Any Baptist, even the president of the Southern Baptist Convention, may recommend a particular book as representative of "the Baptist position." However, that remains his or her opinion, and it must not be seen as an official position of the Convention or all Southern Baptists.

Bailey Smith, while he was president of the Southern Baptist Convention, created a furor with his statement at the National Affairs Briefing, a religious-political rally in Dallas, that "God Almighty does not hear the prayer of a Jew."[22] Smith is entitled to his opinion, for that is all it is. Non-Baptists have assumed that Smith, as president of the Southern Baptist Convention, was stating dogma that all Southern Baptists had to accept simply because of their religious affiliation. There is no requirement that any Southern Baptist accept what another Southern Baptist says, no matter his office or stature, just as there is no requirement that a Mason accept what Masonic writers believe, no matter their office or stature. Southern Baptists believe the freedom inherent in our doctrine of the freedom of conscience and speech carries an equal responsibility.

SEPARATION OF CHURCH AND STATE

A third major contribution, for which the secular world is a debtor to Baptists, is the principle of the separation of church and state. By this, Baptists have meant that the state has no right to interfere with the religious beliefs and practices of individuals or congregations. As we have already seen, Baptists have faced persecution and imprisonment for their insistence of the principles of religious liberty and the separation of church and state. Baptists, from their earliest days, have opposed a state church and any interference of the state in church affairs. Baptist beliefs formed the foundation for the democratic principles of government that we enjoy today.

The 1976 Southern Baptist Convention affirmed the denomination's "long tradition of non-endorsement of any political candidate."[23] The 1981 Southern Baptist Convention in Los Angeles reaffirmed this historic Baptist position,

> that the Southern Baptist Convention, in accordance with and in commitment to the First Amendment to the Constitution of the United States, and to the historic Baptist principle of church and state separation, deplore and reject the arrogation of the right of any group to define and pronounce for all people what is the Christian faith, and to seek through political means to impose this faith upon the American people under a government which is mandated to safeguard and respect the people of all religions and no religion.[24]

One year later, messengers at the 1982 Southern Baptist Convention in New Orleans, Louisiana, reversed the historic Baptist principle and approved a resolution endorsing President Ronald Reagan's proposed amendment to the U.S. Constitution to allow voluntary prayer in public schools: "Therefore, be it *Resolved*, That we messengers of the Southern Baptist Convention is [*sic*] session, June 1982, New Orleans, Louisiana, declare our support of the aforementioned proposed constitutional amendment."[25] The messengers did not resolve the issue of whether the voluntary school prayers would be led by a Baptist, Jew, Jehovah's Witness, Buddhist, Muslim, Mormon, Wiccan or someone from one of the hundreds of other faith groups in the United States.

Francis A. Shaeffer, well-known author and founder of L'Abri Fellowship, has influenced fundamentalists through his two dozen books, such as *Escape from Reason* and *How Should We Then Live?* In *The Great Evangelical Disaster,* Shaeffer points out the danger of confusing Christianity with the United States. He cautioned that Christians must not wrap their faith with the nation's flag.[26]

The Declaration of Independence refers to the Supreme Being four times, once each as "Nature's God," "Creator," "the Supreme Judge," and "divine

Providence." The name of Jesus is not mentioned anywhere in the Declaration of Independence. No reference to a Supreme Being can be found in the Constitution of the United States. The only references to religion are found in [Article VI] where it states that "no religious test shall ever be required as a qualification to any office or public trust under the United States" and in Amendment one of the Bill of Rights where it states that "Congress shall make no law respecting an establishment of religion, or prohibiting the free practice thereof." Anti-Masons John Ankerberg and John Weldon tell us, "Nowhere in Masonic literature will you find Jesus called God or see Him portrayed as the world's Savior who died for men's sins. . . . Masonry completely excludes all particular biblical teachings about Christ such as His incarnation, redemptive mission, death, and resurrection."[27] This, of course, is not true. One illustration will suffice. Albert Pike, in *Morals and Dogma,* refers to Christ as "Him who died upon the cross,"[28] as *"Jesus Christ, the Son of God, the Savior,"*[29] and as "The Christ of the Apocalypse, First-born of Creation and of the Resurrection."[30] At another place, Pike says, "The agonies of the garden of Gethsemane and those on the Cross on Calvary preceded the Resurrection and were the means of Redemption."[31] While the Christian doctrine of Christ is not as clearly stated in Masonic literature as fundamentalists wish, Ankerberg and Weldon are simply wrong to charge that "Nowhere in Masonic literature will you find Jesus called God or see Him portrayed as the world's Savior who died for men's sins. . . . Masonry completely excludes all particular biblical teachings about Christ such as His incarnation, redemptive mission, death, and resurrection." The same charge can be leveled against the Declaration of Independence and the Constitution of the United States. Shall we condemn these documents as Ankerberg and Weldon do Masonic literature?

In 1987, the Public Affairs Committee (PAC), the official name of the Southern Baptist representation to the Baptist Joint Committee on Public Affairs (BJCPA), voted to recommend Judge Robert H. Bork as a nominee to the U.S. Supreme Court. The PAC asked the full BJCPA, which represented seven different Baptist denominations, to endorse Bork. The BJCPA declined. Both moderate and fundamentalist Southern Baptists criticized the PAC vote as a violation of the principle of the separation of church and state, but the fundamentalist movement was well along in its takeover of the convention, and criticism mattered little.

Baptist Press reported in July 1982 that Edward E. McAteer, head of a political organization called the Religious Roundtable, had been encouraged by Morton C. Blackwell, special assistant to President Reagan, to work for the passage of the resolution at the Southern Baptist Convention supporting a constitutional amendment on school prayer. Convention president Bailey Smith appointed Norris W. Sydnor, Jr., a longtime McAteer associate and a director of the Maryland chapter of the Religious Roundtable, as chairman of the resolutions committee. Sydnor, who was attending the Southern Baptist Convention for the first time, asked McAteer to serve as his consultant. Presnall H. Wood asked in his editorial in the *Baptist Standard*, "Are there any Baptists left who doubt the crumbling of the wall of separation of church and state?"[32]

During the 1980s, Southern Baptist leaders began using their influence in a more overt way in the political arena. Judge Paul Pressler explained to Christian Reconstructionist Gary North how the fundamentalists had taken control of the Southern Baptist Convention. (Reconstructionism is the movement to introduce Old Testament laws and regulations into the American legal system.) North urged his listeners to learn from the Southern Baptist fundamentalists so that members of his movement, also called Dominionists, could take control of America. Several SBC leaders openly supported fellow Southern Baptist Pat Robertson's White House bid. Southern Baptists Ed McAteer, Tim and Beverly LaHaye, and Les Csorba worked in the political arena through their own organizations, the Religious Roundtable, Concerned Women for America, or others' organizations, such as independent Baptist Jerry Falwell's Moral Majority. A photograph of President George Bush with a number of Southern Baptist leaders appeared on the cover of the April 1990 *Southern Baptist Advocate*, an independent fundamentalist newspaper. W. A. Criswell, retired pastor of the First Baptist Church of Dallas, Texas, called separation of church and state "an idea invented by an agnostic."[33] This "idea invented by an agnostic" is also found in the Baptist Faith and Message, a statement adopted by the Southern Baptist Convention in 1963.[34]

Southern Baptist fundamentalists regularly invite politicians to speak at their religious services and meetings, abusing the historic Baptist distinctive of the separation of church and state. Bailey Smith's Real Evangelism Bible Conference in Charlotte, North Carolina, in March 1994 featured D. James Kennedy, pastor of the Coral Ridge Presbyterian Church; Adrian Rogers, recent president of the Southern Baptist Convention and pastor of the Bellevue Baptist Church in Memphis; and former United States vice president Dan Quayle.[35] Quayle autographed copies of his new book, *Standing Firm*, at the Southern Baptist Convention exhibit hall during the 1994 Convention in Orlando.[36] Potential presidential candidate Jack Kemp spoke at the 1994 Southern Baptist Pastors' Conference, held immediately prior to the Convention in Orlando.[37]

OPPOSITION TO RELIGIOUS INTOLERANCE

While recognizing and defending the right of others to worship as their consciences dictate, Baptists are also known for their opposition to intolerance by other faiths. For example, Baptists opposed the encyclical *Immortale Dei* by Pope Leo XIII, who declared in 1885 that "the State must not only 'have care for religion, but recognize the true religion.' "[38] Catholics have interpreted "the true religion" as referring to the Roman Catholic Church.[39]

The nation of Italy was formed in the mid-1800s when the numerous city-states joined forces to overthrow and expel their Austrian rulers. Then supported by a national vote, Victor Emmanuel II, king of Sardinia, declared the formation of the Kingdom of Italy in 1861 with himself as the king. The Papal States, a large territory in central Italy ruled by the pope since 756, was reduced to the city of Rome and the immediate surrounding countryside. When French forces, stationed in Rome to protect the Pope, withdrew in 1870, Victor Emmanuel II captured the city, reducing the Pope's temporal control to only 109 acres of Vatican City.

Pope Pius IX could do nothing to stop the loss of his Papal States. Neither could Vatican Council I, which he called in 1869 in the attempt to reverse the loss of his temporal power. Not even the council's proclamation of the pope's primacy of jurisdiction over the Catholic Church and of papal infallibility in 1870 could halt the loss of his earthly power. After Vatican Council I, Pope Pius IX became a self-imposed "prisoner" in the Vatican for the remainder of his reign.

It was in this historical context that Pope Leo XIII, who was named Pope in 1878 when Pius IX died, issued the encyclical *Humanum Genus* in 1884. It is recognized as the strongest and most comprehensive of the seven papal condemnations of Freemasonry. The Pope attacked Freemasonry because Masons believe in religious liberty. The Pope argued that preservation of the true doctrines of God and the means of salvation rested solely within the Roman Catholic Church. Italian Masons were attacked because they called for the separation of the Roman Catholic Church and the state. This had already caused the loss of the Papal States in the Italian peninsula. The Pope decried a state where all religions are "held in the same esteem." He attacked Freemasonry because Masons believed in the education of children by laymen rather than by Catholic priests and nuns. Finally, Pope Leo XIII attacked Freemasonry because Masons believed people had equal rights, extending even to the right to make their own laws and elect their own government, rather than submit to the authority of the Catholic Church.[40]

Albert Pike, in a lengthy response to *Humanum Genus*, charged that the encyclical was an attack on every church, except the Roman Catholic Church, because the encyclical held that all other churches are part of "the Kingdom of Satan."[41]

This so-called "criminal activity by Freemasons" is the reason Baptists revolted against the Church of England to form their own free churches. This activity is that for which Baptists have fought and suffered for nearly four hundred years. This activity is still the driving force of freedom-loving Baptists across our land and around the world.

Freedom of religion, for which Baptists have fought so long, is now openly attacked. Not by the secular world, nor by communism, nor by fascism, but by an alien mindset that has captured the minds of the current leadership of the Southern Baptist Convention. It is called fundamentalism.

2 THE FUNDAMENTALIST MINDSET

"[O]rthodox truth without orthodox love profits nothing."[1]

DEFINITIONS OF FUNDAMENTALISM

A popular definition of a fundamentalist is "an evangelical who is mad about something or at someone." Duke University church history professor George M. Marsden, the author of two books on American fundamentalism, defines a fundamentalist as "an evangelical Protestant who is militantly opposed to modern liberal theologies and to some aspects of secularism in modern culture."[2] However, the media regularly uses the term in a broader sense than just American evangelical Protestantism. It uses the term to refer to any religiously bizarre or fanatical practice, such as the Islamic movement inspired by the late Ayatollah Khomeini in Iran. One can speak of Catholic fundamentalists, Hindu fundamentalists, even Jewish fundamentalists.

Southern Baptist Helen Lee Turner believes "fundamentalism represents a major deviation from the traditional mainline evangelical patterns" and uses the term *fundamentalist* to identify " 'militant conservative evangelicals' who insist upon certain doctrinal uniformity and who have led or supported attacks against what they regard as liberal theology, liberal social issues, and misguided elements of modern science."[3] George W. Dollar defines fundamentalism as "the literal exposition of all the affirmations and attitudes of the Bible and the militant exposure of all non-Biblical affirmations and attitudes."[4]

Southern Baptist sociologist Nancy Ammerman argues that fundamentalism is a mindset or "a way of life that transcends any other institution that might make claims on an individual."[5] With this mindset, fundamentalists have historically developed into an isolationalist subculture with a siege mentality for self-preservation of ideals they have held unchangeable. These ideals have included preservation of the Southern white culture, school segregation, public school prayer, blue laws, and Sunday as a day of rest and worship without the distraction of sports and all other forms of entertainment. It is commonly said that fundamentalists build walls to protect and isolate themselves from the world rather than bridges to reach out to a diverse world. While many fundamentalists reject this interpretation of themselves, their actions betray their protestations. On the other hand, not all those who consider themselves fundamentalists are of that mindset. They hold to the fundamentals of the Christian faith without ascribing to the militant mindset described in this chapter. They can be described as conservatives, rather than fundamentalists. The two terms are not interchangeable.

The fundamentalist subculture tends to reject geographical boundaries where diversity of beliefs is common, emphasizing rather doctrinal agreement. Historically, churches within a geographical area, sometimes with quite diverse beliefs and practices, have united together as associations of churches, for missions and church starting efforts. Much of the Southern Baptist organization has been marked by geographical settings. Baptist associations are an intermediate level of work between the local Baptist churches and the state conventions. They are usually countywide in size.

The director of a Baptist association in Arkansas changed the name of his association to the Northwest Baptist Association. He then asked local churches who shared his fundamentalist theology in other associations to unite with his association as its name no longer suggested a county boundary. Instead of cooperating with all Baptist churches in his association (or county), he sought churches whose members were sympathetic with his fundamentalist mindset.

Fundamentalism is seen as intolerant and extremist by a large number of Americans. A *USA Today*–Gallup poll found that 61 percent of adults consider fundamentalists highly principled and 36 percent view them favorably. Still, 57 percent believed fundamentalists are intolerant and 55 percent called them extremist.[6]

The influence of the fundamentalist mindset extends far beyond its relatively small percentage of the total number of Protestants. A 1990 national survey by Lyman Kellstedt, a professor at Wheaton College, found that 42 percent of Protestants described themselves as moderate to liberal in theology; 24 percent described themselves as evangelical; 21 percent said they were fundamentalist, and 12 percent described themselves as charismatic or Pentecostal.[7] Fundamentalists have been able to rise to power in the Southern Baptist Convention because they have convinced enough people, usually through emotional rather than rational appeals, to support their agenda.

REACTION TO NINETEENTH-CENTURY TRENDS

While fundamentalism presents itself as a return to "the faith which was once for all delivered to the saints" (Jude 1:3) of the first Christian century, it is, in fact, a reaction to religious, scientific, technological, social, and intellectual trends in the nineteenth and twentieth centuries. German theologian Friedrich Schleiermacher (1768–1834) published *On Religion: Speeches to Its Cultured Despisers* in 1799, arguing that true religion is an affection, a feeling, an intuition, a consciousness. Writing in defense of Christianity in a post-Enlightenment world, Schleiermacher rejected the classical philosophical arguments for the existence of God and dependence on creeds and urged that the knowledge of God was to be discovered in a direct, immediate, conscious experience of every person.

Building on the work of earlier scholars, German Old Testament critic Julius Wellhausen (1844–1918) attracted widespread attention with his suggestion that there were four distinct sources in the first five books of the Old Testament. According to Wellhausen and others, these five books, called the Pentateuch, were shaped into their present form by unknown editors long after the death of Moses. The question of Mosaic authorship of the Pentateuch had long been discussed since tradition, not the text itself, claims Moses as the author. It led Mormon prophet Joseph Smith to add the verse "The words of God, which he spake unto Moses at a time when Moses was caught up into an exceedingly high mountain,"[8] at the beginning of his translation of the Book of Genesis in 1830, thus defending the Mosaic authorship of the Pentateuch.

The theory of evolution or "transformism" proposed by Jean-Baptiste de Lamark in 1801 and, later, the publication of Charles Darwin's *Origin of Species by Means of Natural Selection* in 1859, directly challenged the Christian doctrine of the special creation of mankind by a benevolent Creator God. This theory was seen as a direct attack on the Bible and its account of creation in Genesis.

Elements of nineteenth-century Christian modernism included emphases on the immanence of God, rather than His transcendence; an anticreedal bias; an emphasis on human experience as an essential part of knowing God; a recognition of the human, as well as the divine, element in the writing of the Bible; a new interest on the human life of Jesus and His moral teachings; and ecumenism.[9]

A liberal Protestant publication, begun in 1884 as *The Christian Oracle*, was renamed *The Christian Century* in 1900 to reflect the optimism for the twentieth century. It was during this optimistic period, in 1903, that the

Southern Jurisdiction of Scottish Rite Freemasonry, U. S. A., introduced *The New Age Magazine*, decades before the name *New Age* was attached to what is now known as the New Age Movement.[10] Liberals and Masons were not the only groups that held an optimistic hope for the twentieth century. Conservative Southern Baptists, such as B. H. Carroll, the first president of Southwestern Baptist Theological Seminary in Fort Worth, Texas, ascribed to the optimistic postmillennial view, which held that the Kingdom of God would be ushered into existence through the efforts of the Church before Christ's Second Coming.

THE RISE OF FUNDAMENTALISM

Some American Protestants found the optimism of the nineteenth century profoundly disturbing. They saw modernism as a different religion and an attack on the essentials of the Christian faith. The fundamentalist mindset can be traced only as far back as the Princeton Theological Seminary from 1860 to 1890. Princeton theologians Charles Hodge (1797–1878), A. A. Hodge (1823–1886), and B. B. Warfield (1851–1921) are credited with developing what came to be known as the Princeton theology in defense of the Bible. Hodge and Warfield wrote

> that the Scriptures not only contain, but ARE THE WORD OF GOD, . . . all the affirmations of Scripture of all kinds, whether of spiritual doctrine or duty, or of physical or historical fact, or of psychological or philosophical principle, are without any error, when the *ipsissima verba* [*that is, the exact language*] of the original autographs [*the actual manuscripts originally produced by the biblical writers themselves*] are ascertained and interpreted in their natural and intended sense.[11]

Springing from the Niagara Bible Conference in 1895, anti-modernists defined their position with a specific set of doctrinal affirmations: (1) the authority and inerrancy of Scripture; (2) the Virgin Birth and deity of Christ; (3) Christ's substitutionary atonement; (4) Christ's physical resurrection; and (5) the Second Coming. Other doctrines were also affirmed, including the depravity of human nature and the existence of a personal devil and of heaven and hell. But, clearly, the authority and inerrancy of Scripture and the Second Coming were given supreme attention.

A series of twelve small volumes of essays called *The Fundamentals: A Testimony to the Truth* was published between 1910 and 1915, financially backed by two wealthy California brothers. Sixty-four authors were selected to write articles and essays designed to defend fundamental Christian doctrines. Three million copies of the books were sent to every theology student and Christian minister whose address could be obtained.

It was not until 1920 that the term *fundamentalist* was coined by Baptist Curtis Lee Laws, editor of *The Watchman-Examiner*. A group within the Northern Baptist Convention meeting in Buffalo, New York, accepted the title and adopted the name "The Fundamentalist Fellowship." These fundamentalists were conservatives concerned about preserving the fundamental affirmations of the Christian faith. Only later did the fundamentalist movement take on a more closed-minded, belligerent, and divisive nature.

Fundamentalism today has been compared to the fundamentalism of the Pharisees in the first Christian century. In the parable of the Pharisee and the tax collector, we read that Jesus

> also told this parable to some who trusted in themselves that they were righteous, and regarded others with contempt. "Two men went up to the temple to pray, one a Pharisee and the other a tax collector. The Pharisee, standing by himself, was praying thus, 'God, I thank you that I am not like other people: thieves, rogues, adulterers, or even like this tax collector. I fast twice a week; I give a tenth of all my income.' But the tax collector, standing far off, would not even look up to heaven, but was beating his breast and saying, 'God, be merciful to me, a sinner.' I tell you, this man went down to his home justified rather than the other; for all who exalt themselves will be humbled, but all who humble themselves will be exalted." (Luke 18:9–14)

Kendell H. Easley, associate professor of New Testament and Greek at Mid-America Baptist Theological Seminary in Memphis, said of the Pharisees that "obedience to God came to be measured by external conformity to tradition."[12] Fundamentalists have a Pharisee attitude. They measure faithfulness to God by external conformity to parameters, which they have determined set the limits to what is Christian faith and practice.

James T. Draper, Jr., a recent president of the Southern Baptist Convention and now president of the Baptist Sunday School Board, wrote in 1974 that "The Fundamentalist dogma is so mixed with tradition and custom that it is scarcely recognizable as being scriptural."[13] This statement sounds like one that would come from a moderate, not from a person who has been a leader in the takeover of the Southern Baptist Convention.

FUNDAMENTALISM THRIVES ON CONTROVERSY

The feud in the Southern Baptist Convention will continue for many years; it is essential to fundamentalism's survival as a movement. Draper tells of a fundamentalist leader who told his staff, "Be against something. Find something, anything to be against."[14] It will continue because fundamentalists create "satan figures," individuals or institutions they can identify as unbelievers, liberals, or "skunks" who thwart the best efforts of fundamentalism to bring revival to the nation and world. Fundamentalists have a love for conflict and the ability to attract strong and capable soldiers for their cause. Capitalizing on fear and uncertainty about the future and the new millennium, and a feeling of helplessness in the face of perceived threats to families and faith, fundamentalists use emotionally charged words to inflame and draw out the troops.

James Larry Holly, a Beaumont, Texas physician, has been a primary catalyst within the Southern Baptist Convention in the effort to condemn Freemasonry. Holly, in a September 30, 1993 letter to the Home Mission Board directors, the officers and past presidents of the Southern Baptist Convention, Baptist Press, Associate Baptist Press, and editors of the state Baptist papers, reflected the fundamentalist mindset.

> And, if, like the Anabaptists, if, like the Separatists of England, if, like Charles Haddon Spurgeon, this [the Freemasonry issue] causes us to lose members and money, and if this causes us to fall into disfavor with men, let us say with Esther, "If I die, I die," but I will die on the Lord's side.[15]

CATALYST FOR CURRENT RISE OF FUNDAMENTALISM

Many issues have arisen within the past twenty years that can be said to be the catalyst for the current rise of fundamentalism. Fundamentalism is grounded in a conviction that disaster and divine judgment await humankind in the near future. For fundamentalists, the world is getting worse, and nothing, short of the Second Coming of Christ, can stop this deterioration.

Turner cites the movement of large numbers of people from rural to urban settings and the resulting diverse population.[16] Migration has separated families from their ancestral roots and brought them into contact with people whose beliefs and practices are sometimes radically different. Suddenly, people who had never met a Jew, Roman Catholic, Muslim, or Hindu found them living next door, operating a restaurant, laundry, or motel in their towns and cities, or sitting next to their child in first grade. Cable television brought a world of new ideas into living rooms as choices grew to over four dozen channels, with the "information highway" promising even more. (While generally critical of the secular media, fundamentalists and other religion groups recognize the value of cable television in spreading their faith and values.) Old standards for self-identity and self-esteem are called into question or shattered; new standards must be found. Many people attempted to escape this new pluralism by avoiding, as much as possible, anyone holding these new beliefs and practices.

Southern Baptist mega-churches, churches with several thousand members, attract a membership which is dissatisfied with and frightened of the urban setting to which most of them are relative newcomers. In many ways, these mega-churches, with their sports facilities, extensive entertainment, family worship, and private schools function as modern monasteries where people can escape from the Satanic world into a "heaven on earth." They isolate themselves, even for a little while, from complex social changes, from women's changing roles in society and from New Age teachings in public schools. Family reunions and church homecomings formed an important aspect of renewing contact with the familiar.

Another part of the population withdrew from active participation in churches as prosperity enabled them to visit a local tourist attraction on the weekend or travel overseas. For these people, the church became a place to go when they couldn't go somewhere else. To church leaders, this was a sign of growing secularism. However, it was probably a sign that attending church had become a lower priority. These people still considered themselves religious even if they no longer attended church. Besides, they could watch religious programming twenty-four hours a day, seven days a week on cable television.

Fundamentalism has sought divine authority for its movement, as did Pope Pius IX when he announced the doctrine of papal infallibility in 1870 in an effort to prevent the unification of the Italian states into one nation. Satan figures are created to keep the faithful faithful. Some fundamentalists have come to see Satan in everything from Freemasonry to the Supreme Court.

THE FUNDAMENTALIST MINDSET

Fundamentalists require doctrinal agreement; diversity of beliefs is interpreted as a sign of the lack of commitment to the Bible. Draper said, "The basic tenet of Fundamentalism is proper doctrine. The most important thing in the world is to believe the right things."[17] Doctrinal agreement is enforced by an authoritarian leadership using threats of God's judgment against all who waver from the prescribed and narrow path.

Draper's statement is significant in understanding the fundamentalist mindset. Historically, the Southern Baptist Convention emphasized missions, evangelism, and church growth while permitting doctrinal diversity within its ranks. A fundamental shift in priorities has occurred within the denomination since 1979. Doctrinal uniformity is now required at the expense of missions, evangelism, and church growth. Political and social agreement with the fundamentalist agenda has been added to requirements in Southern Baptist life.

Fundamentalism is, by nature, a strongly opinionated mindset. Truth is defined narrowly, with fundamentalists believing they alone "contend for the faith that was once for all entrusted to the saints" (Jude 3). Compromise or even negotiation is not a fundamentalist characteristic. Its aim is nothing less than the unconditional surrender by its enemy or its total destruction. One side or the other must win; there can be no surrender. Draper said of the fundamentalist, he

> is sure that he is the only true follower of Jesus Christ. This belief is bolstered by an intolerance of others. Once you cross him, you can't get back in his good graces. He will never admit to any faults of his own. He is confident and sure that in all things and at all times he is right.[18]

Draper also criticized fundamentalists for their unfairness: "He will never give anyone a fair hearing."[19] Draper said the fundamentalist is quick to act "on first impressions. He is ever quick to accept the worst about everyone and every organization. This makes him a man who has no loyalties, except to himself and his own."[20] Draper, although a recent Convention president and now president of the Baptist Sunday School Board, has hit the nail on the head. He clearly explains the fundamentalist mindset.

Control, from theological to social, is an integral part of the fundamentalist mindset. Moderates repeatedly charged during the 1980s that the real agenda behind the fundamentalist takeover was control of SBC boards and agencies. Fundamentalists repeatedly said the real agenda was the inerrancy of the Bible. James L. Holly apparently agreed with the moderate interpretation when he wrote of "conservatives, who had fought for years to **control** the Convention. . . ."[21]

It is customary for fundamentalists to attack their opponents by casting personal aspersions, by exaggeration and by engaging in scare tactics. Code words are popular with fundamentalists; *modernism* is one such word. Modernism is sometimes used as a synonym for communism, sometimes for liberalism, sometimes for secularism. Modernism always refers to something deemed anti-Christian. Evangelist James Robinson referred to "liberals" in the convention as "spiritual perverts" in his sermon during the 1978 Southern Baptist pastors' conference.[22]

In an April 1994, four-page letter mailed to 39,200 Southern Baptist pastors and directors of missions, Southwestern Baptist Theological Seminary trustees attempted to justify the firing of president Russell H. Dilday the previous month. Dilday's theological conservatism was attacked because he refused to bow down to and support the fundamentalist takeover of the Convention and the Seminary. He spoke out courageously against the toxic nature of fundamentalism and thus became a target for the personal attack. The letter accused Dilday of demonstrating "a commitment to the principles of higher criticism, which spawned theological liberalism (modernism), neo-orthodoxy, the death of God, situational ethics, etc." The Seminary faculty defended Dilday's conservative theology, but the damage was done by the false accusation of "liberalism (modernism)." To be labeled a liberal in the Southern Baptist Convention often results in loss of respect and career.

Fundamentalism succumbs easily and regularly to the cult of personality. Television evangelists attract easy-chair audiences as large as favorite baseball or football teams. In Southern Baptist life, the business model of bigger is better has enabled pastors of successful mega-churches to become the ideals that pastors of smaller churches emulate. Pastors of successful mega-churches are elected to the office of president of the Convention and invited to speak at meetings to draw a crowd. This, in spite of the fact that most Southern Baptist churches have fewer than 300 members and do not have the financial resources or talent among members to put on the more expensive and varied programs of the mega-churches with thousands of members. The median Southern Baptist church had 238 members in 1992.[23]

Statistics are important, especially the number of baptisms. Money given to the Cooperative Program was seen as less important because mega-church congregations typically contributed a smaller percentage of their income to the convention's missions effort. With budgets in the millions, mega-churches took on denominational characteristics, supported non–Southern Baptist mission projects, and directly competed with denominational programs.

The Baptist Sunday School Board canceled a women's conference in Atlanta in February 1994 because the conference conflicted with a similar conference at nearby fundamentalist First Baptist Church, Snellville, Georgia, on the same dates. The church's conference was expected to draw over 2,000 participants; a similar conference sponsored by the Baptist Sunday School Board in 1993 in San Antonio drew only 800 participants.[24] Recent Southern Baptist Convention president Bailey Smith's "Real Evangelism Bible Conferences" typically draw a larger crowd than the state convention's evangelism conferences. Smith's evangelism conference at First Baptist Church, Woodstock, Georgia, in February 1994 featured well-known Southern Baptists Ike Reighard, Rick Gage, and Ed Young, president of the Southern Baptist Convention, among others.[25]

PASTOR AS RULER

With pastors of the mega-churches held up as the ideal, it is not surprising that they have taken on almost superhuman characteristics in the minds of many Southern Baptists, much in the same way that the Bishop of Rome became the Pope of the Roman Catholic Church. At Southern Baptist meetings, it is not uncommon to see young, admiring pastors rushing up to shake hands with pastors of the mega-churches as if some of his aura will rub off. Not only has the person in the pew come to see pastors of the mega-churches as authority figures to whom they looked up, the pastors themselves have begun to see themselves as being bigger than life.

Historically, Baptists have held that the local congregation is a democracy where all members are equal in rank and privilege. There are no rulers within the local congregation. William C. Boone, author of *What We Believe*, says the Baptist position is that the pastor is not the ruler of the church.[26] Rather, the pastor is the shepherd who leads the congregation and ministers to each member's spiritual needs. This historic Baptist teaching has also been attacked in recent years.

Independent Baptist Jerry Falwell, who speaks regularly at Southern Baptist meetings, justified his authoritarian role: "God never intended for a committee nor a board of deacons nor any other group to dominate a church or control a pastor. The pastor is God's man, God's servant, God's leader."[27]

W. A. Criswell, pastor emeritus of the First Baptist Church, Dallas, Texas, recently told a group of pastors in Tupelo, Mississippi, that "The man of God who is the pastor of the church is the ruler." Criswell, who became pastor of the Dallas church nearly fifty years earlier, said he told the church leaders that "The pulpit is mine and I preach what God puts on my mind, and the staff is mine and I run the church." He claimed the authority of God gave him authority as ruler of the church; "They can quarrel with God over that, not me."[28]

FUNDAMENTALISM IS INHERENTLY SCHISMATIC

Fundamentalism is inherently schismatic, even leading those within the movement to separate from each other for what would seem to nonfundamentalists as obscure or inconsequential reasons. Fundamentalist Bob Jones, Jr., president of Bob Jones University in Greenville, South Carolina, called fellow fundamentalist Jerry Falwell, "the most dangerous man in America."[29]

In 1956, fundamentalist Luther Peak returned to the Southern Baptist Convention, saying, "In the Fundamentalist Movement we were usually in a fight of some kind. If we were not fighting Southern Baptists, Northern Baptists, the National Council of Churches, the Catholics, Communism or Modernism, we fought each other."[30] James Draper also refers to the "divisive spirit" of fundamentalists.[31]

Edward J. Carnell, when he was president of Fuller Theological Seminary, said of fundamentalism:

> Fundamentalism is a paradoxical position. It sees the heresy in untruth but not in unloveliness. If it has the most truth, it has the least grace, since it distrusts courtesy and diplomacy. Fundamentalism forgets that orthodox truth without orthodox love profits nothing.[32]

DISPENSATIONALISM

Dispensationalism's roots begin with Margaret McDonald and John Nelson Darby (1800–1882), a Church of Ireland parish priest turned Plymouth Brethren; American Presbyterian James H. Brookes and his protégé, Cyrus Ingerson Scofield (1843–1921). Like Albert Pike, Scofield served in the army of the Confederate States of America where he received the Cross of Honor while serving under General Robert E. Lee. Both Pike and Scofield practiced law after the Civil War, Pike in Little Rock, Arkansas, and Scofield in St. Louis, Missouri.

Unlike other dispensationalists, Darby rejected the theories that the United States would be the "New Israel." Darby, and all dispensationalists who followed him, held that the Jews would play a significant role in the last days. He taught that the nation of Israel would be restored and the Temple in Jerusalem would be rebuilt. According to Darby, history will end with a Tribulation under the rule of the Antichrist. The Tribulation will end with the Battle of Armageddon (Rev. 16:16), when Christ will return to Earth to usher in the millennium, or 1,000 years of peace.

One will encounter different and changing views of dispensationalism today.[33] Classical dispensationalism is a distinct form of prophecy that holds that God's relationship to humanity changed in different periods or dispensations to accomplish his purpose in history. The still popular *Scofield Reference*

Bible, published in 1909 and 1917, is the best known representative of this classical dispensationalism. The *Scofield Reference Bible* had sold in excess of 12.5 million copies by 1990.[34] Scofield proposed seven dispensations: Innocence (before the fall), Conscience (from the fall to Noah), Human Government (from Noah to Abraham), Promise (from Abraham to Moses), Law (from Moses to Christ), Grace (the present Church age), the Kingdom (the future millennium). Annotations in the *Scofield Reference Bible* were revised by a number of dispensational scholars in 1967.

In classical dispensationalism, it is believed God will restore the Old Testament Davidic kingdom as an earthly political kingdom and will redeem a portion of humanity with a heavenly promise. This division of the biblical promise into two covenants, one earthly and one heavenly, is best described by Lewis Sperry Chafer (1871–1952), who founded the independent Dallas Theological Seminary, in his eight-volume *Systematic Theology*.

The support of Southern Baptist J. R. Graves (1820–1893), the founder of the popular Landmark Movement within the Southern Baptist Convention, was crucial in the widespread acceptance of dispensationalism within the denomination. Helen Lee Turner found that 71 percent of self-proclaimed fundamentalists identify themselves as dispensationalists.[35]

Scofield was pessimistic about society's prospects, believing society would degenerate into self-destruction. He believed human institutions, civil and religious, were inherently defective and doomed. His eschatology, or view of the last days, called for a rapture (1 Thessalonians 4:17) of true Christians, while other church members and the world at large followed the coming Antichrist. Scofield's division of true believers and unbelievers within the membership of the Church is a characteristic of the fundamentalist mindset today. Education was criticized by Scofield as both unnecessary and a hindrance to true believers. He believed education was not necessary to correctly interpret biblical prophecy. It is not uncommon to hear fundamentalists attack higher education. Testimonies are heard about ministers who lost their "faith" while attending theology schools where fundamentalist teachings were attacked as narrow-minded.

James Holly, telling his readers that Masons were instrumental in formulating public school education in the United States, says public education "**is founded upon an evil premise, i.e., man does not need God and there are no problems which education and reason cannot solve.**"[36] Holly's criticism of public school education is similar to Roman Catholic objections that Freemasonry called for public school education apart from control of the Roman Catholic Church. It is difficult to blame Masons for the problems in public school education, as Holly implies is the case. Deficiencies that may be found in public school education cannot be blamed on the 2.3 million Masons in this country any more than they can be on the 15.5 million Southern Baptists.

Today, the creation of the nation of Israel in 1948, the coming new millennium, and popular books by authors such as Hal Lindsey, have popularized dispensationalism among millions of individuals.

Millennialism, the belief in a 1,000-year reign of Christ on Earth, is also a driving force in fundamentalism. Lloyd Averill says the cry of the fundamentalist was and is "Back to the once-for-all-delivered word of God in preparation for the imminent end of history!"[37] Millennialism will be discussed more fully in the following chapter.

TOXIC FAITH AND FUNDAMENTALISM

As a postscript to this chapter, a short discussion of toxic faith is in order. There is a fine line between extreme fundamentalism and toxic faith. Stephen Arterburn and Jack Felton in *Toxic Faith: Understanding and Overcoming Religious Addiction*, says "faith becomes toxic when individuals use God or religion for profit, power, pleasure, and/or prestige."[38] They argue that toxic faith is a destructive and dangerous faith that seeks to control a person's life. It is abusive and manipulative, and it reduces family and friends to insignificance as the individual is himself controlled by toxic faith.[39] Certainly, the majority of fundamentalists could not be accused of practicing a toxic faith. However, a few fundamentalists who succumb to toxic faith can hold an entire denomination hostage and terrorize individuals who become their targets.

Individuals controlled by toxic faith are extremely intolerant of different opinions or expressions of faith. They are quick to judge others and attempt to control what they believe and with whom they associate. They reject fellow believers rather than accepting them. They insist on controlling others' lives, especially others' beliefs. They allow no accountability for their actions. Those who recognize the dysfunctional nature of toxic faith, discern right from wrong, and speak out for the truth, usually lose their positions within the dysfunctional organization and are often treated as outcasts or lepers.

3 Southern Baptist Fundamentalism

The only thing to which he was subject was his own undying passion to dominate. Few among his contemporaries could hold their own against his verbal attacks, for his conscience seemingly never interfered with his method. Any tactic was acceptable to him so long as it helped him to achieve his purposes, purposes that, to the consternation of his opponents, he sincerely viewed as synonymous with the purposes of God.[1]

Non-Southern Baptists shake their heads and roll their eyes in disbelief at the political/theological controversy that has torn the Southern Baptist Convention apart since 1979. Many Southern Baptists cannot believe this has happened either. This chapter will attempt to help readers understand some of the background to Southern Baptist fundamentalism.

J. R. GRAVES AND THE LANDMARK MOVEMENT

In many ways, the current fundamentalist movement within the Southern Baptist Convention, with one major exception, can be compared to the Landmark movement of J. R. Graves in the Nineteenth century. The Landmark movement received its name from a tract written by J. M. Pendleton, "An Old Landmark Reset," in 1854. This title refers to Proverbs 22:28: "Do not remove the ancient landmark that your ancestors set up." In the tract, Pendleton attacked the doctrine of pedobaptism and argued that pedobaptist preachers should not be recognized as Gospel ministers.

Alan Neely lists six marks of the Landmark movement: (1) rejection of any New Testament entity beyond the local church; (2) only Baptist churches (and not all of them) are true New Testament churches; (3) only Baptist churches can trace their lineage back to the New Testament; (4) Baptist churches are the only visible signs of the Kingdom of God; (5) all other so-called churches are merely "human societies;" and (6) only a Baptist church has the authority to observe the ordinances of baptism and the Lord's Supper.[2]

Graves, a self-educated minister, was editor of the influential Baptist paper *The Tennessee Baptist*. Through the printed word and his ability as a persuasive preacher, he fought against Campbellism and earned a reputation as a defender of the autonomy of the local Baptist church. Campbellism was the name given to the group following Alexander Campbell, who attacked practically all Baptist beliefs and caused splits in Baptist churches from Texas to Virginia in the early and middle nineteenth century. Today, the Disciples of Christ and the Churches of Christ trace their roots to Alexander Campbell.

Graves, reacting against Campbellism, was seen as the orthodox champion against anyone or anything that would dilute what he held were pure Baptist teachings. He argued that Landmarkism was not unloving since they were simply following the teachings of the Bible. Landmarkism, Graves said, did not deny the right of anyone to believe and preach any view, but it came very close to saying that salvation was impossible outside a local Baptist church.

The major exception to the Landmark movement lies in the fundamentalist use of denomination positions and agencies to promote their beliefs. Landmarkism was very suspicious of any organization that might exist beyond the local church level. Beginning in the late 1970s, fundamentalists realized the power inherent in the office of president of the Southern Baptist Convention. The president's primary responsibility was to name persons to a committee on committees that, in turn, recommended persons to serve as trustees/directors of Southern Baptist agencies and institutions. When the majority of trustees/directors held fundamentalist views, fundamentalists could control policy decisions, appointment of missionaries, and election of denominational staff. Denomination staff and agency presidents who resisted the fundamentalist movement could be forced to take early retirement or could be fired. The strategy would see a majority of fundamentalist trustees/directors elected in as few as five years.

Graves, in an attempt to force the Convention to adopt his views, openly threatened to split the Southern Baptist Convention if R. B. C. Howell were reelected as Convention president in 1859. Howell, pastor of the First Baptist Church, Nashville, Tennessee, where Graves had been excluded as a member by action of the church, then declined the office. Richard Fuller was then elected president. None of Graves's views were adopted by the Convention; he spent the remainder of his years pressing his cause in meetings across the Convention. As Southern Baptists have seen in recent years, a resolution was adopted at the 1859 Convention urging that "personal controversies among pastors, editors, and brethren should, from this time forth, be more than ever avoided."[3] Landmarkism never again threatened to split the Convention after 1859. Increasingly, according to Homer Grice, many of Graves followers "tired of warfare and yearned for peace."[4] Still, Landmarkism had gotten into the bloodstream of Southern Baptists, and it continues to impact the thinking of the Convention in different ways.

J. FRANK NORRIS

While there are exceptions, Southern Baptist fundamentalism in the 1980s and 1990s can also be closely identified with the fundamentalism of sixty or seventy years ago.

John Franklyn Norris (1877–1952), known as J. Frank, was the most colorful and controversial fundamentalist in Southern Baptist history. The son of an alcoholic sharecropper, Norris was shot by Texas cattle rustlers when he was fifteen. During his three-year recuperation, his mother instilled in young Norris a positive self-esteem, confidence, and determination and an aggressiveness that would serve him the remainder of his life. After graduating from Baylor University in Waco, Texas, he completed a three-year course at the Southern Baptist Theological Seminary in Louisville, Kentucky, in two years and was chosen to address his graduating class. He soon acquired majority ownership of the *Baptist Standard*, the official state paper for the Baptist General Convention of Texas, and became its editor, a position where he discovered the power of the pen. Giving up control of the *Baptist Standard* in 1907, he became pastor of the First Baptist Church of Fort Worth, Texas. There, he became known for his sensationalist sermon topics, including "The Ten Biggest Devils in Fort Worth, Names Given." When the church trustees attempted to fire Norris, he dismissed all of the trustees and deacons. Six hundred members left the church, a move Norris viewed as a "purification process."[5]

Fire destroyed the church sanctuary in 1912, and Norris was indicted for arson by a grand jury, but he was acquitted. Norris turned his attention in 1926 to exposing corruption in the city government. H. C. Meacham, the Roman Catholic mayor, was his principal target. Norris declared Meacham unfit to be "manager of a hog pen." When a friend of the mayor visited Norris in his church office, Norris shot him three times. Indicted for murder, Norris pleaded self-defense and was acquitted.

Norris believed he was called to reform the Southern Baptist Convention. He started his own newspaper in 1917, originally called the *Fence Rail*, and later called the *Searchlight* and then the *Fundamentalist*. At one time, its circulation exceeded that of the *Baptist Standard*. The two issues that Norris saw as being most critical were denominational control of the local church and infiltration of "modernism" into the convention. Baylor University was a primary target. When George W. Truett, pastor of First Baptist Church, Dallas, and a Mason, resisted his attack on Baylor, Norris accused Truett of being under the control of modernists, a derogatory term referring to those who accept modern science and historical research rather than traditional Christian teachings.

L. R. Scarborough, president of Southwestern Baptist Theological Seminary in Fort Worth, and S. P. Brooks, president of Baylor University, accused Norris of accepting "alien immersion" and permitting non-Baptists to preach in his church. "Alien immersion" is the practice of accepting baptism by means other than immersion after a profession of faith in Jesus Christ. "Alien immersion" would include the sprinkling of infants practiced in many Protestant churches. The Tarrant County Baptist Association, in which Fort Worth is located, then expelled Norris and his church. Two years later, in 1924, the Baptist General Convention of Texas, also expelled Norris.

For many years, Norris was pastor of both the First Baptist Church of Fort Worth and the Temple Baptist Church in Detroit, Michigan. Under his autocratic leadership, both congregations grew, First Baptist from 1,200 members to 13,000 and Temple Baptist from 800 to 12,000. He started his own denominational organization, the World Fundamental Baptist Mission Fellowship, in 1938. The Fellowship founded its own seminary, the Baptist Bible Institute in Fort Worth, in 1939. John R. Rice, fundamentalist editor of the *Sword of the Lord* newsletter, and John Birch, after whom the John Birch Society is named, attended the seminary. Norris's denomination suffered a schism when certain pastors tired of his dictatorial leadership. Because of his continued public attacks on the schismatic pastors, the Temple Baptist Church voted 3,000 to 7 to fire Norris as pastor.

Mark Toulouse says of Norris, "Anyone who differed in any way with Norris immediately became a likely candidate for a tongue-lashing, if not something worse."[6] Also, "The only thing to which he was subject was his own undying passion to dominate. Few among his contemporaries could hold their own against his verbal attacks, for his conscience seemingly never interfered with his method. Any tactic was acceptable to him so long as it helped him to achieve his purposes, purposes that, to the consternation of his opponents, he sincerely viewed as synonymous with the purposes of God."[7] J. Frank Norris clones are still with us.

WHAT DO SOUTHERN BAPTISTS WANT TO BE CALLED

Many Southern Baptist fundamentalists today don't like the term *fundamentalists* applied to them, probably in the attempt to disassociate themselves from J. Frank Norris. Paul Pressler, one of the two primary architects of the fundamentalist takeover of the Convention, said it is a synonym for being narrow-minded, bigoted, and redneck.[8] After the Scopes trial in 1925, the term became synonymous with anti-intellectualism, although many Southern Baptists fundamentalists are well-educated and produce scholarly works.

In 1986, the Baptist Press announced that it had adopted the terms *fundamental-conservative* and *moderate-conservative* to identify the two parties within the Convention. The terms correctly defined both parties as being conservative in theology, but they proved too cumbersome to use in print and have been generally replaced by "conservative" and "moderate."

Southern Baptist fundamentalists,[9] such as Pressler, would prefer to be simply called conservatives, but so would moderates in the Convention. The overwhelming majority of Southern Baptists could correctly be called conservative in theology; they also accept the five fundamental statements of earlier fundamentalists. The difference between moderates and fundamentalists within the Southern Baptist Convention does not revolve around differences in theology, although there are exceptions. The difference is one of attitude toward those who differ in theology or practice and control over another's theology and practice.

Robinson B. James distinguishes between the "fundamental-conservatives" and the "moderate-conservatives." Fundamental-conservatives, he says, are Southern Baptists in sympathy with the plan "to gain control of and redirect Southern Baptist agencies by electing governing boards of those institutions that are more or less fundamentalist."[10] Moderate-conservatives are those Southern Baptists opposed to this takeover of the Convention's agencies and institutions. For many Southern Baptists, this is the primary division between those who call themselves fundamentalist and those who call themselves moderates.

Instead of speaking of a "fundamentalist takeover," Pressler would prefer the phrase *conservative resurgence*. Many fundamentalists refer to moderate Southern Baptists as "liberals." Moderates reject this appellation since few, if any, accept the classical liberal religious teachings, such as rejecting the divinity of Jesus or the inspiration of the Bible.

Southern Baptist liberals are so few in number that they are more a curiosity than a threat to conservative theology. David Montoya of Arkansas said, "finding a liberal Baptist in Arkansas is like hunting snipe with a youth group. Some believe snipes exist, but no one has caught one."[11] When asked to name five "liberals" in denominational agencies, Jerry Vines, newly elected president of the Southern Baptist Convention, admitted, "If you're talking about classical liberalism, that is not the real theological issue in our denomination. You're getting closer to the matter when you think in terms of neo-orthodoxy."[12] Vines did not name anyone he thought was a Southern Baptist liberal or who was neo-orthodox.

INERRANCY

The doctrine of biblical inerrancy held by nineteenth-century Princeton Presbyterians has been adopted by Southern Baptist fundamentalists who have made "inerrancy" the rallying cry in their takeover of the Southern Baptist Convention. Inerrancy, meaning "no error or mistakes," is the belief that the original writings or autographs of the Bible are without error, although fundamentalists sometimes simply speak of the Bible as inerrant, without regard to the original writings of the biblical authors. Inerrantists insist the original writings or autographs were without error in all matters: theology, philosophy, history, science, geography, and mathematics. For example, 2 Chronicles 4:2 states, "Then he made the molten sea; it was round, ten cubits from rim to rim, and five cubits high. A line of thirty cubits would encircle it completely." This verse has been used to argue that the Bible is mathematically accurate.

Bailey E. Smith, former president of the Southern Baptist Convention, said, "inerrancy is not a side issue. It is a very vital issue."[13] Adrian Rogers, who immediately preceded Smith as the convention president, stressed that the inerrantists' position is that the Bible is "historically, philosophically, scientifically and theologically without error."[14]

Related to the word *inerrancy* and loosely synonymous is the term *infallible*, meaning "incapable of error." While Roman Catholics use infallibility to speak of the words of a Pope when he speaks ex cathedra, or "out of the chair," conservative evangelicals and fundamentalists use the term solely for the Bible. *Ex cathedra* refers to Papal pronouncements on matters of faith and morals that are considered infallible among Catholics.

Theologian Kenneth S. Kantzer has stated that "The proof of an error in Scripture would . . . destroy our confidence that the Bible is a completely trustworthy authority and guide to the teaching of Christ."[15] He says that "puzzling passages" in the Bible, such as passages that seem "to give different accounts of the same events," are merely "unsolved problems." He admitted that he has had "a freight-car load of unsolved problems" that when resolved have led him to "a new freight-car."[16] He admitted in another article on inerrancy, that while the Bible is infallible, our interpretations and application are not.[17] Others refer to "apparent discrepancies, verbal differences, seeming contradictions, and so forth."[18]

David S. Dockery, vice president of the Southern Baptist Theological Seminary in Louisville, Kentucky, defines inerrancy as

> the idea that when all the facts are known, the Bible (in its autographs, that is, the original documents), properly interpreted in light of the culture and the means of communication that had developed by the time of its composition, is completely true in all that it affirms, to the degree of precision intended by the author's purpose, in all matters relating to God and His creation.[19]

Dockery, a conservative theologian, adds too many qualifications to his "balanced" definition for many fundamentalists. They hold a position called "absolute inerrancy," which allows for human involvement in writing the biblical text but insists that all assertions about science and history are true.

Between 1977 and 1987, the International Council on Biblical Inerrancy, a series of summits of conservative Bible scholars, proposed to restore confidence in the "total trustworthiness of the Scriptures."[20] One conclusion of this council was that God has nowhere promised "an inerrant transmission of Scripture"; therefore, "the authority of Scripture is no way jeopardized by the fact that the copies we possess are not entirely error-free. . . . no translation is or can be perfect."[21] Not all inerrantists agree with this conclusion. Jerry Vines, a recent president of the Southern Baptist Convention, said, "I just could not look Southern Baptists in the face and appoint people who believe there are errors in the Bible."[22] In the same interview, however, Vines said he would only appoint persons to SBC boards and committees who are sympathetic with the fundamentalist movement, leaving observers wondering whether the issue was inerrancy or politics.

THE PEACE COMMITTEE

An ad hoc committee, called the Southern Baptist Convention Peace Committee, was formed in 1985. Approximately two dozen men (two women were later added) were chosen, theoretically one half from the fundamentalist camp and one half from the moderate camp. However, the fundamentalists were able to set the tone for the committee, which met in secret fourteen times over a period of two years. Turner speaks of the Peace Committee report, which was approved with little discussion by messengers to the Southern Baptist Convention (SBC) in St. Louis in 1987, as "almost entirely a document of formal institutionalization for the fundamentalist philosophy."[23] The document spoke of theology that "most Southern Baptists" believe, such as the belief that "Adam and Eve were real persons" and that "the named authors did indeed write the biblical books attributed to them by those books."[24] The Peace Committee Report was adopted at the Convention in St. Louis in 1987. Turner says that after the 1987 convention, the "fundamentalists were ecstatic. To many of them, it was almost as though the Kingdom of God had come." One fundamentalist leader said the victory was perhaps more important than the Reformation begun by Martin Luther.[25]

Theological conservative Daniel Vestal, who eventually aligned himself with the moderate movement in the convention, summarized his experience on the Peace Committee: "I realized the Fundamentalists only desired control, total control, absolute control, and that they wanted no participation except with those who had that same desire."[26]

THE COOPERATIVE PROGRAM AS A WEAPON

Resentful that several seminary presidents were speaking out against the fundamentalist takeover, W. A. Criswell said, "It isn't right for them to take our [Cooperative Program] money and damn us."[27] Bailey Smith, pastor of First Baptist Church, Del City, Oklahoma, cut his church's Cooperative Program gifts from $175,000 annually to $125,000 in 1985 to protest Southwestern Baptist Theological Seminary president Russell Dilday's effort against Charles Stanley as president of the convention.[28]

The word was put out that thousands of churches might withhold financial support of the Convention if Stanley was defeated, when it appeared the moderates might have the strength to defeat fundamentalist Charles Stanley for president of the Convention in 1985. He won the election.

In 1986, Adrian Rogers, three-time president of the Southern Baptist Convention, affirmed his satisfaction with the fundamentalist proposal to end the theological controversy in the Convention by allowing churches to select which Southern Baptist institutions they wanted to contribute to, an idea called "negative designation."[29] Paige Patterson argued that no money should be shifted to compensate for "negative designation."[30] In a proposal for peace in the convention, Patterson called for designation of Cooperative Program gifts away from agencies in which they in "good conscience" could not support.[31] This theme was repeated by many fundamentalists during the early and mid-1980s. "Negative designation" has not been mentioned by these leaders since they gained control of the Convention.

Rogers said it was not "only illogical, it is immoral to ask a man to support with his money and with his influence . . . things that are theologically repugnant to him." Rogers claimed that Southern Baptists "have made a golden calf of the program," meaning the Cooperative Program.[32]

Patterson, now president of Southeastern Baptist Theological Seminary and one of the two men credited with formulating the fundamentalist strategy to take control of the Southern Baptist Convention, compared giving money to SBC institutions that don't accept the fundamentalist point of view with giving scrap metal to the Japanese during World War II. "It's the same situation as before World War II when we shipped scrap metal to the Japanese and they shot it back at us," Patterson said.[33]

Jerry Johnson, pastor of the Central Baptist church in Aurora, Colorado, and a trustee of the Southern Baptist Theological Seminary, published a sixteen-page attack, *The Cover-Up at Southern*, in 1990 charging that seminary professors had doubts about supernatural events in the Bible, among other heresies. Johnson repeated an often-heard statement from fundamentalists during the 1980s, "We give them our money to teach what we do not believe in."[34]

Cooperative Program offerings, volunteer offerings from local churches, to support the ministries and agencies of the Southern Baptist Convention peaked at $140,710,282 in fiscal year 1989–1990. The offering dropped to $136,537,730 in fiscal year 1992–1993. By contrast, offerings received by the Cooperative Baptist Fellowship, the moderate organization formed in 1991 within the Southern Baptist Convention, grew from $4.5 million in 1991 to $11.2 million in 1993.

The success of the Cooperative Baptist Fellowship and the failure of the Cooperative Program offerings to continue their percentage increases of the past indicates that moderate Southern Baptists are following the suggestions of the fundamentalists prior to their takeover of the convention. As long as Southern Baptists talk about each other rather than to each other, this trend can only continue and accelerate as more moderate Baptists decide to designate their money for local church use only or for the Cooperative Baptist Fellowship to avoid giving their money to a Convention that rejects them as fellow Southern Baptists.

In 1988, SBC president Jerry Vines said he would appoint the "very best Southern Baptists I can find" to the SBC boards and agencies, but he qualified that by saying they would have to be sympathetic with the fundamentalist movement in the Convention.[35] After his election in 1988, Vines announced that his church, First Baptist Church, Jacksonville, Florida, had increased its Cooperative Program gifts to 2.7 percent of an annual budget of approximately $8 million.[36] The average Southern Baptist church gives eight percent of its annual budget to the Cooperative Program.

THE RUSE OF A WIDENED TENT

Several fundamentalist leaders floated a proposal for a "widened tent of leadership" in the Southern Baptist Convention as they solidified their hold on the convention. In March 1990, fundamentalist leader Joel Gregory, then pastor of First Baptist Church of Dallas, Texas, affirmed a plan proposed by John Bisagno, pastor of the First Baptist Church of Houston, to broaden the tent to give moderates, who affirmed a "perfect Bible," leadership positions within the Convention. Gregory said that Morris Chapman had "publicly and privately" agreed that he would "be far more encompassing in his appointments than has ever been" if he were elected president of the Convention the following June in New Orleans. Moderate candidate Daniel Vestal said the endorsement of Chapman was a "very clear political strategy." Vestal said Chapman was selected as the candidate by Convention president Jerry Vines and four of his immediate predecessors while on a Caribbean cruise. Richard Jackson, now pastor emeritus of the North Phoenix Baptist Church in Phoenix, was quoted as saying that if the goal is "inclusiveness," the selection of a candidate by a small group of Convention presidents on a Caribbean cruise was hardly the way to go at it.[37]

Richard Lee, pastor of the Rehoboth Baptist Church in Atlanta, Georgia, disagreed with Chapman's reported plan and expressed his opinion that "It's not people, but God's literal word that is important. . . . And there can be no reconciliation with the moderates unless they repent."[38]

Nothing came of the proposal; ruses are just that, and it died a quiet death.

THE FUNDAMENTALIST STRATEGY

The annual pre-Convention Pastors' Conference, long dominated by pastors of well-known fundamentalist churches, was a major factor in the fundamentalist takeover of the Southern Baptist Convention. Using slogans, catchphrases, appeals to emotional issues like liberalism and abortion, calls for revival, and just plain good preaching, fundamentalist preachers appealed to Southern Baptist messengers who appreciated their populist rhetoric.

Speaking at the Old Forest Road Baptist Church in Richmond, Virginia, in 1979, Pressler announced fundamentalists were "going for the jugular" to win control of the SBC. In 1984, moderate Roy Honeycutt described the SBC controversy as a "holy war." One writer described the moderate-fundamentalist controversy in the SBC as being like a wolf and bear chained together.[39] Harold Lindsell, former editor of *Christianity Today*, attacked what he called the rise of theological liberalism in the Southern Baptist seminaries as an "infection." In February 1985, Paige Patterson announced that the fundamentalists wanted only three of the six seminaries. It now is apparent that Patterson and others were paying lip service to this principle until they could take control of all six seminaries.

Criswell denounced Baptist seminary professors as infidels in an address at the June 1985 Pastors' Conference. Some fundamentalists believe academic freedom means professors can only teach what the fundamentalists regard as truth. Adrian Rogers made the absurd statement that "If the majority of Southern Baptists say that pickles have souls, then professors in Southern Baptist seminaries should teach that pickles have souls."[40] Fundamentalists like Rogers have long argued that their views reflect those of a majority of Southern Baptists.

In October 1991, trustees of the Southern Baptist Foreign Mission Board defunded the Baptist Theological Seminary in Ruschlikon, Switzerland. The seminary, founded by Southern Baptists in 1949, had been accused of liberalism and not emphasizing evangelism enough. The $365,000, one third of the operating expense of the seminary, was diverted to Eastern European schools believed more sympathetic to the fundamentalist movement.[41]

CALLS FOR REVIVAL

Repeated calls for revival were heard from the preachers at the annual Southern Baptist Pastors' Conference, held the day before the opening of the Southern Baptist Convention. Jack Taylor, of Fort Worth, Texas, preached on revival at the 1980 Pastors' Conference, saying, "Revival is the only answer."[42] Criswell, in 1985, asked those in attendance at the Pastors' Conference, "Why not America and why not now," in his call for revival.[43] Calls for a Holy Ghost revival were made. Revivals were held simultaneously in churches across the Convention in 1986 and 1990. Books were written by well-known fundamentalist pastors calling for revival. Bailey Smith began holding "Real Evangelism" conferences to compete with the annual state convention evangelism conferences. The theme of the 1988 Southern Baptist Convention was "Pour Out Revival."

James Holly blames the lack of revival, at least in part, in the Southern Baptist Convention to the lack of a condemnation of Freemasonry by the convention. Holly and Charles Burchett, pastor of the First Baptist Church, Kirbyville, Texas, stated in a spring 1992 letter accompanying Holly's first volume on Freemasonry, *The Southern Baptist Convention and Freemasonry*, that

> Revival only awaits Southern Baptists demonstrating to God how absolutely serious they are about being His people. The unshackling of the Southern Baptist Convention from any fellowship with the occultism of the Masonic Lodge by the Convention's declaring of Freemasonry to be incompatible with Christianity and with the ministry and mission of Southern Baptist churches would be a major step in that direction.

On the back cover of this book, Holly cites an unnamed African pastor who said "rebellion . . . ignorance of the supernatural (spiritual warfare not charismatic gifts) . . . and the toleration of Freemasonry in the church" were hindering revival among Southern Baptists.

Holly, in a September 16, 1992, letter, stated his opinion that "No conservative, Christ-honoring, Bible-believing Southern Baptist, who wants to see revival, can afford to be ignorant of the teachings and practices of the Masonic Lodge."

In an unpublished document titled "S.B.C. Resolution and Its Relationship to Freemasonry," Holly said that the Home Mission Board

> is charged with the evangelization of America, with promoting church growth, and with seeking revival among Southern Baptist church members. There is nothing more directly and specifically related to that responsibility than the exposure of the true nature of Freemasonry.[44]

Goals were set for baptisms of converts. The goal for the year 2000 is 500,000 baptisms, but there has been no dramatic climb in the number of baptisms reported by Southern Baptist churches since the fundamentalist takeover began in 1979. In some years the statistics have been flat or even declined slightly. Southern Baptist churches reported 429,742 baptisms in 1979–1980, the first year of the fundamentalist takeover. These churches reported 349,073 baptisms in 1992–1993.

ATTACK ON BAPTIST PRESS

When Houston Judge Paul Pressler was elected to the Southern Baptist Executive Committee in 1984, he began to bring charges of bias, lack of balance, and unfairness in the *Baptist Press*, especially on stories about him. Wilmer C. Fields, director of the *Baptist Press* and the Executive Committee's vice president for public relations, retired in 1987. Alvin C. Shakleford was elected to fill Fields's position, in spite of Pressler's vigorous opposition.[45] Pressler continued his efforts to silence Shakleford and news editor Dan Martin because of their alleged bias against him and the fundamentalist movement. Finally, on July 17, 1990, the Executive Committee met in a special session to dismiss Shakleford and Martin. Executive Committee president Harold Bennett had refused to carry out an earlier order by the officers of the Executive Committee to demand their resignations. Behind closed doors guarded by armed, off-duty Nashville police officers, the two long time Southern Baptist journalists were fired. They were given six months' salary and accrued vacation in their severance package. No specific charges against the two journalists were released by the committee.

Moderates incorporated the Associated Baptist Press on the same day "to serve as a trusted source of Baptist information."[46] Spokesmen for the Associated Baptist Press said they would be a "free" press, an obvious reference to the fact that reporters for the Baptist Press are employed by and responsible to the persons, agencies, and trustees who hired them and pay their salaries.

Baptists Today, an independent Baptist periodical that had begun as *SBC Today* in 1983, became known as a source where Baptists could receive an unbiased and fuller account of news within the Southern Baptist Convention and the wider Baptist family.[47]

John E. Brymer, in a 1993 editorial in the *Florida Baptist Witness* titled "The Denominational Press: Imagemaker or Truthseeker," said many people believe the role of the "religious press" more as imagemaker than truthseeker. He cited Edwin Young, president of the Southern Baptist Convention, who questioned the value of "investigative reporting" in the religious press. Brymer cautioned Southern Baptists not to succumb to the desire to report only the good news.[48]

Larry Lewis, then president of Hannibal-LaGrange College in Hannibal, Missouri, wrote in the foreword to James Hefley's second volume of *The Truth in Crisis*, "A free press goes hand in hand with soul freedom and the priesthood of the believer. We who are heads of denominational institutions may not always appreciate the media, except when they are saying good things about us, but we need press scrutiny from all side. . . . A free press keeps us on our toes and aware of that responsibility."[49] Lewis had obviously changed his mind, when, as Home Mission Board president, he began deleting portions of and radically changing the Home Mission's Board *A Study of Freemasonry*.

ELDER FORCED TO TAKE EARLY RETIREMENT

Baptist Sunday School Board president Lloyd Elder was forced to take early retirement in January 1991 rather than face being fired after several years in a feud with board trustees. Associated Baptist Press reported that James Larry Holly, a trustee for the Sunday School Board, wrote a letter to all board trustees critical of Elder, which resulted in an hour-long discussion of a motion to fire Elder in August 1969. The motion was withdrawn.[50] In a letter to Interfaith Witness Department missionary William E. Gordon, Jr., after Gordon wrote a critique of Holly's first volume of *The Southern Baptist Convention and Freemasonry*, Holly stated that he "wrote the syllabus which ultimately resulted in Lloyd Elder's resignation."[51] Elder was charged with: (1) fiscal irresponsibility even though Sunday School Board assets increased from $133 million to $180 million during his presidency; (2) unethical conduct for allegedly tape-recording phone conversations, a charge Elder denies; and for (3) bias in a centennial history of the Sunday School Board written by Leon McBeth, a thorough researcher and distinguished Professor of Church History at Southwestern Baptist Theological Seminary in Fort Worth.[52] Elder was specifically criticized for allowing McBeth to examine all of the board's records, including those involving lawsuits against the board, during the past one hundred years. McBeth was accused of writing an unbalanced manuscript that would fan the flames of controversy in the convention. McBeth's book was also said to present Elder's administration in a light too favorable for the trustees. They paid McBeth for writing the manuscript and then ordered all copies, except one, destroyed.

TRUSTEES FIRE RUSSELL DILDAY

At their March 1994 meeting, trustees abruptly fired Russell Dilday, 63, president of Southwestern Baptist Theological Seminary, after he refused to accept early retirement. Rumors had circulated for more than a week that Dilday would be fired if he refused the offer of early retirement. Two letters had been prepared by trustees, one if Dilday took early retirement and one if he were fired. The vote came on preprinted ballots in a closed-door meeting. After the vote Dilday was escorted off campus and the locks on his office door were immediately changed.

Dilday was quoted as asking on "what charges, what rationale" was he being fired. He said trustee chairman Ralph Pulley told him, "We don't need a reason. We can do it. We have the votes and we will." Later, Pulley said, "We just felt like the institution needed new leadership to move into the twenty-first century."[53]

Dilday's firing led columnist Roddy Stinson to write,

There may be a group meaner than Southern Baptist fundamentalists but you would have to go to jackal/hyena/wild dog country to find it.

First, the fundamentalists single out their prey.

Then, they attack in a pack.

Most of them—particularly the ministers—seem emotionally and psychologically incapable of anything other than mob action.

The pattern is so predictable that the fundamentalists' savaging of Russell Dilday hardly is news.

Whether on an African savanna, on an urban street or in a Southern Baptist boardroom, a gang is a gang is a gang.[54]

FORMATION OF THE COOPERATIVE BAPTIST FELLOWSHIP

In May 1991, after twelve years of fundamentalist victories at the annual meeting of the Southern Baptist Convention, moderate Southern Baptists formed their own organization, the Cooperative Baptist Fellowship.[55] Cecil Sherman, pastor of the 2,300-member Broadway Baptist Church in Fort Worth, was elected executive director in May 1992.[56] The Fellowship gives Southern Baptists and Southern Baptist churches a vehicle to support missionaries, schools, and agencies while remaining within the Southern Baptist Convention. It has experienced phenomenal growth since its incorporation. Its receipts totaled $12,219,752 in 1993 and the Fellowship had commissioned forty-one missionaries by May 1994.

Citing his concern about the Foreign Mission Board's direction and his freedom to lead it, president Keith Parks retired in October 1992. A month later, Parks, with over thirty-eight years experience in Southern Baptist missions, announced he had accepted an offer to direct the global missions program of the Cooperative Baptist Fellowship.[57]

The Cooperative Baptist Fellowship holds an annual assembly each year. Moderate Baptists in several states have formed active statewide fellowships.

In reflection, Sherman and Baptist theologian Walter Shurden gave reasons why they believe the moderate movement failed in the Southern Baptist Convention.[58] Even as fundamentalist presidents and trustees were elected each year, moderate Southern Baptists continued to believe that the fundamentalist takeover attempt would collapse before it succeeded in taking control of the Convention and its institutions. Their attitude was that this new movement would soon pass into history; it was best to wait until that happened. They remembered that other groups have arisen with grand schemes, only to die a quick death. After all, the pendulum had always swung back. Denial was in vogue. Many moderates felt they could handle the fundamentalists. Others wanted to avoid any hint of what might be perceived as an organized political movement, even though the fundamentalist movement was such an organization. Politics was repugnant; it was somehow less than morally right within the Christian church. Others, knowing that fundamentalists never saw a fight they didn't enjoy, thought the fundamentalists would eventually turn on each other and self-destruct. Too many influential pastors remained silent; in the Southern Baptist Convention influential pastors receive a larger hearing than any other group of people. Too many thought the fight for control of the national organization would never affect them in the local church. The few moderates willing to organize were ill-prepared and ill-equipped to lead such an effort. A deaf ear was turned to those few leaders willing to lead; followers did not follow well. The effort was divided because of different interests. Moderates were naturally to the left of the fundamentalists. In Southern Baptist life, to be to the left is to be liberal. Even the most conservative Southern Baptists were said to be somehow demoniacally influenced by "liberals" if they supported the moderate movement. Some thought the fundamentalists would mellow once they got control of the Convention. They tried to make peace with the new fundamentalist leadership. It was an uneasy peace because trust had been an early casualty in the controversy. Increasingly, moderates were forced out of leadership positions by early retirements, resignations, or outright terminations. As history shows, the fundamentalists had a sophisticated and effective plan, using computer networks, local church rallies often with an evangelistic theme, and busing to get voters to the annual conventions. Sensational rhetoric about liberals who didn't believe the Bible and the coming judgment were powerful motivators. Baptist historian Bill Leonard summed up the fundamentalists' success, "Southern Baptist fundamentalists are masters of populist rhetoric, learned in brush arbors and tent meetings but perfected under the bright lights of Christian broadcasting."[59] The fundamentalists' victories proved the obvious: that a well-organized, well-orchestrated, well-financed, well-defined campaign with catchy slogans can turn public opinions and win elections. By the time the moderates realized the pendulum would not swing back,[60] the fundamentalist train was at full steam; nothing could stop it.

Sherman summarizes his discussion of why the moderate movement failed:

> Moderates did not have enough moral energy to win. We could not bring ourselves to use moral language to describe our cause. Truth was butchered. We said nothing. Good people were defamed. We were silent. Baptist principles were mangled and Baptist history was replaced, rewritten. All the while, teachers who could have written about the problems in calling the Bible inerrant, did not. And preachers who could have called us to arms said nothing. The want of moral energy was the undoing of the Moderate movement.[61]

Fundamentalists saw this lack of moral energy as indicative of no clear vision.

The Cooperative Baptist Fellowship supports a number of moderate Baptist organizations. Southern Baptist Women in Ministry was formed in 1983 to affirm women ministering in Southern Baptist churches. Smyth & Helwys was founded as a moderate publishing house in 1990 to provide books by Baptist authors and age-graded Sunday School literature, called *Formations*. The Baptist Center for Ethics, was formed by former Christian Life Commission staff member Robert Parham, in 1991. The Baptist Theological Seminary at Richmond, Virginia, opened in 1991 with thirty-two students. The George W. Truett Theologial Seminary was incorporated in 1991 on the Baylor University campus in Waco, Texas; classes opened in 1994. The Whisitt Baptist Heritage Society was formed in 1992. The Fellowship supports the Baptist Joint Committee for Public Affairs in Washington, D.C., which was defunded by the Southern Baptist Convention in 1991. The Fellowship continued the funding of the Baptist Theological Seminary in Switzerland, whose Southern Baptist support of $365,000 had been eliminated by Foreign Mission Board trustees.

While resisting efforts to become a new Baptist denomination, the Cooperative Baptist Fellowship has become an avenue for Baptists, dissatisfied with the fundamentalist control of the Convention, to support missions, education, and evangelism around the world.

THE FUTURE

With control of the Southern Baptist Convention agencies and institutions realized, fundamentalists have begun a strategy of seeking to elect people sympathetic to their cause in the Baptist state conventions. The first of these "forums" was held in Memphis, Tennessee, in April 1992. A second meeting was held in Nashville, Tennessee, in February 1993. Another meeting was held in Louisville, Kentucky, in October 1993, a few weeks prior to the annual meetings of the Baptist state conventions. Spokesman Perry Ellis of Dallas, executive director of the Texas Baptist Conservative Fellowship, said the meeting was "for fellowship and understanding what we're facing in our convention." He denied there was a concentrated effort to strategize in each state convention. Ellis specifically criticized the Cooperative Baptist Fellowship who, he said, "are spiriting away our Southern Baptist churches."[62]

Churches leaving the Southern Baptist Convention, or at least redirecting their mission offerings, has been a concern of fundamentalists for years. Fundamentalist Sam Cathey said that those who did not believe in the inerrancy of the Bible were not true Southern Baptists. He challenged those who disagreed, "Why don't you just get out . . . and as you go, don't take any of our churches with you!"[63]

These statements about "our" Southern Baptist churches support George W. Cornell's observation that the historical principle of the autonomy of the local Baptist church is being replaced by a more authoritarian hierarchy. Every Southern Baptist and every Southern Baptist church is completely free to contribute to any cause that they wish and to redirect their contributions if they choose.

The Associated Baptist Press reported that at least fifteen of the top Southern Baptist Convention fundamentalist leaders held a private meeting at a downtown Atlanta hotel on April 21, 1994. The meeting was called because of concern about fallout over the firing of Southwestern Seminary president Russell Dilday in March and the announced that Jim Henry, pastor of First Baptist Church, Orlando, would run for Southern Baptist Convention president against the fundamentalists' handpicked candidate, Fred Wolfe, pastor of Cottage Hill Baptist Church, Mobile, Alabama. Paul Pressler, Paige Patterson, and four recent Convention presidents were among those present for the seven-hour meeting.[64] Bailey Smith, one of the recent presidents in attendance, said sympathy for Dilday likely would translate into votes for Henry, but added that he did not think it would change the outcome of the election.[65]

The question "Will there be a split?" has been asked thousands of times. As early as the mid-1920s, T. T. Martin of Mississippi called for a split in the Southern Baptist Convention to avoid "fearful division and strife."[66] In the mid 1970s, some fundamentalist pastors threatened to pull their churches out of the Southern Baptist Convention unless their concerns about liberalism in the denomination were addressed. Preparing for the 1981 Southern Baptist Convention in Los Angeles, the Baptist Press spoke of a "blood-letting," a "shootout," an "angry, knock-down battle" that would "produce a split or further polarization."[67]

Although not new, discussion about a split in or "splintering" of the Southern Baptist Convention can be heard at denominational meetings and in hallways of agency headquarters. No one knows if or when this will occur. The success of the Cooperative Baptist Fellowship and the at least temporary stagnation of offerings to the Cooperative Program, Lottie Moon Offering for Foreign Missions, and the Annie Armstrong Offering for Home Missions suggests that many Southern Baptists are withholding or redirecting their mission offerings. Whether these Baptists would be willing to leave the Southern Baptist Convention is a question which they may be forced to answer in the near future.

A much more likely scenario is that persons and churches contributing to the Cooperative Baptist Fellowship will be expelled by action of the Southern Baptist Convention. Messengers at the 1994 Southern Baptist Convention in Orlando voted to "direct" SBC agencies to decline funds from the Cooperative Baptist Fellowship, an action which will force Baptists to make difficult decisions.[68]

CHRISTIAN RECONSTRUCTIONISM

As a postscript to this chapter, one other growing movement should be discussed. Christian Reconstructionism, also called dominion theology or "theonomy," began as a movement in the early 1960s among Calvinist Presbyterian evangelicals and has attracted a growing, dedicated following. It is a continuation of the "New Israel" motif that has been an undercurrent throughout the history of this nation. Dominion theology is based on Genesis 1:28: "God blessed them, and God said to them, 'Be fruitful and multiply, and fill the earth and subdue it; and have dominion over the fish of the sea and over the birds of the air and over every living thing that moves upon the earth.' " Theonomy, meaning "God's law," is the belief that a Christian must obey "every jot and tittle of God's law" in both the Old and New Testaments.[69]

Founded by Rousas John Rushdoony (1916–   ), Reconstructionism proposes "Christianizing America" by inaugurating the sovereignty of God and His Old Testament laws into every aspect of individual and corporate life. The death penalty would be required of a number of offenses: murder, kidnapping, adultery, incest, homosexuality, premarital sex with virgins, witchcraft, incorrigible delinquency in children, blasphemy, propagation of false doctrines, and sacrificing to false gods.[70] Career criminals would be executed and thieves would repay victims through the reinstitution of "biblical slavery" until the theft was repaid; there would be no need for prisons. Atheists and adherents of other religions would not be tolerated. Home schooling and/or Christian schools should replace public schools, which are said to be filled with "humanists" and "humanistic teachings." The federal government would be abolished; democracy is "heresy."[71] The U.S. Constitution is a pagan document. Tithing will replace taxes. If someone disagrees with Reconstructionism, they are liberals or "perhaps not even Christian."[72] Gossip would be illegal, as would unisex fashions. There "is no middle ground, no neutral point between saints and sinners."[73] These goals will be accomplished as Christians are educated about the issues and then take control through the political process.

As one might suspect, Reconstructionism is well received by persons in the extreme religious right. Rousas Rushdoony, an ordained Presbyterian minister, and his son-in-law, Gary North, have repeatedly appeared on television programs with Jerry Falwell, Pat Robertson, and D. James Kennedy. Robertson's CBN University uses a number of Reconstructionist books as textbooks.[74] William Hatfield, writing in *Southern Baptist Public Affairs*, finds Reconstructionism is "not inherently anti-Baptistic."[75]

Most fundamentalists, including Falwell, Robertson, and Kennedy, cannot be called Reconstructionists because dominion theology is postmillennial, while most fundamentalists are premillennial. Postmillennialism is the belief that the Church can usher in the millennial (thousand-year) Kingdom of God prior to Christ's Second Coming. Premillennialism is the belief that society will continue to turn against God until Christ Himself returns to end human history as we know it and usher in the millennium. Still, Fundamentalists and Reconstructionists agree on a number of issues concerning public schools, crime and punishment, morality, and lack of toleration of those who disagree with them. Much of Reconstructionism is appealing to a growing number of fundamentalists within the Southern Baptist Convention.

4 Millennialism and Apocalyptism

Said John Bisagno, pastor of the First Baptist Church in Houston, Texas, in 1978, "Ecologically, sociologically, politically, financially, prophetically, everything points toward the next few years as the end of time."[1]

Millennialism has been a hope within the Christian community since Christ's disciples asked Him if He would then restore the Davidic kingdom to Israel (Acts 1:6). Christians in every generation since then have found hints, real or imagined, in apocalyptic literature and historical events that the end was near. For some, it was and is an obsession. The end of the present millennium and the arrival of a new millennium has raised new interests in the persistent millennial hope.

APOCALYPTIC LITERATURE

The word *apocalyptic* is a transliteration of the Greek word *apokalyptein*, meaning to uncover, disclose, or reveal. The word describes writings employing symbolic language to speak of divine truth. Apocalyptic literature has been a popular type of literature since as early as the sixth century B.C. The most famous piece of apocalyptic literature for Christians is the Revelation to the Apostle John, where apocalypse, or revelation, is the first word in the text.

Ezekiel and Daniel are other well-known apocalyptic books. Most apocalyptic writings date from 200 B.C. to A.D. 300. They include the extrabiblical 1 Enoch, 2 Enoch, 4 Ezra, 2 Baruch, and the Apocalypse of the Virgin Mary.[2]

Characteristic of symbolic literature, apocalypses use coded speech, in which animals, numbers, and natural events are given special meaning. Later writers redefine the symbols and give them additional meanings, thus piling meanings on top of meanings. This practice has led popular author Hal Lindsey to interpret Ezekiel 39:6, "I will send fire on Magog and on those who live securely in the coastlands," as referring to a nuclear war between Russia (Magog) and the United States (the coastlands).[3]

Apocalypses may instruct individuals how to live based on secrets revealed within the texts. For example, 4 Ezra speaks of "secret" works for the last days. Apocalyptic eschatology, or teaching about the "last days," tends towards dualism, this age and the age to come, good and evil, God and Satan. The immense popularity of recent books on end-time theories stems from the fact the people "have been obsessed with the desire to know what is going to happen in the future."[4]

Many scholars believe apocalyptic thinking arises in societies or subcultures within larger societies when those individuals feel challenged or threatened by external attacks or persecutions. The Revelation to John, for example, was written in the last decade of the first Christian century when Christians faced persecution and death at the hands of Roman authorities. The Revelation offered hope for the future in the form of a millennial Kingdom of God.

EARLY MILLENNIALISM

In the second half of the second century, a Phrygian convert to Christianity named Montanus began proclaiming the immediate advent of the New Jerusalem predicted in the Revelation to John (Rev. 21:2). As the self-appointed prophet for the last days, Montanus encouraged his followers to expect persecution, to separate from the world, to practice an ascetic lifestyle, and to purify the church so she would be a fit bride for the returning Christ. Although his millennialism was condemned and his followers virtually excommunicated in A.D. 230, Montanism, as his millennialism came to be known, was influential across much of the Mediterranean world for more than a century.

The preeminent theologian of the early church, Augustine (354–430) rejected the millennialism of his day. His *The City of God*, written between 413 and 426, was free of end-time prophecies and predictions of a literal, earthly, millennial reign of Christ. Using an allegorical interpretation, Augustine argued that millennial fulfillment was a present reality for Christians. His vision was accepted by the Council of Ephesus in 431 when earlier millennial views of a sensual, earthly reign of Christ were condemned.

The approach of the year 1000 generated a renewed interest in popular millennialism, just as the approach of the year 2000 has generated the current interest in end-time prophecies. The year 1260 was another popular apocalyptic date. Using the forty-two months mentioned in Revelation 13:5, it was calculated that forty-two months equaled 1260 days, if a month is thirty days. Using the popular transposition that a day refers to a prophetic year, the year 1260 was believed to be the beginning of a new age, called the Age of the Spirit, by the monk Joachim of Fiore (c.1135–1202). The recapture of Jerusalem in 1229 contributed to the popularization of this prediction. King Frederick II (1194–1250) was called *Stupor Mundi* ("The Amazement of the World"); he was named king of Germany at age 2 and king of Italy at age 4. He was named Holy Roman emperor in 1215 and king of Jerusalem in 1229. He was widely believed to be the "Emperor of the Last Days." Some held that Frederick II, who died in 1250, would return in 1260 to reform the government and establish righteousness.[5] Later, the myth arose that Frederick II would return as the Antichrist.

Apocalypticism was used to fuel support for the Crusades between 1097 and 1270. Driving the Muslims out of Jerusalem and the Holy Land was seen as essential to prepare for the New Jerusalem and the Second Coming of Christ. Both Muslims and Jews were said to be agents of Satan and the Antichrist; campaigns against both faiths were conducted to prepare for the end time.

Like modern apocalypticists, who point to AIDS as a sign of divine judgment, apocalypticists in the mid-fourteenth century pointed to the Black Death as a sign of divine judgment.

The Anabaptist movement, which began in Zurich in 1523, stressed the rebaptism of adult believers, personal piety, toleration, pacifism, separation from the world, separation of church and state, and the primacy of Scripture. Some Anabaptists were millennialists and militant in their beliefs concerning the end times. One Anabaptist, Melchior Hoffman, came to believe that the New Jerusalem would arise in Strasbourg. Another Anabaptist, Jan Matthys, proclaimed Munster as the site of the New Jerusalem. Matthys prophesied that the end of the world would occur on Easter Sunday, April 5, 1534. The end of the world came on that day for Matthys and a small company of followers when they were killed while attacking a stronger force besieging the city.

John of Leyden (Jan Beukelszoon) (1509–1536), who had been rebaptized by Matthys, announced he was the king of the "New Zion" and Messiah after Matthys's death. He instituted a community of goods where property and possessions were shared equally by the entire commune and, at God's command (so he said), polygamy. He took Matthys's widow and several teenage girls as wives and executed men and women who resisted his teachings. Beukelszoon was later captured by the Bishop of Munster. He and two followers were publicly tortured and killed with red-hot irons after being paraded about in chains. After Beukelszoon's death, Anabaptists turned to more peaceful and moderate leaders such as the Dutch Anabaptist Menno Simons (1496–1561), eventually taking the name *Mennonites* after Menno Simons.

While opposing the Anabaptists' attempt to usher in the Kingdom of God by force and their emphasis on millennialism, Martin Luther (1483–1546) and John Calvin (1509–1564) linked the Pope with the Antichrist. This alleged link is found in current apocalyptic literature.[6] Christopher Angelos of Oxford University identified Mohammed as the Antichrist in 1624. Puritans identified the Antichrist with Church of England bishops. Others identified Charles I or the Archbishop of Canterbury, William Laud, as the Antichrist. A 1640 pamphlet calculated that "Will Laud" totaled 666, the number of the beast in Revelation 13:18. Still later, Oliver Cromwell was given the number. The year 1666 was given apocalyptic significance; every thunderstorm in 1666 brought expectations of the end. John Napier, the inventor of logarithms, predicted the end of the world in 1688.

EARLY AMERICAN MILLENNIALISM

Millennialism has been an inherent part of the settlement and expansion of the American republic since its beginning. It brought a growing sense that the New World and, more specifically, the United States was "a new Israel," "a new Eden," "the Lord's Chosen Nation," and mankind's great hope. The Puritan migration to Massachusetts, the First and Second Great Awakenings, the expansion of the nation to the Pacific, the Union victory in the Civil War, the defeat of Germany in World War I, and the defeat of Germany, its Allies, and Japan in the Second World War convinced many people of the "Manifest Destiny" of this nation.

This millennial hope led John Cotton (1584–1652), minister of Boston's First Church, to predict the end of the Antichrist's reign in 1655. Boston minister Increase Mather suggested King Philip's War (1675–1676) between the colonists and the Indians was foretold in the red horse in Revelation 6:4. Increase Mather's son Cotton (1663–1728) predicted the end of the world in 1697 and that the New Jerusalem would be located in New England. When 1697 passed, Mather selected 1716 and then 1736 as the end of the world.

Historians record two great revivals in this nation. The first, simply called the Great Awakening, began in New Jersey in 1726 under the preaching of Dutch Calvinist T. J. Frelinghuysen (1691–1747). Later, revival was experienced in 1734–1735 under the quiet, but penetrating, Calvinist preaching of Jonathan Edwards (1703–1758), minister of the Northampton Congregational Church in Massachusetts.

The one man credited with uniting these and other regional outbreaks of revival into a "Great Awakening" was the itinerant evangelist George Whitfield (1714–1770). Unlike Edwards, who spent up to thirteen hours a day preparing two sermons a week, Whitfield preached up to twenty sermons a week. If Edwards was a scholar and thinker, Whitfield was an actor who relied on his gifted voice, gestures, and style to overcome his lack of preparation.

As expected, these revivals brought apocalyptic speculation. In 1723, Edwards began a journal on the apocalypse. About six dozen New England ministers hailed the Awakening as a sign that the Kingdom of God was at hand in 1743. The French surrender in Canada in 1760 led Samuel Langdon of Portsmouth, New Hampshire, to announce that "Babylon the great is fallen" (Rev. 18:2). Someone else predicted earthquakes and wars in the 1750s with the end of the world coming in 1763; another thought the end would come in 1766, while Yale's Timothy Dwight speculated that the world wouldn't end until the year 2000. King George of England replaced the pope as the Antichrist during the Revolutionary War, when it was announced that the words *Royal Supremacy in Great Britain* totaled 666 in both the Greek and Hebrew languages.

Postmillennialism, the belief that the Church could usher in the millennium peace prior to Christ's Second Coming, generally held sway during the Great Awakening. But, the revivals of the Great Awakening ended in 1760. They were followed by forty years of "spiritual deadness, a period of religious and moral indifference."[7] Baptist church historian Robert Baker says that only seven percent of Americans were professed Christians at the close of the Revolutionary War in 1783.[8] Was this lowest and most critical period in American religious life caused by exhaustion from or in reaction against the excesses of the Great Awakening? Does evangelical fundamentalism today face the same verdict?

The Second Great Awakening (1797–1825) had a more lasting effect. The first missionary societies sprang into existence as a result of the Second Great Awakening. Bible societies were formed beginning in Philadelphia in 1808 to promote Christian knowledge and education.

Moral reform, beginning among students at Yale College, was stressed as a necessary part of true conversion. Using alcohol and profanity and breaking the Sabbath (Sunday) were primary targets. Temperance societies were formed in dozens of cities to fight for total abstinence from alcohol. Joseph Smith, founder of the Mormon Church, gave the prohibition against the use of alcohol the weight of Scripture in his *Word of Wisdom* in 1833. Dancing and going to theaters became suspect. Lotteries, which had financed the erection of many church buildings, were banned.

Humanitarian efforts were begun. Concern for the poor, the physically handicapped, mentally ill, and those in slavery were a direct result of the Second Great Awakening.

Two other outgrowths of the Second Great Awakening and the growing sense of the new Israel motif inherent in the founding of the American Republic must be mentioned: growth of popular denominations and rise of sectarian groups.

A number of sects emphasizing millennial themes sprang up during and immediately after the Second Great Awakening. Church historian Sydney Ahlstrom cites Leland Jamison who found four emphases in these millennial sects: (1) perfectionism or the belief that a person can or must achieve complete holiness for salvation; (2) universalism or the belief that Christ's sacrifice provided ultimate salvation to all mankind; (3) illuminism or the belief that God would give additional revelation in the latter days; and (4) millennialism or the belief in the immediate return of Jesus Christ and the advent of his Kingdom.[9] Millennialism is the most important emphasis in this discussion.

Although living before the Second Great Awakening, Emanuel Swedenborg's (1688–1771) influence is seen in many sects and movements that appeared after his death, including Transcendentalism, the Brook Farm commune, Joseph Smith, Mary Baker Eddy, and dozens of other lesser known, short-lived religious experiments. Swedenborg's influence extended far beyond his relatively few followers in his Church of New Jerusalem. Swedenborg, who believed he enjoyed "perfect inspiration,"[10] saw himself as an eschatological figure proclaiming that the Second Coming was found in his allegorical interpretations of the Bible.

Ann Lee Staley (1736–1784) brought the United Society of Believers in Christ's Second Coming—commonly known as the Shakers because of their practice of ecstatic dancing—to the United States in 1774. Among her unique teachings was that she was the feminine Second Coming of Christ. The sect reached its greatest size between 1830 and 1850 when about 6,000 members were found in nineteen communities. Because of "Mother" Ann Lee's interpretation of Mark 12:25, celibacy was required of all members, which adversely affected the continued growth of the sect.

Alexander Campbell (1788–1866) founded the Campbellites or Disciples of Christ in 1827. The imminent Second Coming of Christ was a central tenet, reflected in the name of one of his periodicals, *The Millennial Harbinger*.

Joseph Smith (1805–1844) founded the most successful millennial sect in Fayette, New York, in 1830. First called the Church of Christ, his movement soon took the more millennial-sounding name the Church of Jesus Christ of

Latter-day Saints, reflecting his belief that he was living in the last days prior to Christ's return. Smith was influenced by the Second Great Awakening as a teenager in western New York. Surrounded by strong anti-Catholic and anti-Masonic feelings and questions about Indian origins (Were American Indians part of the "ten lost tribes of Israel?"), Smith claimed to have discovered a lost Scripture, called the Book of Mormon, which dealt with those issues most on the minds of his contemporaries. *The Book of Mormon*, first published on March 26, 1830, claims Indians are descendants of Jews who sailed to America about 600 B.C. Repeatedly in the Book of Mormon, Smith speaks of "secret combinations," saying God does not "will that man should shed blood, but in all things hath forbidden it, from the beginning of man. And now I, Moroni, do not write the manner of their oaths and combinations" (Ether 8:19–20). "And it came to pass that they did have their signs, yea, their secret signs, and their secret words; and this that they might distinguish a brother who had entered into the covenant" (Helaman 6:21). At another place in the *Book of Mormon*, Smith speaks of the "secret society of Gadianton" who are "wicked and abominable robbers" (3 Nephi 3:9–11). In an apparent reference to Masonic penalties, Smith has Satan telling Cain to "Swear unto me by thy throat, and if thou tell it thou shalt die; . . . that they tell it not; for if they tell it, they shall surely die" (Moses 5:29).[11]

While Smith was writing the Book of Mormon, one of the most famous anti-Masonic uprisings was taking place in western New York. This uprising centered around the disappearance of William Morgan on September 12, 1826, in Canandaigua, New York, less than fifteen miles from Smith's home. In an interesting side note, Morgan's wife later became the plural wife of Mormons George W. Harris and Joseph Smith.[12]

Later, while enjoying relative peace in the Mississippi River town named Nauvoo by Smith, a lodge was established by Illinois Grand Master Abraham Jonas on October 15, 1841.[13] This, in spite of objections from Bodley Lodge No. 1 in Quincy, about forty miles south of Nauvoo. It is speculated by some historians that Jonas needed the large Mormon vote to run for governor of the state.

Joseph Smith was raised a Master Mason on March 15–16, 1842. Some speculate Smith desired a Masonic lodge in Nauvoo in an effort to bind his followers together after word leaked out concerning his newly introduced polygamist practices. The requirement of secrecy within Freemasonry, Smith hoped, would prevent husbands from complaining when he made advances on their wives.[14] It would appear that Jonas and Smith used each other to further their own goals.

Joseph's older brother, Hyrum, had been raised a Master Mason in the Mount Moriah Lodge No. 112 in Palmyra, New York. Other Mormons, such as

John C. Bennett, had been raised Master Masons prior to the move to Nauvoo. The Nauvoo lodge received 345 petitions between March 15 and August 11, 1842, when it was suspended. By August 1842, the Nauvoo lodge was the largest Masonic lodge in Illinois.[15] The suspension was lifted in November 1842.

The Nauvoo lodge, along with the Helm, Nye, and Keokuk lodges, was again suspended in October 1843 for "gross un-Masonic behavior." The Nauvoo Masons refused to suspend their Masonic work, having already incorporated several Masonic signs, grips, symbols, and rituals into the Mormon temple ceremonies in May 1842, two months after Smith was raised a Master Mason. Smith later claimed that Freemasonry had been corrupted, had lost its original goals, and that he had been appointed by God to lead "Masonry to the higher degrees."[16]

Baptist William Miller (1782–1840), after studying the Book of Daniel, became convinced that Christ would return in 1843, began another millennial sect. Hundreds of thousands accepted Miller's computation and began to prepare for the Second Coming of Christ. However, the Millerite movement collapsed on October 22, 1844, the last date set by the leadership. In the chaos of the "Great Disappointment," a Portland, Maine, teenager, Ellen G. Harmon (1827–1915), began to receive heavenly visions that reorganized the movement, which took the name *Seventh-day Adventists*. Harmon, who married James White in 1846, was believed by her followers to be endowed with inspired counsel from God. She wrote over 5,000 articles and fifty-three volumes on most Adventist teachings, among them texts on following the Jewish dietary regulations concerning the use of pork. John H. Kellogg, an Adventist vegetarian, made Battle Creek, Michigan, the breakfast food capital of the nation.

A Methodist minister, Fountain Pitts, delivered a day-long sermon at the U.S. Capitol in February 1857 detailing his understanding of biblical prophecy. Pitts argued that Russia would invade the United States and that the Battle of Armageddon or Harmagedon (Rev. 16:16) would be fought in the Mississippi River valley. According to Pitts, the United States, with God's intervention, would be victorious. With the victory, the millennium would arrive.

Wars often bring images of apocalyptic urgency. The Civil War was no different. The words of Julia Ward Howe became Union rallying words, but they could have been used by the Confederacy as easily.

I have seen him in the watch-fires of a hundred circling camps;
They have builded him an altar in the evening dews and damps;
I have read his righteous sentence by the dim and flaring lamps;
His day is marching on.

I have read a fiery gospel, writ in burnished rows of steel,
"As ye deal with my contemners, so with you my grace shall deal";
Let the Hero, born of woman, crush the serpent with his heel,
Since God is marching on.[17]

TWENTIETH-CENTURY MILLENNIALISM

Both World War I and World War II brought tremendous impetus to end-time prophecy, date setting, and numerology. The European wars were seen as a prelude to Armageddon and the Second Coming of Christ. An avalanche of books, articles, and pamphlets poured out to make Armageddon a household word.

Wilhelm II (1859–1941) was the German Kaiser during World War I. That he might be the Antichrist was bolstered by the fact that *Kaiser* is the German form of the Latin word *caesar*, or emperor.

Dispensationalists are notoriously famous for changing their predictions as world events dictate. The capture of Syria and Palestine in 1917–1918, including Jerusalem, by British Field Marshall Lord Edmund H. H. Allenby and Major T. E. Lawrence (Lawrence of Arabia) produced a tidal wave of end-time prophecies. Darby's and the fundamentalists' dream of a long-awaited Jewish state was now a possibility. The use of combat planes during World War I was seen as fulfillment of Ezekiel 38:16: "You will come up against my people Israel, like a cloud covering the earth." In the 1950s, the "cloud" came to be seen as intercontinental ballistic missiles raining down on the earth. With the invention of television in the 1920s, dispensationalists found a fulfillment of the prophecy that "every eye" will see Christ when he returns (Revelation 1:7).

When Germany surrendered in 1918, the attention of the dispensationalists turned to the League of Nations, formed in 1920 with its headquarters in Geneva, Switzerland. To dispensationalists, the League of Nations was the forerunner, if not a fulfillment, of the apocalyptic ten-nation Roman Empire ruled by the Antichrist foretold in Daniel 7:1–28.

The Scopes "Monkey Trial" in Dayton, Tennessee in 1925 is one of the most famous and controversial legal cases in American history. High school teacher John T. Scopes was accused of violating Tennessee law prohibiting the teaching of evolution in public schools. The trial became a rallying point for dispensational fundamentalists, whose position in the trial was represented by William Jennings Bryan. The Scopes trial had little lasting effect, except in the minds of fundamentalists. Scopes's fine of $100 was overturned on appeal. The

Tennessee law prohibiting the teaching of evolution remained in effect until 1967, when the legislature abolished it.

The rise of Adolf Hitler to power in Germany in the 1920s caused some to see him as the Antichrist. Some numerologists found that the name *Hitler* added up to 666 if *A* was given the value of 100, *B* the value of 101, and so on. Hitler outlawed freedom of the press, labor unions, and political parties except his Nazi party when he was named chancellor in 1933. The Masonic fraternity in Germany was suppressed with the decree, "Jews, Freemasons and the ideological enemies of National Socialism."[18] People were imprisoned or shot on suspicion alone.

The favorite nominee for role of the Antichrist prior to and during World War II was the Italian fascist dictator Benito Mussolini. He urged the Italian people to rebuild the glories of ancient Rome. To dispensationalists, Mussolini's plan was nothing short of a fulfillment of biblical prophecy. The "icing on the cake" for many dispensationalists was Mussolini's compact with the Pope in 1929. Others contended that Hitler, Mussolini, and Soviet dictator Joseph Stalin were merely forerunners of the Antichrist.

The detonation of a nuclear weapon near Alamogordo, New Mexico, on July 16, 1945 brought on the nuclear age and a whole new scenario for dispensationalists. Suddenly, prophecies concerning nuclear weapons were found in the Bible (Joel 1:19–23, 31; Zechariah 14:12; 2 Peter 3:10; Revelation 6:12). For example, 2 Peter 3:10 reads, "But the day of the Lord will come like a thief, and then the heavens will pass away with a loud noise, and the elements will be dissolved with fire, and the earth and everything that is done on it will be disclosed." Prophecy conferences, radio programs, and books spelled out in excruciating detail the aftermath of a full-scale nuclear war as the fulfillment of biblical prophecy. While dispensationalists contended that only the Second Coming of Christ would end the nuclear threat, schoolchildren practiced ducking under their desks during nuclear drills. Families dug fallout shelters and local governments identified and stocked basements of buildings to house the general population when the nuclear exchange happened.

Popular author Hal Lindsey believes a leader of a ten-nation European Common Market will be the Antichrist who will usher in a one-world government. Lindsey wrote in 1980 that he believed the Antichrist is already living in Europe awaiting his opportunity to reveal himself.[19]

The former Soviet Union or Russia has played an essential part in end-time scenarios in the past seventy-five years. According to the conspiracists, Rosh (Ezekiel 28:2, NASV)[20] is an old spelling of modern Russia; Meshech and Tubal, in the same verse, refer to Moscow and Tobolsk, both Soviet cities.

Gog, also in the same verse, has been identified with Russia since John Nelson Darby proposed the connection in 1840. The Scofield Reference Bible, used by many Southern Baptist ministers, identified Gog with Russia. The fact that the Soviet Union was a major nuclear power that lay directly north of Israel fit well the biblical argument that Israel's enemy lay in "the remotest parts of the north" (Ezekiel 38:6). The Soviet Union has not always been cited as the biblical Gog. Early Christians considered Scythians, an Indo-European power centered northwest of the Black Sea from 600 B.C. until A.D. 100., as Gog. The Scythians were skilled horsemen (Ezekiel 38:4) whose attacks ranged south through Palestine into Egypt. Later, the Ottoman Turks were given the role.

That Israel's enemies are found in the north is commonly stated in the Bible. Jeremiah says Israel's adversaries will come from the north, "Out of the north disaster shall break out on all the inhabitants of the land. For now I am calling all the tribes of the kingdoms of the north" (Jeremiah 1:14–15), "for evil looms out of the north" (Jeremiah 6:1), and "Hear, a noise! it is coming—a great commotion from the land of the north to make the cities of Judah a desolation" (Jeremiah 10:22).

The directions of the compass are prominent in Masonic ritual, as they are in the Bible. The directions of the compass are cited in a discussion of the walls and gates of the chambers of the Temple (Ezekiel 40:20–41:12). The *Louisiana Masonic Monitor* says

> A Lodge has THREE SYMBOLIC LIGHTS. One of these is in the East, one in the West, and one in the South. There is no light in the North; because King Solomon's Temple, of which every Lodge is a representation, was placed so far North of the ecliptic that the sun and moon, at their meridian height, could dart no rays into the Northern part thereof. The North, therefore, we Masonically call a place of darkness.[21]

Referring to the Masonic reference to the north as "a place of darkness," Masonic critic A. Ralph Epperson cites Isaiah 14:13 and claims Masons associate the north with darkness because "the God of the Bible sits in the north."[22] Likewise, Cathy Burns says that "the Bible shows us that God's throne is in the NORTH."[23] She cites three verses to prove her argument: Psalm 48:102 [*sic*], 75:6–7, and Isaiah 14:12–14. Psalm 48:102 [*sic*] does not exist. Psalm 75:6–7 states, "For not from the east or from the west and not from the wilderness comes lifting up; but it is God who executes judgment, putting down one and lifting up another." The direction north is not mentioned in any context.

Epperson and Burns completely misinterpret Isaiah 14:12–16:

How you are fallen from heaven,
O Day Star, son of Dawn!
How you are cut down to the ground,
you who laid the nations low!

You said in your heart,
"I will ascend to heaven;
I will raise my throne above the stars of God;
I will sit on the mount of assembly on the heights of Zaphon;

I will ascend to the tops of the clouds,
I will make myself like the Most High."

But you are brought down to Sheol,
to the depths of the Pit.

Those who see you will stare at you,
and ponder over you:
"Is this the man who made the earth tremble,
who shook kingdoms."

Zaphon is a town situated north of Succoth in the Jordan Valley (Josh. 13:27). Zaphon can be translated as "north" as it is in Judges 12:1: "And the men of Ephraum gathered themselves together, and went northward." Compare that translation in the King James Version with Judges 12:1 in the New Revision Standard Version: "The men of Ephraim were called to arms, and they crossed to Zaphon." While Zaphon is translated as "north" or "northward" in the King James Version, the context of the verse does not support the interpretation that God's throne is in the north.

Biblical scholars are convinced that Isaiah made use of a myth from Canaanite religion to portray the fall of the king of Babylon. The myth speaks of a minor Canaanite deity, *Helal ben Shahar* (Day Star, son of Dawn), who tried to make himself like *'Elyon* (Most High), the chief Canaanite god who sat in the far north. The original inspiration for this myth probably came from the observation of the planet Venus rising as the morning star, only to be extinguished by the brighter sun.

Many Christians today believe Day Star is a reference to Satan or Lucifer. Italian biblical scholar Jerome (345–419) introduced the name *Lucifer* when he revised the Latin language Bible. His Vulgate became the official Roman Catholic Bible in 1546. The name was borrowed by Protestant translators and erroneously placed in the King James Version of the Bible. Modern translations, such as the New American Standard Version, the New Revised Standard Version, and the New International Version, have corrected this error. The name *Lucifer* has received additional support from Dante's *Inferno*, written in the early fourteenth century, and John Milton's *Paradise Lost*, written in 1667. Even the Douay version of the Roman Catholic Bible says, concerning Isaiah 14:12, "All this, according to the letter, is spoken of the king of Babylon. It may also be applied, in a spiritual sense, to Lucifer the prince of devils, who was created a bright angel, but fell by pride and rebellion against God."[24]

There is no biblical justification for arguing that "the God of the Bible sits in the north," as Epperson claims, or that "God's throne is in the NORTH," as Burns claims. An untruth repeated does not become truth. The reference to the "north," translated "Zaphon" in the New Revised Standard Version, refers to a mountain viewed as home of the gods in the Canaanite religion.[25] Psalm 48:3 speaks of Mount Zion or Jerusalem as the city where Yahweh can best be praised, as opposed to the north, probably a reference to Zaphon. The Psalmist asks, "Is Mount Zion in the far north?" The rhetorical answer is no; Mount Zion is Jerusalem.

Television evangelist Jerry Falwell, citing Ezekiel 38:12, "to seize spoil and carry off plunder," pointed out that if "sp" is removed from "spoil," one gets "oil." In 1979, Falwell speculated that an oil shortage would be the catalyst for the Soviet invasion of the Middle East.[26] Israel, of course, has few natural resources and only small amounts of oil and natural gas. "Spoil" in Ezekiel 38:12 could not refer to Israeli oil; crude oil and coal must be imported to meet energy needs. Russia, by contrast, has vast reserves of oil and natural gas. Falwell didn't think through his creative interpretation.

Gomer in Ezekiel 38:6 is believed by some apocalyptists to refer to Germany. The "kings from the east" in Revelation 16:12 are said to refer to China and perhaps Japan. China is currently said to be able to raise an army of two hundred million troops, exactly the number given in Revelation 9:16.

Television evangelist and former U.S. presidential candidate Pat Robertson predicted in a May 1982 broadcast, "I guarantee you by the fall of 1982 there is going to be a judgment on the world."[27] When he began looking at campaigning for the U.S. presidency in 1985, Robertson dropped his end of the world predictions.

Edgar Whisenant is the author of the two-million-copy best-seller, *88 Reasons Why the Rapture Will Be in 1988*. Unlike most end-time prophets, Whisenant set a specific date for the end of the world. Even though Jesus said no one knows the "day and hour" (Matthew 24:36), Whisenant argued it is possible to know the day and year. He dated the rapture between September 11 and 13, 1988, during the Jewish Rosh Hashanah. World War III would begin at sunset on October 3, 1988, when the Soviet Union invaded Israel. Using Psalm 90:10, "The days of our life are seventy years," Whisenant said the Soviet Union would be annihilated one hour later (Revelation 18:10), or exactly seventy years after the Bolshevik Revolution in the fall of 1917. Like other end-time prophets, Whisenant predicted nuclear winter, worldwide starvation, and millions of unburied bodies.

Whisenant's date (1988) was exactly forty years or "one generation" after the founding of the nation of Israel. Other date setters use the 1948 date to predict the end of the world. One obviously mistaken prophet predicted that the rapture, the time when Jesus would return to claim his followers, would occur in 1981. He arrived at 1981 by adding forty years to 1948 and subtracting seven years. Another date setter gave successive dates of 1976, 1980, 1988, 1989, and 1992, all said to be based on the 1948 date.[28] Whisenant's second effort to guess the end of the world was *The Final Shout–Rapture Report 1989*, published in 1989 after he admitted he had miscalculated the end of the world.

Rebuilding the Temple in Jerusalem is an integral part of dispensational fundamentalist apocalyptism. A significant barrier to building the Temple is the Mosque of Omar, which is situated on the original Temple site. Various theories have been given about how the mosque might be eliminated. Earthquakes, a misfired missle from Syria or Jordan, zapping the mosque with a laser, bombing by Jewish zealots have all been proposed. Unfortunately for dispensationalists, few Jews share this fantasy for a Temple. Muslims like the idea even less.

Reports have circulated for years that materials and money were being collected to build the Temple. The Baptist Record, published by the Mississippi Baptist Convention, reported in 1974 that construction was scheduled to begin that summer on "the first large, central Jewish house of worship in the Holy City since the destruction of the Temple 1,904 years ago."[29]

THE NUMBER OF THE BEAST: 666

The number "666" (Revelation 13:18) figures prominently in dispensational fundamentalist apocalyptism. Fanciful and imaginative mathematics have been and continue to be used to identify "the beast" of the Book of Revelation. The pope has most often been assigned the number by numerologists. In 1612, numerologists claimed the numerical value of *Romischer Papst* ("Roman Pope") equaled 666.[30] Napoleon's name was also said to total 666 "in Arabic if two letters were omitted."[31] Benito Mussolini, Adolf Hitler, Henry Kissinger, Anwar as-Sadat, and dozens of other political figures' names have been said to total 666.[32] John Kennedy received 666 votes in the 1956 Democratic convention.[33] The last names of the three 1968 Apollo 8 space mission (Lovell, Anders, and Borman) each had six letters, or 666.[34] The numerical value of former president of the Soviet Union Mikhail S. Gorbachev's name is said to be 1,332, or two times 666;[35] the birthmark on his forehead has reminded some of the mark on the forehead mentioned in Revelation 13:16. Another numerologist determined that the numerical value of the Visa credit card was 666.[36] Still another creative numerologist found that the numerical value of the word *computer* totaled 666, as does *New York City*.[37] Peter and Paul LaLonde, of *This Week in Bible Prophecy*, offered their new book, *Racing Toward the Mark of the Beast: Your Money, Computers and the End of the World*, to readers for $19.95. The advertisement announces, "Nearly 2,000 years ago the prophet John was told of a time when every man, woman and child on earth will be numbered and tracked . . . when every person will receive the Mark of the Beast . . . or face death!"[38] Another conspiracist added the digits of a Social Security number and the nine-digit ZIP code and found there were eighteen digits, or 6 + 6 + 6.[39] Others wondered aloud and in books if the Universal Product Code, a bar code using eleven digits and lines instituted in 1973, might be the mark of the beast.

Popular sensationalist Texe Marrs tells of an alleged NASA experiment where six rats were beheaded on a space shuttle mission "using a miniature guillotine." Marrs wonders if this "hellish demonstration" has anything to do with Revelation 20:4, "I saw the souls of them that were beheaded for the witness of Jesus?" Is Marrs saying mice have souls? He tells his readers that NASA is "riddled with evil Freemasonry." And then, he says, "In Revelation 13, we discover that the satanic number of the beast is triple 6's 666. Is it a coincidence," he asks, "that exactly six rats were chosen by NASA to be sacrificed under the bloody, space guillotine?" Marrs goes on to ask if this "grotesque experiment" is "a sadistic and arrogant boast of antichrist forces," "the shadow of things to come," or "some type of occultic cosmic theater?"[40]

THE SECOND COMING OF CHRIST

The immediacy of the Second Coming of Christ has been an integral part of fundamentalism from its beginning. Fundamentalism is essentially a millennial movement. Given fundamentalism's negativity toward society as a whole, the belief in the immediate return of Christ validates their values in the face of overwhelming secular inroads in society and the church. This belief affirms that the world will not continue to get worse and that the faithful will soon be rewarded for their faithfulness to the inerrant Word of God.

Christian apologist Francis A. Schaeffer, a popular writer among fundamentalists, speaks of the period since the 1920s as "a post-Christian world in which Christianity, not only in the number of Christians but in cultural emphasis and cultural result, is no longer the consensus or ethos of our society."[41]

Historian Sydney Ahlstrom speaks of the present period in American religious history as the "post-Protestant era." He contends the "Great Puritan Epoch in American history" came to an end in the 1960s.[42] The assassinations of John and Robert Kennedy and Martin Luther King, Jr., the Civil Rights Bill, the American withdrawal from Vietnam, the threat of nuclear war, the drug culture, the awakening of environmental awareness, the alleged death of God, the Beatles and Elvis Presley, the cancellation of the Asian Exclusion Act, television, the rise of movements from homosexual rights to women's rights, and dozens of other critical issues took their toll on Protestant America. Protestant America did not surrender in the face of these events; it simply became irrelevant in too many people's minds. It no longer provided answers to questions being asked of it. It refused to adapt its presentation to changing needs.

Millennialism appeals to individuals with a sense of alienation. This alienation may be political in which government is seen as anti-family, anti-Christian, anti–law and order. The alienation may be social, where fear that immigration has brought people with new ideas, habits, beliefs, and lifestyles into previously familiar neighborhoods. This alienation may be economic with conflict arising between socio-economic groups. Millennialism appeals to those who cannot or are not willing to adapt to the changes brought about by changing political, social, or economic realities.

Millennialism has been a popular theme within Southern Baptist life, as it has been in secular society, for nearly seventy-five years. But it has reached a crescendo in the past twenty-five years. Well-known pastor of the Bellevue Baptist Church in Memphis, Tennessee, R. G. Lee, now deceased, ended the 1969 Southern Baptist pastors' conference with his sermon "The Second Coming of Christ." The annual pastors' conference, held in connection with the annual Southern Baptist Convention, became a platform for end-time sermons.

At the 1978 Southern Baptist pastors' conference, John Bisagno, pastor of the First Baptist Church in Houston, told the crowd of 20,000 that "Ecologically, sociologically, politically, financially, prophetically, everything points toward the next few years as the end of time."[43] Bisagno repeated his belief that the time was right for the Antichrist's appearance in a sermon at the Southern Baptist Pastors' Conference in 1980.[44]

With this conviction of the approaching of the millennium, it became more important to give every person the opportunity to learn of the salvation available through Jesus Christ. Many religious groups recognized the power of television in reaching millions with their messages. One of the largest is Vision Interfaith Satellite Network (VISN). VISN, which advertised itself as the national faith and values cable TV network, began transmitting in 1988, and by 1992 VISN was available to over 12.8 million U.S. households. VISN is supported by fifty-four diverse faith groups, including the Church of Jesus Christ of Latter-day Saints (Mormons), the Episcopal Church, the Unitarian Universalist Association of Congregations, the United Methodist Church, the Christian Holiness Association, and the National Council of Churches of Christ in the USA.[45]

The Southern Baptist Convention's American Christian Television System (ACTS), troubled by financial difficulties since its inception, joined with VISN to share a single channel in October 1992. The combined network, known as VISN/ACTS, reached more than 20 million households. VISN/ACTS changed its name to the Faith and Values Channel in 1994.[46] The largest religious network is the Roman Catholic Eternal Word Television Network, which reaches 23 to 27 million households.[47]

In spite of this monumental effort, many dispensational premillenialists were and are convinced that the world can never be Christianized. Rather, the church will never be more than the faithful remnant. The anti-Masonic movement within the Southern Baptist Convention can be seen as an effort to force out those who are not a part of the "faithful remnant." Even the optimistic and worthy Southern Baptist goal of baptizing 500,000 people in the year 2000 is an admission of less than full victory because the U.S. population will increase by a number greater than the baptism goal in 2000.

To most people, all of the talk about the Antichrist, Gog and Magog, 666, and the sacrifice of six rats in space is too much. Paul Boyer says "twentieth-century prophecy popularizers often portray God as a cosmic playwright stage-managing a vast melodrama, shifting about a huge cast of puzzled and unwitting actors."[48] But to fundamentalists and dispensationalists, these everyday events and symbols in the Bible point to the fact that the stage is set for the final apocalyptic event that will occur in the immediate future.

5 Conspiracy Theories and Anti-Masons

There is an old saying that a lie (or rumor or hoax) can travel around the world before the truth can get its boots on.[1]

A CHAPTER ON CONSPIRACY THEORIES WAS REMOVED FROM *A STUDY OF FREEmasonry* during the editing process by Home Mission Board president Larry Lewis. Several of the individuals discussed in this chapter were included in the chapter removed from the original manuscript of the *Study*.

CONSPIRACY THEORIES

Conspiracy theories are popular with individuals seeking sensational answers to difficult or ambiguous issues in life, or to discredit an individual or organization. Conspiracy theories have been around since the beginning of recorded history.

Historian Justo Gonzalez finds that early Christians were accused of committing incest, eating their children, drinking blood, worshipping the sexual organs of their priests, and many similar things. For example, some critics claimed that after their *agape*, or love feasts, Christians held orgies. Other critics claimed a child was covered with flour during the Eucharist, as if a loaf of bread, before a neophyte was ordered to cut the child; its blood was then eaten. Since all present participated, they were forced to remain silent. Others critics argued that Christian teachers were ignorant people belonging to the lowest strata of society. They were said to appeal to others in the lowest strata of society.[2] To counter these sensational stories, Christian apologists such as Aristides, Justin Martyr, Athenagoras, and Theophilus of Antioch wrote "apologies" in defense of the Christian faith.

Early Baptists, who practiced immersion of converts, were accused by their critics of baptizing converts in the nude. To counter these falsehoods, Baptists added these words to their 1651 confession, "as many eye-witnesses can testify."[3]

Editor Bob E. Mathews reminds us of an old saying that a lie, a rumor, or a hoax can travel around the world before the truth can get its boots on. One such rumor is the report that atheist Madalyn Murray O'Hair has been granted a hearing before the Federal Communications Commission to remove religious broadcasts from radio and television. Smudged, poorly typed petitions asking people to make ten copies and send them to the FCC protesting the purported threat to religious broadcasts appear as regularly as back-to-school sales. The petitions claim that O'Hair "successfully eliminated the use of Bible reading and prayer from all public schools fifteen years ago." The U.S. Supreme Court ruled on school board–written prayers and required Bible reading in 1963, over thirty years ago. The petition has been circulating, basically unchanged, since 1978, which was fifteen years after the ruling. The petition was untrue in 1978, and it is still untrue. Even so, the FCC has received over twenty-one million letters from individuals concerned about this hoax. Mathews says, "Many pastors have been wise to check out the false story before allowing the petitions to be spread among church members."[4]

Since 1982, the Fortune 500 Procter & Gamble Company has been fighting a persistent rumor that the president of the company appeared on a television program, usually said to have been "Donahue," and announced that the company's profits were going to the Church of Satan. Poorly copied offsets have been distributed in churches across the nation warning readers not to buy an P&G products. Procter & Gamble's moon-and-stars trademark, which was registered in 1882, is said to be a Satanic symbol. The conspirators argue that by connecting the thirteen stars the numbers "666" can revealed. Procter & Gamble, frustrated in its attempt to stop the spread of the false rumor, has successfully sued dozens of people found distributing copies of the offset or otherwise spreading the rumor. The company sued a Kansas couple, who were independent Amway distributors, and won $75,000 in damages.[5]

John Broderick of Red Cloud, Nebraska, wrote to the editor of *The Red Cloud Chief* in March 1993 claiming that "the end of the world will fall upon mankind sometime between Sept. 15 and Sept. 27, 1994. Just prior to that, Sept. 6, 1994, the salvation plan of God will end, that is, there will be no hope of ever being accepted into God's grace every again." Broderick claimed the final tribulation began May 21, 1988, when Satan was loosed from the bottomless pit for a brief period.[6]

Helen Lee Turner found that 84 percent of Southern Baptist dispensational premillennialists surveyed had a positive response to Hal Lindsey's *Late Great Planet Earth*. Nearly 85 percent believed its prophecies should be regularly used in preaching and 83 percent said they occasionally referred to the terrors facing the unsaved at the end of time.[7] Lindsey is the author of eleven books, with more than 35 million copies in print worldwide.

In his books, dispensationalist Hal Lindsey states his belief that the Council on Foreign Relations and the Trilateral Commission are part of a worldwide conspiracy. Lindsey claims the Trilateral Commission groomed Jimmy Carter to be president. He states that George Bush is a member of the Trilateral Commission, as are other leaders in government, business, and media. The Trilateral Commission, a private group that promotes cooperation between the United States, Japan, and Western European countries, was formed by David Rockefeller and Zbigniew Brzezinski.[8]

Lindsey believes the Council on Foreign Relations, a private organization established in 1921, is an integral part of the efforts to undermine the sovereignty and independence of the United States and usher in one world government.[9]

Texe Marrs is one of the most popular conspiracists today. A retired U.S. Air Force officer, Marrs is president of Living Truth Ministries in Austin, Texas, and the author of over twenty-five books. His ministry also sells books by his wife and other authors, as well as audio- and videotapes. One of his books is entitled *Dark Majesty: The Secret Brotherhood and the Magic of Thousand Points of Light*. Marrs claims there is a worldwide conspiracy of well-known men whose goal "is to accumulate most all of this planet's wealth and power under their wings. *They intend to become our masters, our benefactors, and our gods.*"[10] These men are said to be super-rich, greedy, and deadly. He states that this conspiratorial group is called the Great Brotherhood or the Illuminati. Under the Illuminati are dozens of other secret groups, including Freemasonry, Skull & Bones, the United Nations, the Vatican, UNESCO, the Bilderbergers, the World Bank, multinational corporations, and "some TV evangelists."[11] He claims there are "thousands of groups acting either knowingly and in concert with or unwittingly supporting the Secret Brotherhood."[12] He believes these group number 25,000.[13] Marrs claims he gained access to the secret plan "only after I was able to unlock the deepest secrets of their *illuminist code* and decipher their cryptic special language."[14] Former presidents Ronald Reagan and George Bush are involved in this conspiracy, according to Marrs. Others include Bill Clinton, Dan Quayle, Henry Kissinger, Gerald Ford, Jimmy Carter, "and just about every other major political and social leader in America."[15]

Marrs claims to have found a pattern to the assassinations of many world leaders, including John F. Kennedy. In an audiotape entitled "Murder Made to Order," Marrs "unmasks a startling *Masonic connection* and the *hidden ties* of the *Council on Foreign Relations*. Also exposed is the little known role of the *Mafia*."[16] In an audiotape on the Skull & Bones Society, he claims that that organization and the CIA also conspired to assassinate Kennedy.

Marrs says he has uncovered "new evidence that the *Council on Foreign Relations*, the *Trilateral Commission*, and the *World Federalists*, under the direction of the *Bilderbergers*, are conspiring to terminate American sovereignty and deliver the United States' armed forces into the hands of a U.N. bureaucracy."[17]

In the October 1993 issue of his newsletter, *Flashpoint*, Marrs promoted a book by G. A. Riplinger entitled *New Age Bible Versions*. The book argues that the King James Version of the Bible is "the only reliable and trustworthy version." All other versions, including the New International Version, the Revised Standard Version, Today's English Version, and The Living Bible. are "tainted" by New Age philosophy. Recognized biblical scholars reject Riplinger's position as being totally without foundation.

In another audiotape, Marrs predicted a "colossal financial collapse" of America's economy and suggests how "patriots and Christians can survive and even prosper during what may soon become the bleakest period in American history."[18]

In a "Special Report" entitled "The Great Southern Baptist Cover-up," Marrs attacked the Home Mission Board study on Freemasonry. He says Larry Lewis, "who heads up the Home Missions [*sic*] Board, has complained, whined, and moaned for almost a solid year now about having to do this [study]." Besides attacking Lewis, he recommended to Southern Baptist messengers that they "go in droves to the Houston conclave, and there, . . . demand the *immediate resignation* of your denomination's president, Dr. Ed Young, your Home Missions [*sic*] Board boss, Dr. Larry Lewis, and every other spiritually corrupt person involved in this sordid attempt to cover up the manifest evils of Freemasonry." Marrs attacked my "secret connections with Masonic leaders" and reprinted my letter of January 17, 1993, to Southern Baptist Mason D. L. Talbert of Chattanooga. Marrs credits Talbert with being a "well known Masonic leader in Tennessee." In truth, I doubt if many of the Masons in Tennessee even know Talbert. Marrs refered to Holly as a "courageous layman whom God had mightily used to force a reluctant Southern Baptist leadership to study the evils of Freemasonry in the first place" and bragged that his newsletter, *Flashpoint*, is "a powerful and influential newsletter that goes out to tens of thousands around the world."[19]

In a book offered for sale by Marrs, J. R. Church suggests that the United States might be the end-time Babylon the Great prophesied in Revelation 17:1–5. As proof, he calculates that the numerical value of New York, New York, is 666. If further proof is needed, a suburb on Long Island is called Babylon. The United Nations Building in New York City is a modern "Tower of Babel." Church believes sending rockets into space and men to the moon is a fulfillment of Jeremiah 51:53: "Though Babylon should mount up to heaven." In addition, he reminds his readers that more Jews live in New York City than in the entire nation of Israel.[20]

According to Church, a secret European organization believes its 9,000 men are literal descendants of a "sacred lineage" born to Jesus and Mary Magdalene. According to the conspiracy, Mary Magdalene fled to France in A.D. 70, with the Holy Grail and the sword used to pierce the side of Jesus as he hung on the cross. In France, her children married into the royal family and produce a king named Merovee. According to the theory, Notre Dame Cathedral in Paris was named after Mary Magdalene, not Mary, the mother of Jesus. Church even wonders if the Statue of Liberty might not be a representation of Mary Magdalene. Church states that an astrological book links Mary Magdalene with the Egyptian goddess of fertility, Isis.[21]

Church says Merovee's offspring were noted for a small red cross birthmark above the heart. The Knights Templar adopted the birthmark as their symbol. The Knights Templar fled to Scotland in the fourteenth century after Jacques de Molay was killed; there they developed into the Scottish Rite. This is a strange claim by Church since none of the Scottish Rite degrees originated in Scotland or were developed by any regular Masonic body in Scotland.[22]

The Habsburg dynasty in Austria is reportedly part of the lineage of Mary Magdalene and Jesus. Could the Antichrist come from this line? According to Church, Karl von Habsburg (1961–) will become the next "King of Jerusalem" and his numerical number is 666. If that is not convincing, Church tells his readers that Kabbalists believe the number 9, the symbol of imperfect man, is sacred. The suspense is almost unbearable. If the numbers of Karl von Habsburg's name are combined two different ways, the number 9 comes up both times. Church asks, "Just coincidence? . . . perhaps . . . perhaps not!"[23]

Church's "conspiratorial FACT," not theory, involves the Illuminati, The Priory of Sion, the New Age Movement, the Federal Reserve System, international bankers, the Masonic lodge, and so forth. And who is behind this "very real conspiracy"? "His name is Lucifer."[24]

Gary H. Kah, in *En Route to Global Occupation*, argues that Freemasonry is the "hidden catalyst" to usher in the new world order. He includes a diagram to show the relationship between Freemasonry, the New Age movement, the World Council of Churches, Kabbalism, the Ancient Mystery Religions, the Rosicrucians, and so forth.[25] Like Marrs, Kah believes Marxism, American and European secret political societies, the international banking elite, the World Council of Churches, the Theosophical Society, and many cults are involved in this conspiracy. He quotes Albert Mackey describing the Illuminati as a "secret society, founded on May 1, 1776, by Adam Weishaupt."[26] Kah failed to quote Mackey's statement that the Illuminati "has thus become confounded by superficial writers with Freemasonry, although it never could be considered as properly a Masonic Rite."[27] Kah lists many of the same government leaders who are allegedly involved in this conspiracy as does Marrs. They include Gerald Ford, Jimmy Carter, George Bush, Ronald Reagan, Colin Powell, Henry Kissinger, Richard Nixon, and dozens of others.[28] Kah believes that Freemasonry founded the Soviet Union[29] and that the United States and the Soviet Union, now nonexistent, will eventually merge.[30] He believes that the Universal Product Code will soon be made invisible and then "it will only be a matter of time before humans are tattooed with a similar mark."[31] In a strange twist, Kah calls for prayer for Senator Jesse Helms, a 33° Scottish Rite Mason, who is trying to expose the plot concerning global economics.[32]

Promoting another popular fraud, Salem Kirban, author of *Satan's Angels Exposed*, believes that Italian patriot Giuseppe Mazzini (1805–1872) and Albert Pike wrote a blueprint, allegedly on display in the British Museum Library in London "until recently,"[33] for three world wars. The First World War enabled Communism to destroy the Czarist government of Russia. The Second World War enabled Communism to destroy other governments, while Christianity was outlawed in China. The Third World War will be fought between the Jews and the Muslims as a prelude to Armageddon.[34] Stating we are living in the Last Days before the Rapture, Kirban believes Russia will align with Islamic countries and invade Israel. As with other conspiracy writers, the Council on Foreign Relations, the Bilderbergers, the Trilateral Commission, and the European Common Market figure prominently in Kirban's scenario.

Southern Baptist Pat Robertson, the son of a Mason and founder and chairman of the Christian Broadcasting Network and author of *The New World Order*, claims the Council on Foreign Relations "has been able to control the results of elections" and "promote the communist takeover of Russia, China, Eastern Europe, and parts of Central America and Africa."[35] The influence of the Council on Foreign Relations is said to extend to and control the Central

Intelligence Agency, American universities, and the U.S. presidency.[36] According to Robertson, the Council on Foreign Relations chairman David Rockefeller rejected George Bush and turned to Jimmy Carter for president in 1973.[37]

A. Ralph Epperson, author of another book titled *The New World Order*, describes himself as a investigator on "the Conspiratorial View of History." Leaders in Epperson's conspiracy include the New Age movement, Humanism, Communism, and Freemasonry. Epperson believes the New World Order, which is based upon the worship of Lucifer, will begin in 2000. Former President George Bush will help usher in the New World Order, according to Epperson.[38] Epperson, as do other conspiratorial writers, believes the "all-seeing eye" above the pyramid on the back of U.S. one-dollar federal reserve notes represents the sun god Lucifer.[39] Epperson did not state whether he has given up use of one-dollar federal reserve notes.

William T. Still also proposes a conspiratorial view of history. Still begins his book, *New World Order: The Ancient Plan of Secret Societies*, by telling of a "rumor" that a committee was seeking to repeal the 22nd Amendment to the United States Constitution limiting American presidents to two terms so that Richard Nixon could run for the U.S. presidency for a third term. A second committee was charged with keeping "Mr. Nixon in office by any means: – INCLUDING A MILITARY COUP BY HIGH RANKING OFFICERS."[40] Still's conspiracy includes antiwar disruptions during the 1972 Republican National Convention "in San Diego [*sic*]," after which Nixon would "declare a state of national emergency, and essentially suspend Constitutional rights."[41] Freemasonry is one of Still's secret societies.

Stories in these and dozens of other conspiratorial books belong in the same category as stories in supermarket tabloids such as the *Weekly World News*. The May 17, 1994, issue informed its readers that "The Sun Will Burn Out in 1999," "Space Aliens Hang Out at Nevada Bar," and "Farmer Shoots 23-lb Grasshopper." The issue also told that an angel's six-foot-long wing had been found in Arizona after the angel flew into a helicopter's spinning blades. Experts are reportedly examining the wing at an undisclosed location. The article said scientists now have evidence that proves the existence of heaven.

ANTI-MASONS

James D. Shaw's and Tom C. McKenney's *The Deadly Deception: Freemasonry Exposed . . . By One of Its Top Leaders* is popular among anti-Masons. It is a biography of Jim Shaw's life beginning when his father abandoned the family when Jim was a few months old. His mother remarried when Jim was two years old. The stepfather abused Jim and ordered him to leave home at the age of thirteen. Jim says he remembered his mother's advice, "Try to be like your Uncle Irvin (her brother); he is a good man and a Mason."[42] Jim, who had begun working as a newspaper boy at age five, worked at a drug store, a job he had had while living at home and going to school. When he married, Shaw joined the Loyal Order of the Moose and then the Masonic lodge. Shaw provides details of his initiations into the three degrees of the blue lodge in his book. The lodge became the family he longed for and assisted him to overcome his negative self-image. He received special honors and served in most "chairs" in his Blue Lodge. Shaw also joined the Scottish Rite, the Eastern Star, and the Shrine.

Not a Christian, Shaw made the Masonic fraternity his religion, but he found it failed to satisfy his deepest spiritual needs. After a friend witnessed to him, Shaw became a Christian.

Shaw resigned from the fraternity on October 25, 1966, saying, "This is being done with deep regret, but I am devoting my spare time to attending bible college, [*sic*] and Bible study. The material that I have pertaining to the Twenty Fifth [*sic*] degree I will turn over to the assistant degree master Mr. Jack Harris also [*sic*] give him any help he needs to confer the degree this fall. I am resigning only because I find that as long as I belong to Masonic work it interferes with my studies in the Lords' [*sic*] work. I could never just be a card carrier so I am turning it in."[43]

Shaw clipped his 1966 Miami Consistory membership card to the letter of resignation. It clearly shows that Shaw was a 32° K.C.C.H., or Knight Commander in the Court of Honor, in the Scottish Rite, not a 33° as he claims in his book, *The Deadly Deception*. A 32° K.C.C.H. must serve in that rank, which is an honorary position between the 32° and the 33°, for a minimum of forty-four months. Shaw claims he had been a 32° K.C.C.H. for four years,[44] but his investiture as a 32° K.C.C.H. occurred on December 18, 1965, only ten months prior to his letter of resignation.[45]

There are thirty-three men who hold the position called Sovereign Grand Inspector General or S.G.I.G. The heads of the Scottish Rite in other states in the Southern Jurisdiction are referred to as deputies. Each of the other 33° Scottish Rite Masons in the Southern Jursidiction is referred to as "Inspector General Honorary." Ed Decker, director of Saints Alive/Free the Masons in Issaquah, Washington, wrote in his May 1991 issue of the *Free the Masons* newsletter that "Brother Shaw was actually a Sovereign Grand Inspector General (33°) in the Scottish Rite." Shaw was neither a 33° Scottish Rite Mason nor a S.G.I.G. as Decker claims.

Art deHoyos and Brent Morris, in *Is It True What They Say About Freemasonry?*, cite a number of other false claims by Shaw. On the cover of his book, Shaw claims he was a Past Master of a Blue Lodge. Morris and deHoyos found Shaw was "appointed Junior Deacon" of the Allapattah Lodge No. 271 in Florida, but was never elected to any office, much less Master of the lodge.[46] Shaw, on the cover of his book, claims he has revealed the 33° initiation ceremony for the first time in history. Authors deHoyos and Morris respond that the 33° ceremony has been "exposed" for 165 years and catalogued thirteen times since 1829 when the 33° ceremony had been published. Shaw claims the cost of going through the thirty-two degrees is "well into the thousands of dollars."[47] Morris and deHoyos include a copy of Shaw's member's record card indicating he paid only $217.50 to receive the thirty-two degrees.[48] Shaw refers to all of the drinking done in Masonic life. However, the Grand Lodge of Florida and the Scottish Rite Bodies of Miami, where Shaw was a member, prohibit use of alcoholic beverages in any form.[49]

Edward C. Decker is president of Saints Alive in Jesus, formerly known as Ex-Mormons for Jesus, of Issaquah, Washington. He is also the president of Free the Masons Ministries. Decker says he was reared in a lukewarm Episcopalian family and joined the Church of Jesus Christ of Latter-day Saints in 1961 after five years of marriage to a Mormon convert. The marriage ended in divorce in 1969. Decker continued to attend Mormon services periodically until he says he became a Christian in 1976.[50] Decker is currently a member of the Assemblies of God.[51]

Because he sees an inverted five-pointed star in a map of the streets of Washington, D.C., with the bottom point resting on the White House, Decker can quote Bill Schnoebelen, a former Satanist and Mason, "We have been under siege from the first day our first president walked into the Oval Office."[52] Inverted five-pointed stars are well-known symbols both in witchcraft and Satanism. Decker also shares a "staggering" bit of news that the Medal of Honor, our nation's highest military award, consists of an inverted five-pointed star within a circle. This, Decker asserts, "is the highest form of satanic expression."[53]

Schnoebelen's *Masonry Beyond The Light* is one of the more colorful anti-Masonic books with headings such as "Mirror, Mirror on the Wall—Who's the Most Worshipful One of All?"[54] "A 'Mr. Potato-Head' God,"[55] "Mickey Mouse Money,"[56] and "A Pig in the Poke!"[57] Schnoebelen says he received the 90° in the Egyptian rite of Masonry, "a level few U.S. Masons are even aware of!"[58]

Charles Z. Burchett, pastor of the First Baptist Church, Kirbyville, Texas, and James L. Holly introduced a resolution at the 1985 Southern Baptist Convention in Dallas, Texas, titled "Freemasonry Not Compatible with Baptist Faith and Message, Bold Mission Thrust, or Cooperative Program."[59] Outside the Dallas Convention Center, individuals passed out to messengers a pamphlet including the resolution and portions of a booklet by Decker entitled *Question of Freemasonry*. Decker's name and the address of his ministry, Free the Masons Ministries, were printed on the back of the pamphlet.

Southern Baptist John Ankerberg, president of The John Ankerberg Evangelistic Association and the Ankerberg Theological Research Institute, and host of the nationally televised "The John Ankerberg Show," is one of the most prolific anti-Masonic writers with several books on the subject. His books are usually coauthored with John Weldon.

In one of their books, *The Facts on the Masonic Lodge*, Ankerberg and Weldon make the following absolute statement: "This is why Masonry completely excludes all particular biblical teachings about Christ such as His incarnation, redemptive mission, death, and resurrection."[60] The words "completely excludes all" makes this an absolute statement. In other words, according to Ankerberg and Weldon, statements about Christ's incarnation, redemptive mission, death, and resurrection never appear in Masonic literature. Ankerberg and Weldon are mistaken. A number of Masonic sources can be cited. *Morals and Dogma*, often the target of anti-Masons, is one of several of such sources; Pike wrote, "To the Christian Mason they [*Iota*, *Eta*, and *Sigma*] are the first three letters of the name of the Son of God, Who died upon the cross to redeem mankind."[61] On page 307 of the same book, Pike says, "The agonies of the garden of Gethsemane and those of the Cross on Calvary preceded the Resurrection and were the means of Redemption."

Masons may not refer to Christ as often as Ankerberg and Weldon would wish, but it is a falsehood to say Masons never refer to Christ's incarnation, redemptive mission, death, and resurrection.

Southern Baptist Larry Kunk, director of Ephesians 5:11, Inc., has worked closely with Holly[62] in an effort to get the Home Mission Board to adopt an anti-Masonic position. Kunk mailed a copy of his study, *What Is the Secret Doctrine of the Masonic Lodge and How Does It Relate to Their Plan of Salvation?* to (Home Mission Board evangelism vice president) Darrell Robinson and me. Holly included a copy of Kunk's study in his notebook presented to the Interfaith Witness Department staff in September 1992. Kunk claims to have discovered a secret doctrine in Masonry: Masons become a Christ or a god:

> Initiation is a process in which a Mason goes into trance [*sic*] by passive meditation and attains conscious union—that is, he establishes communications with the Masonic god. By attaining conscious communion, he becomes a Christ. The process of Initiation reoccurs over months and years and after each conscious union with the Masonic god he has new understandings about himself and about the god. The process is evolutionary; the Mason evolves into a god himself.[63]

A number of anti-Masonic ministries, including Kunk's Ephesians 5:11 and C. D. A. Oxley's In His Grip Ministries, Inc., held a "National Leadership Conference on Ministry to Masons" in 1993 and 1994.

The hysteria of the anti-Masons takes on the absurd. Wayne Lela, of Downers Grove, Illinois, wrote to announce his "as-yet-unpublished book on Freemasonry" which "is easily one of the most revealing works on this secret society." Lela charged, "the leaders of Masonry are amoral or immoral and libertarian/anarchistic" and "the leaders of Masonry are homosexuals or bisexuals who are behind the modern homo/bisexual 'revolution.'"[64]

Eleanor Snyder of Bronson, Texas, charged the Southern Baptist Convention's failure to condemn Freemasonry was because of the fear that the Convention would lose "$700 million annually."[65] Contributions to the Cooperative Program, the Annie Armstrong Offering for Home Missions, and the Lottie Moon Offering for Foreign Missions totals approximately $250 million. Snyder's "$700 million annually" is nearly three times the actual receipts for the three major Southern Baptist Convention offerings.

Kenneth Cornn of London, Kentucky, wrote to tell me of a paper he had written arguing that the Jews in Jerusalem were not really Jews, but Edomites. He claims that when a Mason read his paper, Cornn was told he "had been the only one who had figured out the master plan of 1776." He further claims that the unnamed Mason wrote him a letter detailing the alleged master plan. Cornn sent me the first page of the plan. The letterhead was "Royal Order of the Illuminati." It told of a meeting allegedly held at the House of the Temple in Washington, D.C., on "February 23, 2482 A.L." [*sic*]. As any Mason knows, "2482 A.L." corresponds to 1518 B.C., or 3,512 years ago. The master plan spoke of the "distinguishment [*sic*] of raceism [*sic*]."[66] I think someone was trying to pull something over on Cornn, or he on me.

The original manuscript of the Study concluded the chapter on conspiracy theories with the following advice:

> The Apostle Paul cautioned Titus, his "loyal child in the faith," concerning "many rebellious people, idle talkers and deceivers" (Titus 1:10) who destroy church fellowship rather than build it up. In his commentary on this passage, Herschel H. Hobbs wrote, "Amazingly, many otherwise sensible people are led astray, or else disturbed, in their faith by such [false teachers]. By the time they get through, people who listen to them are so mixed up that they do not know what to believe."[67]

Hobbs's words are especially relevant as the year 2000 approaches. There are dozens of conspiracy-oriented books on the market today. Taking liberties with fact and outright misrepresentation are typical of conspiratorial theorists. They write for emotional impact, not to share truth. Given the popularity of supermarket tabloids such as *The National Enquirer*, it is not surprising that these books attract the curious and appeal to the fears of uninformed people. Unfortunately, the popularity of conspiracy-oriented books will certainly mushroom as the new century approaches. Both old and new conspiracy theories of all kinds will appear or be revised as "new secrets are revealed" and cause terrible confusion among God's people. Church leaders need to prepare their people now for this with clear **biblical** preaching.[68]

6 The Present Southern Baptist Investigation of Freemasonry, Part I

"[M]ore damage has been done to the cause of Christ and that of Southern Baptists by those who raised the controversy than the Masons have done in 150 years."[1]

1985 RESOLUTION AGAINST FREEMASONRY

The Southern Baptist Convention has been embroiled in an attack on Freemasonry since 1985. James Larry Holly, a Beaumont, Texas, physician whose father and father-in-law are Masons,[2] and Charles Z. Burchett, pastor of the First Baptist Church of Kirbyville, Texas, introduced a resolution at the 1985 Southern Baptist Convention titled "Freemasonry Not Compatible with Baptist Faith and Message, Bold Mission Thrust, or Cooperative Program."[3] Copies of the resolution were passed out at the convention center doors and included a reprint of "The Question of Freemasonry" by J. Edward Decker, Jr., director of Free the Masons Ministry of Issaquah, Washington. Decker's address was provided for more information.

The Resolutions Committee, chaired by Larry L. Lewis, then president of the Hannibal-LaGrange College in Hannibal, Missouri, referred the resolution to the Interfaith Witness Department of the Home Mission Board "for their study and recommendation."

In a letter to William Tanner, then president of the Home Mission Board, on August 5, 1985, Lewis clarified the position of the Resolutions Committee, saying,

> The committee neither favored or [*sic*] opposed the text of the resolution but felt the serious nature of the subject and the concerns

> expressed in the resolution deserved thorough study by the Interfaith Witness Department. The Interfaith Witness Department and the Home Mission Board are at liberty to dispose of the matter in whatever way they feel most appropriate.

Holly responded to this letter, a copy of which had been sent to him, on August 9 by saying he understood that the Resolutions Committee had "a strong sense of agreement" with his resolution. He told Lewis he would be pleased to poll the members of the committee in order to establish that fact.

Richard W. Harmon, assistant director of the Interfaith Witness Department, was assigned the task of conducting the study. He met with Holly, Burchett, and others who opposed Freemasonry, as well as Masons. He read books by anti-Masons and Masons, as well as letters received.

HARMON'S CONCLUSIONS

Harmon concluded,

(1) no one authority speaks for Freemasonry;
(2) some Masonic teachings reflect strongly the moods of the eras in which they were written;
(3) the Interfaith Witness Department does not recognize Freemasonry as a religion, although he stated that for some Masons, Freemasonry may have become a pseudo-religion;
(4) and finally, that Freemasonry, and other fraternal orders do not fall within the scope of the department's assigned responsibility.

The Home Mission Board directors adopted a response meeting to the resolution on Freemasonry during their March 1986 meeting: "It is the Board's conclusion that Freemasonry does not fall within the scope of assigned responsibility of the Home Mission Board." Messengers to the Southern Baptist Convention in June 1986 approved the Home Mission Board response.

1991 RESOLUTION AGAINST FREEMASONRY

Holly and Burchett brought a similar resolution to the 1991 Southern Baptist Convention. The resolution was again referred to the Home Mission Board for response. As director of the Interfaith Witness Department, Lewis asked me to assume responsibility for the research and to prepare a report for him.

As part of my research, I asked Lynn E. May, Jr., executive director and treasurer of the Historical Commission of the Southern Baptist Convention, whether the Southern Baptist Convention has considered the Freemasonry issue during the Convention's more than 140 years of existence. After examining an index of SBC annuals from 1845, May reported, "We cannot say with absolute certainty that the subject of Freemasonry does not appear in the Convention annuals in the past, but that appears to be the case."[4] About this time, well-known anti-Mason Edward C. Decker, an Assembly of God layman from Issaquah, Washington, wrote in his July–August 1991 *Saints Alive in Jesus Newsletter* that "reliable sources within the [Southern Baptist] Convention estimate that there are anywhere from 40 to 65 percent of Southern Baptist pastors who are involved in the Masons!"[5] Decker estimated that the number of laymen involved in Freemasonry "almost certainly [is] an even higher percentage." Decker did not identify his (so-called) reliable sources. The exaggeration of facts has long been the practice of many groups when such a practice helps accomplish their goals. A November 1991 poll, conducted by the Corporate Planning and Research Department of the Sunday School Board of the Southern Baptist Convention at my request, found that only 14 percent of pastors were or had been Masons. Only 18 percent of deacons were or had been Masons.[6]

The Baptist VIEWpoll also found that most church leaders—60 percent of pastors, 56 percent of ministers of education, 72 percent of directors of missions, 63 percent of deacon chairmen, and 74 percent of church clerks—felt that an official statement on Freemasonry by the Convention was either "not very important at all" or had no opinion about whether a statement was needed.

In a memo dated January 16, 1992, Lewis asked me to contact his secretary to schedule a time for an oral report on my study of Freemasonry. He specifically said he did not want a written report. Lewis and I later met in his office, at which time I gave an oral report.

Holly's statement in his second volume that he became involved in the current controversy over Freemasonry only after receiving a letter from an unnamed associate pastor on March 4, 1992 is puzzling.[7] His name appears on the 1985 and the 1991 resolutions against Freemasonry offered at the annual meetings of the Southern Baptist Convention.

During the regular spring meeting of the Home Mission Board directors on March 11, 1992, the directors declined the request from the Southern Baptist Convention to study the teachings of Freemasonry and referred the issue back to the Southern Baptist Convention for action in June 1992. Director chairman Johnny Jackson was quoted as saying that most Southern Baptists have no opinion about Freemasonry.

Jackson said, "It's those who are extremist or militant on either side of the issue who have caused whatever divisiveness that has occurred."[8]

Several directors disagreed with the motion to refer the issue back to the Southern Baptist Convention, but it passed easily. (Those directors who disagreed believed the Home Mission Board should proceed with the study.) Lewis later expressed hope that an ad hoc committee would be appointed by the Convention president to study the issue.

HOLLY CALLS FOR AN AD HOC COMMITTEE AND MAILS BOOK

Holly was quoted as saying he also wanted "an ad hoc committee to study the Masonic Lodge and to report back to the Convention in 1993 with a recommendation for action by the Convention."[9] He said he hoped he would be among the members of the committee investigating Freemasonry.

Prior to the June 1992 Southern Baptist Convention in Indianapolis, Holly mailed 5,000 copies of his fifty-seven-page book, *The Southern Baptist Convention and Freemasonry*, to leaders and trustees of all of the SBC agencies and commissions, state convention leaders, association directors of missions, every Southern Baptist pastor in Indiana and some 1,500 people on his ministry's mailing list. Holly said he planned to distribute another 5,000 copies during the Convention in Indianapolis.[10]

Holly called for the following "as a start" in his book.

- No Mason should be allowed to serve as a deacon or other leader in any Southern Baptist church.
- No Mason should be called as a pastor unless he publicly renounces Freemasonry and burns his apron and other Masonic paraphernalia.
- Converts should be counseled about the incompatibility of membership in Freemasonry and membership in a Baptist church.
- No pastor should participate in a funeral service conducted by Masons.
- Churches with cornerstones dedicated by Masons should hold public ceremonies of repentance and prayer.[11]

1992 SOUTHERN BAPTIST CONVENTION

On Tuesday morning during the 1992 Southern Baptist Convention, Holly introduced the following motion:

> The Southern Baptist Convention in annual session June 9–11, 1992, at Indianapolis, Indiana, directs the president elected at this convention to appoint an ad hoc committee for the study of the compatibility with Christianity and Southern Baptist doctrine of the organization known variously as the Masonic Lodge, Masonry, Freemasonry and/or Ancient and Accepted Rite of Freemasonry. This study is to encompass any and all branches and/or lodges thereof. Furthermore, the Convention directs the president to appoint this committee within thirty days of the conclusion of this convention and to charge this committee with the responsibility of bringing a report with recommendation to the convention which is to meet in Houston, Texas, June 1993.[12]

John M. King of Georgia then presented the following motion, which was ruled out of order, "I move that the committee or persons to which the motion to investigate Freemasonry is directed, take no action and no committee to study or investigate be appointed."[13]

Debate on Holly's motion was held the following day. Holly and Randy Day of Texas spoke for the motion. Fred McPeake of Knoxville, Tennessee, spoke against the motion. Then Alvin Rowe of Rockledge, Florida, moved to amend the motion, by offering the following:

> The Southern Baptist Convention in annual session June 9–11, 1992, at Indianapolis, Indiana, directs the Interfaith Witness Department of the Home Mission Board to study the compatibility with Christianity and Southern Baptist doctrine of the organization known variously as the Masonic Lodge, Masonry, Freemasonry, and/or Ancient and Accepted Right [*sic*] of Freemasonry. The study is to encompass any and all branches and or lodges thereof. Furthermore, the convention charges the Home Mission Board with the responsibility of bringing a report with recommendation to the Convention which is to meet in Houston, Texas, June 1993.[14]

After approval of Rowe's amended motion to send the issue back to the Interfaith Witness Department, a series of resolutions were adopted, one of which was titled "On Christian Witness and Voluntary Associations." Although this resolution did not mention Freemasonry, a number of people, including Holly,[15] concluded its intended target was Freemasonry. The resolution stated:

> WHEREAS, We are called to be in the world but not of the world; and
>
> WHEREAS, We are called to maintain biblical standards of holiness and to avoid compromise of our Christian witness, or cooperation which would threaten that witness; and
>
> WHEREAS, We are called to maintain Christian witness openly before the world; and
>
> WHEREAS, We recognize the value of many social, fraternal, and philanthropic organizations.
>
> Therefore, Be it RESOLVED, That we, the messengers to the 135th session of the Southern Baptist Convention, call upon all Christians to maintain personal purity in all activities, associations, or memberships; avoiding any association which conflicts with clear biblical teaching, including those teachings concerning the taking of oaths, the secrecy of activities, mystical knowledge, or racial discrimination; and
>
> Be it further RESOLVED, We affirm that biblical doctrine is to be open and public knowledge and that the Christian faith is to be a clear and public expression of the truth that Jesus Christ is the only means of salvation, that the Bible is our infallible guide, and that salvation comes by the Gospel of grace and not by works; and
>
> Be it finally RESOLVED, That we urge all Southern Baptists to refrain from participation or membership in organizations with teachings, oaths, or mystical knowledge which are contrary to the Bible and to the public expression of our faith in the gospel of Jesus Christ, which must be above all reproach.[16]

Ankerberg and Weldon erroneously concluded that this resolution "prohibited a Christian from joining groups or organizations such as the Masonic

Lodge."[17] The resolution did not prohibit Southern Baptists from joining any organization, although it urged them to refrain from doing so. Resolutions represent the opinion of messengers present and voting for the resolution. They are not binding on any church or individual in the Southern Baptist Convention. Fundamentalists have attempted to enforce resolutions as if they are authoritative on all Christians, but this has never been the intent of resolutions.

RESEARCH FOR THE *STUDY*

As director of the Interfaith Witness Department, I was given overall responsibility for conducting the research and writing a study of Freemasonry. The *Baptist Press*, reporting on the July 1992 meeting of the Home Mission Board directors, said the directors authorized a three-month study leave while I conducted the study so I could be relieved of some of my duties as department director. Home Mission Board evangelism vice president Darrell Robinson was quoted as saying I would "be personally responsible for researching and writing the study." Robinson said, "He can involve others as he sees fit."[18]

Robinson, Lewis, and I met on July 29, 1992, at the Baptist Conference Center at Glorieta, New Mexico, to discuss response to Holly's criticism that I was doing the Freemasonry study alone. I received a six-and-a-half-page fax from Holly on August 13. Lewis received an eighteen-and-a-half-page fax from Holly on August 26.

The Interfaith Witness Department invited James Holly and Charles Burchett to Atlanta for a meeting with the department staff to discuss their concerns about Freemasonry on September 17, 1992. Bill High of Beaumont, Texas, and Ron Sutherland of Atlanta also attended the meeting as Holly's guests. The Interfaith Witness Department reimbursed Holly, Burchett, and High for travel expenses, which included airfare, lodging, and meals. Others attending were Brad Allen, then chairman of the evangelism committee of the board of directors; Larry Lewis; Darrell Robinson; and the following department staff: Jimmy Furr of Mt. Juliet, Tennessee; Ken James of Manhattan, Kansas; Bill Gordon of Lilburn, Georgia; Tal Davis of Snellville, Georgia; and me. Joyce Johnson, lead secretary for the department, attended to record the meeting. David Winfrey, from *Baptist Press*, attended a portion of the meeting.

I worked an average of five days each week on the *Study* and two days each week either in the office or out of town leading Interfaith Witness conferences from early September until early December 1992. I reject Home Mission Board director J. Walter Carpenter's statement that "The HMB Administrative Committee recognized early on that it was patently unfair to let denominational employees at a middle management level be left to fend for themselves in this highly charged atmosphere."[19] I agree it was "patently unfair," but the administrative committee had little or no involvement in the process until after the *Study* was submitted to them in February 1993. I agree with Carpenter that the issue became politicized, but I reject his argument that the issue was not a moderate-fundamentalist issue. Moderate Southern Baptists did not push for condemnation of Freemasonry; the push came solely from fundamentalists.

Robinson, Lewis and I met on December 8 to discuss the progress of the Freemasonry study. We agreed I would submit the findings to them on January 25, 1993. We would forward the study to the members of the HMB administrative committee prior to our meeting with them on February 8th. I met with the administrative committee at their luncheon meeting on December 8 to discuss my progress and plans for sharing the findings with them.

Pierce Dodson of Lebanon, Tennessee, who resigned as pastor of his church because of his strong anti-Masonic stand, wrote to Larry Lewis on December 30, 1992, expressing his concern that the study would focus "on James L. Holly's little book," referring to Holly's fifty-seven-page book on Freemasonry. Dodson wrote, "I am writing to ask you please not to allow the report on Freemasonry to be sidetracked by focusing on James L. Holly's little book. The convention voted for the Interfaith Witness Department to report on Freemasonry, not on James L. Holly's little book." Dodson sent copies to SBC president Ed Young, Albert Mohler, Jr., editor of the Georgia *Christian Index*, and me.

I sent the following memorandum to Robinson and Lewis on January 18, 1993:

> The Freemasonry Report[20] is nearly completed. I am waiting for responses to two letters requesting additional information and for a reader to return the manuscript. Two of my staff (Tal Davis and Ken James) have read the manuscript and made comments, all of which we incorporated into the text. In addition, [department missionaries] Jimmy Furr and Bill Gordon worked with me at different times throughout these past six months with specific assignments to read books or conduct personal research. I plan to give you the report on Friday, the 22nd.
>
> I know Dr. Holly is worried that the study will make an issue of his "little book," to quote Pierce Dodson. My opinion and Bill Gordon's, who did a critique of his [Holly's] book at my request, is that Dr. Holly's book is poorly researched and full of errors. Still, we did not make it

> "the issue" of the report, although I felt we had to respond to some of his more blatant errors as his book was the one used last year in the call for this study. I believe we referred to his book thirteen times out of a total of over 315 footnotes in the report. We certainly did not personally attack him as he fears. My staff and I are scholars; we do not have to resort to *ad hominem* attacks.
>
> I want to say that the **only**[21] pressure we felt during this study was from people like Dr. Holly, Texe Marrs, Pierce Dodson and other Masonic critics. The tone of their letters was that we had better agree with them. We did not sense this kind of intimidation from Masonic writers.
>
> I am pleased with the report. I believe it is as factual and objective as is humanly possible.

I felt the study was balanced with both affirmation and criticism of both Masons and anti-Masons. I felt I had done what Lewis urged James C. Hefley to do in his books on the controversy within the Southern Baptist Convention: "Tell both sides and let readers decide."[22] Hefley says Lewis never asked him to take sides.

THE FIRST DRAFT OF THE *STUDY* COMPLETED, CHANGES MADE BY LEWIS

The study on Freemasonry was completed on January 21 and copies given to Robinson, Lewis, and each of the department staff the following day. I met with Lewis for two hours and twenty minutes on January 26 to discuss my study. It was obvious he did not like much of the study. He mentioned receiving a phone call from Holly the previous day and asked me to remove all of the quotes from Holly's "little book" as well as the section on conspiracy theories. Lewis's cuts constituted major surgery on my study, not simply the "massage" that Robinson spoke about in his phone call to me on January 25. Lewis also rewrote and put in bold print anti-Masonic statements to make them more anti-Masonic. He commented that I might not want my name on the study because of the many changes.

I made the changes as directed by Lewis and removed my name from the cover and text of the study. The study was reduced from eighty-one pages to sixty-six pages. I gave Lewis the edited version on January 28. I was angry at myself for not resisting more forcefully Lewis's changes to the study. A friend on the Home Mission Board staff reminded me that Joshua's and Caleb's report was not accepted either (Numbers 13:25–33).

Lewis made other significant changes in an hour-long meeting on February 2, removing statements he thought were pro-Masonic. Evidently someone had called him and mentioned Rex Hutchen's *A Bridge to Light* because Lewis asked me if I had read Hutchen's book. I got the impression Lewis had not read the book, but was influenced by what the caller had told him. I said I had read the book.

In a thirty-minute meeting with Robinson and Lewis on February 5, I was told that the vice presidents thought the edited study was still too biased toward the Masons. They didn't think it would be approved by the administrative committee on February 8. I was asked if I or one of my staff could rewrite the paper; I responded that neither I nor my staff had time. They discussed having an editor from the evangelism section of the Home Mission Board rewrite the study to remove any hint of "bias" and to reduce the study to twenty-five or thirty pages. They cited my use of the word *unfortunately* in the manuscript, which they said implied bias. They also cited my naming of Southern Baptists who were Masons, while not naming any Southern Baptists who were anti-Masonic. They specifically mentioned anti-Masons Charles Stanley, pastor of the First Baptist Church, Atlanta, Georgia, and Paige Patterson, president of Southeastern Baptist Theological Seminary, Wake Forest, North Carolina. I responded that I used only the names of deceased Southern Baptists and had not discussed names of living Southern Baptists who were Masons or anti-Masonic. I said I doubted Stanley and Patterson would want their names used in the study. Lewis said he might have to call a special meeting of the directors at the Southern Baptist Convention in June to approve a report and recommendation if the administrative committee did not approve the study. Lewis asked that my staff attend the meeting with the administrative committee on February 8. Copies of the study were mailed to the members of the administrative committee so they could read it prior to the meeting.

I remembered reading a statement by Reinhold Niebuhr in *Leaves from the Notebook of a Tamed Cynic:* "the ministry is the only profession in which you can make a virtue of ignorance."[23] I struggled with obedience to ecclesiastical authority and the integrity of my conscience. Perhaps Mormon scholar Russell Nelson was correct when he said, "Some truths are best left unsaid."[24]

STUDY ACCEPTED, LEWIS MADE ADDITIONAL CHANGES

Department staff Tal Davis, Bill Gordon, Maurice Smith, and I met with nine members of the administrative committee on February 8. In addition, Lewis; five vice presidents; Joan Redford, administrative assistant to the president;

and Martin King, director of the office of public relations and development, attended. Chairman of the Board of Directors Ron Phillips, a former Master Mason, strongly affirmed the study as accurate. Although opposed to Masonic rituals, Phillips did not believe the Home Mission Board should take a strong stand against Freemasonry. He volunteered that he had received 1,581 letters on Freemasonry; only 9 were from persons opposed to Freemasonry. I had received over 2,100 with fewer than 30 from persons opposed to Freemasonry.

During the discussion, director Brad Allen asked if I had critiqued Holly's book as there were no references to the book. The minutes of the administrative committee meeting taken by Redford report that "Dr. Lewis explained that in Leazer's original, this was done, but Dr. Lewis did not feel the HMB should critique individuals and that part of the study was omitted. Allen said he appreciated this thinking, but questioned the wisdom of doing it from one side of the issue. If we are going to do a scholarly study, both sides of the issue should be reported, but in a kind way."[25]

Nelson Price, HMB director and pastor of the Roswell Street Baptist Church, Marietta, Georgia, read from several anti-Masonic books he brought to the meeting. He obviously was not in agreement with the study but voted for it. Steve Hammack, HMB director and pastor of the Clarkston Baptist Church, abstained. The final vote was 8 for, 0 against, 1 abstention. According to the minutes, a motion was made by Brad Allen "that the conclusion as given by Leazer be adopted. The motion was seconded and passed." It was agreed that no further changes would be made in the study, except for minor changes suggested by the directors in the meeting and outlined in the minutes.

The administrative committee asked me to write a one- to three-page summary that would constitute the Home Mission Board report to the Southern Baptist Convention. Lewis and Robinson, along with directors Ron Gaynor and Brad Allen, would form a subcommittee to approve the summary before it was presented to the administrative committee for approval.

On February 10, Robinson told me the administrative committee had approved a $1,500 writer's fee as well as an additional two weeks of vacation because of my work on the study, both of which I later received. Lewis also called to ask me to meet with him the next day to make more changes to the study. I was surprised as I understood the vote of the administrative committee was that no more changes would be made to the study. Brad Allen, one of the directors at the meeting on February 8, agreed that was also his understanding. Individuals could accept or reject it, but they couldn't change it.

Robinson, Redford, and I met with Lewis on February 11 for four hours, and ten minutes to make additional changes in the study. Lewis said Holly had called him the previous day and talked for an hour. Holly then faxed Lewis a three-page letter. I wondered if Holly had been sent a copy of the study. I again submitted the often-edited study to Lewis on February 16, hoping that was the last of the editorial changes. Lewis is quoted by Associated Baptist Press as saying that "radical revisions" were made to the study after I had completed my work.[26]

Lewis would later claim he made the "radical revisions" to remove "potentially libelous" statements.[27] However, no one who has read the original manuscript said they found any "potentially libelous" statements. Lewis did not respond to my request to cite those portions of the original manuscript that he believed were potentially libelous. A characteristic of toxic faith is to create a victim upon which to cast aspersions and to direct attention from oneself. A comparison of major portions of the original manuscript with the published *Study* is found in the Appendix; other changes are cited throughout this book.

7 The Present Southern Baptist Investigation of Freemasonry, Part II

One by one
they throw us from the tower
and we spread our wings
and fly.[1]

REMOVAL FROM MASONIC STUDY FOR "DAMAGE CONTROL"

On February 22, 1993, I traveled to Lexington, Kentucky, to preach at a state evangelism conference. Upon arrival at my motel, I was given a telephone message from my secretary that Home Mission Board president Larry L. Lewis was trying to contact me. James Larry Holly had received a copy of a personal letter I had written to D. L. Talbert, a Southern Baptist Mason friend in Chattanooga, on January 17. Evidently Talbert made copies for some of his friends and a copy had been passed on to Holly. Lewis expressed fear that the study was now compromised. He related that he was waiting to talk to Darrell Robinson and Bob Banks, executive vice president, before deciding what course of action to take, which he called "damage control."

Lewis was upset that I had encouraged Masons to attend the Southern Baptist Convention in Houston in June to vote their conscience. A number of Masons had written asking how they could help with the study. I responded that there was nothing they could do to help with the study. I told a few, including Talbert, that, if they felt strongly about the matter, they could attend the convention as messengers elected by their churches and vote when the issue came up for discussion. While I was repeatedly criticized for this action, others regularly encouraged people to attend the convention and vote for particular candidates. In the two years prior to the 1979 convention, Paul Pressler and Paige Patterson held rallies in twenty-five states to encourage people to take the maximum number of messengers to the convention and vote for the fundamentalist candidate.[2] Patterson was reported to have provided the name of a travel agent and urged pastors in a meeting at First Baptist Church of Dallas, Texas, to find five other pastors to go to the 1986 Southern Baptist Convention in Atlanta, which he called "the second battle of Atlanta."[3] Southern Baptists who happen to be Masons have as much right to be present and vote at the convention as any other properly elected messenger.

Lewis was especially upset that I had allowed two Masons, Southern Baptist Abner McCall, president emeritus of Baylor University, and Disciples of Christ layperson Jim Tresner, editor of *The Oklahoma Mason*, to read advance copies of the study. I had written each man on January 7 stating that:

> My primary concern, since I am not a Mason, is that Masonic critics will find obvious misstatements about Freemasonry which will call into question my conclusions. I would hope you will check that carefully. I know Masons will not agree with all of my report but believe it to be fair and objective. I am still waiting for documentation on several points I want to include and am not satisfied with the wording of the conclusion so there will be minor changes and additions to the report.

I thanked each man for his willingness to help on such short notice.

McCall returned the manuscript with no marks or comments. Tresner made several corrections. For example, I had stated that a candidate for initiation could be rejected when any Mason cast one black ball. Tresner said Texas and perhaps other Grand Lodges required two black balls for rejection. As an editor, Tresner pointed out a number of typographical errors. I retained complete editorial control until I submitted the manuscript to Lewis on January 22.

REPRIMAND

Robinson called me at 12:45 A.M. the following morning, February 23, to tell me I was being "strongly reprimanded" for writing the letter to Talbert. Lewis called at 7:20 the same morning to repeat Robinson's statement that I was being reprimanded. He said Holly had "widely distributed" copies of the letter along with his "diatribe."

In a letter to the Home Mission Board directors on February 23, 1993, Holly stated directors should reject the study and ask me to resign. He is quoted by the *Associated Baptist Press* as saying that he "blames Masons for the fact his father, a Mason, rejects Christianity."[4] Holly's father is a member of the Episcopal Church.

I did not meet face-to-face with either Robinson or Lewis until March 9, a week before the board of directors' spring meeting, when I had a meeting with Robinson in his office to discuss my future with the Home Mission Board. He was very cool. He sat behind his desk rather than his usual practice of sitting in a chair in front of his desk next to his guest. He did not ask about my family or offer to pray, as was his custom. Robinson mentioned several options that were being considered for me. He said a demotion and transfer to a field staff position was his first choice. He said other options were to fire me or to leave me in my present position as director of the Interfaith Witness Department. I think he was hoping I would offer to take a field staff position. I didn't.

MATERIALS REMOVED FROM HOME OFFICE

The next morning, March 10, Lewis called me to his office. Bobby Sunderland, special assistant for promotion and project development, was present. Lewis said he, along with Charles Stanley, Adrian Rogers and Art Tolston, had received a fax from Holly, who claimed to have learned of another letter that I had written to a Mason. Lewis asked me to sign a release to allow the administration to read all Freemasonry correspondence in my home. I signed the release but later regretted doing so. Sunderland accompanied me to my Home Mission Board office and personally removed three boxes of correspondence, mostly the 2,300 letters I had received since the previous July, and carried them to executive vice president Robert T. Banks's office. Then, Sunderland and Banks went with me to my home. Banks rode with me while Sunderland followed in his car. They removed another box of correspondence from my home. I had an engagement that evening to speak in a local church promoting the annual Annie Armstrong Offering for Home Missions. Knowing that in my present emotional state I could not make an effective presentation, I called the pastor and canceled the engagement.

TRANSFER TO FIELD STAFF POSITION

I received a formal written reprimand from Lewis on March 12. On March 15 while in a staff meeting, I received a note that Lewis wanted to meet with me at

5:00. Robinson was also in the meeting. They said they wanted me to ask to be moved to a field staff position as assistant director with my office in my home. No other options were discussed. I asked to discuss the request with my wife and promised an answer the next morning. We agreed that I would speak to the administrative committee in the morning and the full board of directors the following evening and ask their forgiveness. I was specifically told not to defend myself or my actions.

Robinson called me to his office at 9:00 the next morning, March 16, and I said I would accept the transfer. He emphasized that I had to say I had requested a transfer to the field staff position. I was asked to write a proposed position description. Robinson then called Tal Davis to his office to offer him the job of interim director of the Interfaith Witness Department.

I met with the administrative committee at 10:45 on March 16 and said exactly what Lewis asked me to say. I asked their forgiveness and left. It was over in ten minutes. I spoke to the Board of Directors at 8:00 P.M. Prior to speaking to them, Brad Allen, newly elected chairman, told me I could say anything I wished without fear of recrimination. I spoke for fifteen minutes, apologized for any embarrassment I caused the Home Mission Board, and left. Several directors responded with "amens" as I left. Rex Holt, a director from Arkansas, hugged me. Lewis, in a letter to me on March 18, called my appearances "magnanimous."

I met with Robinson and Ken Carter, associate vice president of the evangelism section, on March 19, 1993, to discuss my new field staff position. They accepted my position description as I had written it. Robinson again reminded me I had to say I "asked" for the field staff position. I remembered that Mormon apostle Bruce R. McConkie said, "It is my province to teach to the Church what the doctrine is. It is your province to echo what I say or to remain silent."[5]

SEVEN-PAGE "REPORT" APPROVED

Holly credits Nelson Price, a Home Mission Board director and pastor of the Roswell Street Baptist Church in Marietta, Georgia,[6] and the "courage" of one or two other directors, for the stronger recommendation adopted by the Home Mission Board and eventually the Southern Baptist Convention. The original statement said, "In light of the fact that many tenets and teachings of Freemasonry are compatible with Christianity and Southern Baptist doctrine. . . ."[7] The word *not*, that is, *are not compatible*, was added to the statement in an effort to gain the support of anti-Masons.

Holly correctly states that "the HMB Board meeting [March 17, 1992] at which this motion [on the "Report"] was acted upon allowed absolutely no discussion of the matter. Immediately, upon the motion being made, the question was called, the vote was taken."[8] However, the "Report" was discussed by the board of directors in a sixty- to ninety-minute meeting the previous evening. Directors had ample opportunity to discuss, debate, and offer changes to the "Report."

The Board of Directors approved the seven-page report, allegedly drafted by Larry Lewis,[9] with only one dissenting vote, on March 17. The Baptist Press reported that "Within minutes of the board's adjournment, Holly released a prepared statement supporting the report's recommendation," saying, "I plan to do nothing but support the [HMB] motion." Holly said his hope is that the recommendation "will be overwhelmingly approved" at the Southern Baptist Convention in Houston and that he planned to expend no more effort on the issue. Holly expressed appreciation to Bill Gordon, the Interfaith Witness Department missionary whom Holly had earlier criticized for writing a critique of his "little book," Lewis, and me.[10]

However, within a week, Holly, upset that the *Study* would be made available along with the seven-page "Report," sent a letter to all of the Home Mission Board directors and the news media calling for the directors to "disclaim the study . . . before the Southern Baptist Convention."[11]

ADDRESS TO STATE INTERFAITH WITNESS COORDINATORS

My last official act as department director was to address the annual meeting of the State Interfaith Witness coordinators meeting at the Hilton Plaza Inn in Kansas City, Missouri, on March 21. The speech was as follows:

> There is a strong, unbroken tradition in the history of the Interfaith Witness Department. It doesn't appear in our program statement, but I know it must be written in stone somewhere. That tradition is that no director in the twenty-seven years since the department was formed has lasted long enough in that position to retire. I was director five years and five months. That is a good record. The previous director served about fourteen months.
>
> I first stood before you as department director on this weekend in 1988 in this very hotel. Today, I stand before you as a former director. I am not going to talk about the details of this change. I am still too close to that event to talk about it without becoming emotional. I will

say that in light of an almost certain motion by Dr. Holly's supporters on the Board to fire me, I asked to be reassigned. I am experiencing the same emotions now that I experienced after my mother's death ten years ago. You can ask Ken Carter for additional details or read about it in the press releases which Joyce Johnson will pass out later.

You are hearing and will, no doubt, continue to hear much about my actions during the Freemasonry study. Last August, James Larry Holly called for my removal from the study after Craig Branch of Watchman Fellowship forwarded a letter I wrote to him on to Dr. Holly.[12]

The most infamous letter and the catalyst for the change in department leadership was a letter of January 17 that I wrote to D. L. Talbert, a Southern Baptist Mason friend in Chattanooga. He made copies, one of which Dr. Holly somehow received. The rest has been well publicized by Dr. Holly and others. Ed Decker, of *Saints Alive in Jesus*, has sent a letter to his supporters calling me a "Wolf in sheep's clothing" and offering to send my letter of January 17 to anyone wanting a copy. Texe Marrs has also indicated he will do an article on me.

In the January 17 letter I mentioned I had sent the manuscript to two Masons, one a Southern Baptist and one a non–Southern Baptist. I also sent a manuscript to a Southern Baptist who is not a Mason; that fact was of no interest to *Baptist Press*. My action was unusual but not unique. It is common for scholars to send manuscripts to others to critique. I have read manuscripts sent to me and have sent manuscripts to others in the past. I sent a Roman Catholic manuscript to a Catholic scholar a few years ago when Pope John Paul II visited the United States. I have even sent a manuscript on Mormonism to both the Mormon and RLDS Church headquarters for their critique.

In response, Southern Baptist Mason Abner McCall made no comment on the manuscript; it was returned without marks. Jim Tresner made a number of comments updating Masonic teachings and making editorial corrections. Any scholar will consider all sources for his research. I have worked in this area for fourteen years and know if and when an individual or group is trying to influence me. The Masons did not try to influence me but were open to me, providing access to their libraries and answering my questions.

There was absolutely **no** collusion on my part. I showed the Home Mission Board administration Talbert's letter of January 5 to me. It was a very personal letter with only one mention of Dr. Holly and none specifically of the study.

I want to remind you that Masons are not our enemies. Five hundred thousand of our pastors, church staff, and laymen are Masons. You arrive at four million when you add spouses, children, brothers, and sisters to that figure.

I mentioned in the letter that I had previewed the February 1993 issue of the *Scottish Rite Journal*. Because of professional courtesy, I was asked to check facts on the Southern Baptist Convention. I made several comments on the manuscript: the date of the Southern Baptist Convention in June was incorrect; one writer confused the 1992 motion with the 1985 resolution on Freemasonry; a writer indicated my doctorate was in religious philosophy rather than philosophy of religion; Morris Chapman's title was incorrect.

Two thousand three hundred Masons wrote letters to me between July 1 and December 31, 1992. The overwhelming number of them were from Southern Baptist Masons. They asked how they could have input into the "investigation" as they put it. I responded to only a few of the letters as time was too short. I said they could not have any input into the writing of the study and that their only recourse was to attend the Southern Baptist Convention as duly elected messengers of their local church as is their right as Southern Baptists. I also told that to anti-Masons, but not many anti-Masons wrote. There was no outpouring of anti-Masonic sentiment in the form of letters. Ron Phillips, chairman of the trustees, received fewer than a dozen anti-Masonic letters out of a total of about 1,800 letters.

I don't know what God has in store for me. I know that when men close one door of ministry, God always opens another one. I have taken the promise in Isaiah 55:8–9, "My thoughts are not your thoughts, neither are your ways my ways, . . . For as the heavens are higher than the earth, so are my ways higher than your ways, and my thoughts than your thoughts."

For the time being, I am an assistant director serving as a field staff. I no longer have an office in the Home Mission Board building, so you will not reach me if you call the Home Mission Board building. Joyce will pass out my address and phone number later.

There are some good things about this new assignment. One Home Mission Board staffer asked his supervisor what he could do to be punished like Leazer. I will be able to conduct more research and writing; that is where my interest lies. I have several books in my head that I have not had time to put on paper. I will still accept conferences as in the past.

The first person I brought on board after becoming director was a young man from Tallahassee, Florida. I chose well, and I am pleased he is now interim director. If I had made the choice of the person to succeed me, I would have chosen Tal Davis. For five years, Tal has effectively, but quietly, done a super job as associate director.

I have kept a journal for over twenty years. I use it as therapy to work out my stress. I wish I had followed that practice rather than expressing my frustration in the January 17 letter to Talbert.

On several occasions in my journal, I expressed amazement at Tal's understanding of interfaith witness. He has exceeded my every expectation. I know you join me in affirming Tal as the interim director. He assumes that role during what is probably the most difficult time in the history of our department. I commit myself to do everything in my power to help him do the best possible job.

In closing, let me say, I was ordained specifically to this ministry, not to the general church ministry. Glenn Igleheart, who is here today, participated in my ordination. Until God calls me into another ministry, I will be involved in interfaith witness. Thank you.

HOLLY RELEASED SECOND BOOK ATTACKING FREEMASONRY

In the spring of 1993 Holly released the second volume of *The Southern Baptist Convention and Freemasonry*. Much of its content came from the 630-page notebook Holly presented to the Interfaith Witness Department staff in September 1992. The first volume of *The Southern Baptist Convention and Freemasonry* was placed behind the second volume within the same cover. Even though Holly would argue his first volume was "irrelevant," he chose to reprint it with the second volume.

"REPORT" ACCEPTED AT SOUTHERN BAPTIST CONVENTION

I was concerned that the administration would withdraw the *Study of Freemasonry* from circulation. My concern received a boost on April 22 when Martin F. King, director of the office of public relations and development, wrote a memo to Lewis and five others at the Home Mission Board recommending that the study not be sold in the Baptist Book Store at the Southern Baptist Convention in Houston in June. I quickly sent Lewis and the other five persons recommending it be sold. Fortunately, the *Study* was sold at the bookstore in Houston.

Larry Lewis, in a letter to the editors of the state Baptist papers immediately preceding the June 1992 Southern Baptist Convention, said the *Study* was "a scholarly examination of the teachings of and charges against Freemasonry" and that it was "a fair and accurate review of the issues which Southern Baptist should find interesting and enlightening." Lewis stated that the "Report" prepared by the Home Mission Board administration and trustees was not a "cop-out," but its approach was "Baptistic." He expressed hope that Southern Baptists could return to the primary focus of planting and growing churches.[13]

Messengers approved the $111,000 Home Mission Board "Report on Freemasonry" at the Southern Baptist Convention in Houston, Texas, on June 16, 1993, by an overwhelming vote after a forty-five-minute discussion. Estimates ranged from a 4 to 1 approval to as high as 9 to 1 approval. Many Masons and non-Masons breathed a sigh of relief that the long nightmare was finally over.

RELIEF OVER ADOPTION OF "REPORT" SHORT-LIVED

However, almost immediately Richard O. Pierce of Cedar Park, Texas, introduced a resolution, which was referred to the Home Mission Board for response. The resolution read,

> Whereas the Home Mission Board of the Southern Baptist Convention has reported its investigation of Freemasonry shows the teachings of Freemasonry are incompatible with the teachings of the Holy Bible,
>
> Be it resolved: that the Southern Baptist Convention, in its 136th annual convention, desires all Christian men everywhere to know that the teachings of Freemasonry are in conflict with the teachings of the Holy Bible.[14]

Editors of the Baptist state convention papers and Grand Lodge periodicals voiced hope that the Freemasonry issue was finally settled. In his editorial in the South Carolina *Baptist Courier*, John E. Roberts wrote,

> The question of Baptists and the Masonic Order was settled and the chapter was closed. But it won no friends and made nobody happy. The good news is that it is over. A committee assigned last year to

> study the issue made its report and it was adopted. The report says any conflict in being both a Baptist and a Mason is a matter for each individual and each church to decide and is not a concern of the Convention. The bad news is that we bothered with the study in the first place, spending $111,000 on it, annoying each other while amusing the public.[15]

The editor of Iowa's *Grand Lodge Bulletin* expressed the hope that "it appears the matter of a 'conflict' between the two groups has finally been put to rest."[16]

As expected, Masons and their critics interpreted the conclusion in the Home Mission Board conclusions and the vote of the Convention differently. Craig Branch, director of the Birmingham, Alabama, office of Watchman Fellowship, Inc., an anticult ministry, called the report "a compromise."[17] Greg Warner, writing for *Associated Baptist Press*, had earlier spoken of the report as a "compromise."[18]

SPEECH AT SOUTHEAST MASONIC CONFERENCE

Shortly after the Southern Baptist Convention, Earl D. Harris, a Past Grand Master of the Grand Lodge of Georgia, invited me to give the keynote address to the thirty-third annual Southeast Masonic Conference on August 6 to summarize the conclusions of the *Study of Freemasonry* and explain the meaning of the vote on Freemasonry at the Southern Baptist Convention in Houston. I agreed because I felt Southern Baptists owed Masons an explanation of the vote. I felt it would be a good opportunity to reiterate the conclusions of the study and emphasize to Masons the need to take seriously the criticisms listed in the study. The speech was well received and, afterward, a request was made that my speech be published in the October 1993 issue of the Grand Lodge of Georgia quarterly *Masonic Messenger*. Permission was granted.

HOLLY CHARGES HMB KNEW "REPORT" NOT TRUE

In a September 30, 1993, letter to the Home Mission Board trustees, the officers and past presidents of the Southern Baptist Convention, *Baptist Press*, *Associated Baptist Press*, and the editors of the state Baptist papers, Holly charged the Home Mission Board of publishing "a report which they knew was not true." Holly was referring to a statement in the Home Mission Board Report on Freemasonry approved by the Southern Baptist Convention, which read, "To be sure, not all Grand Lodges affirm Christian doctrine, and many do not declare Jesus as the unique Son of God; but many do, and for this we commend them." He cited a letter from Tal Davis, interim director of the Interfaith Witness Department, to Jennifer Falk of Northfield, Minnesota, on September 15. Falk had written Lewis to ask for clarification on the statement in the report. Lewis asked that Davis respond to Falk's inquiry. Davis clarified the statement in his response to Falk:

> Our research did not find any local Masonic lodge nor any Grand Lodge which have [*sic*] taken a position for or against the biblical teaching affirming the uniqueness of Jesus Christ as the Son of God. . . . The sentence you cited from the report might have been stated more clearly, " . . . but many [Masons] do, and for this we commend them."

In his September 30 letter Holly called upon Home Mission Board president Larry Lewis to issue a statement "emphasizing the cautions contained in the concluding statement of your recommendation to the Convention, which states:

> In light of the fact that many tenets and teachings of Freemasonry are not compatible with Christianity and Southern Baptist doctrine . . . we exhort Southern Baptists to prayerfully and carefully evaluate Freemasonry in light of the lordship of Christ, the teachings of Scripture, and the findings of this report, as led by the Holy Spirit of God.

Home Mission Board president Larry Lewis countered, "Any implication that the Home Mission Board deliberately attempted to mislead Southern Baptists is patently untrue and certainly unfortunate."[19] Lewis continued, "It would be impossible to write any document which could not be misinterpreted, misunderstood or misapplied by those who wish to do."[20] Lewis never made a more truthful statement. Masons have learned this truth defending themselves from attacks by anti-Masons who have misinterpreted, misunderstood, and misapplied Masonic writings and writings by Masons. In my opinion, the sentence in the Home Mission Board Report on Freemasonry that Falk questioned is poorly written as no Grand Lodge affirms Christian doctrine. This is not their prerogative, just as it is not the prerogative of the Lions Club, Boy Scouts of America, the Fraternal Order of Police, or other similar organizations. The Home Mission Board Report on Freemasonry can arguably be said to have been poorly written by people largely ignorant of Freemasonry, but there was no conspiracy to hide the truth as Holly charges.

MISSOURI CHURCH PROHIBITS MASONS AS MEMBERS

The Missouri Baptist Convention's *Word and Way* reported in September 1993 that the Pulaski Baptist Association had tabled a recommendation that Briarwood Baptist Church, Dixon, Missouri, be granted membership in the association after reviewing the church's constitution and bylaws. (An association consists of Baptist churches in a limited area, usually one or more counties.) The church prohibited persons belonging to a "secret organization" from becoming a member of the church. The pastor, Floyd Stewart, said the provision in the constitution and bylaws is an "intensely bold statement on Freemasonry" that he believed is incompatible with Christianity. The church and the association were caught on the horns of the dilemma that each is an autonomous organization with the rights to determine its own internal affairs. The church, in Baptist life, is free to include prohibitions against Freemasonry or any other fraternal group. The association, in Baptist life, is free to grant or deny membership to any church.

In his third volume, Holly expressed his opinion that the "original intent of the motion to study Freemasonry was for the Convention to establish the truth about the Masonic Lodge in order to assist pastors who are being attacked and oppressed by Masons."[21] The "truth" was established in the Study. Nothing prevented nor now prevents any church from taking any action its membership so chooses, as we see with the action by the Briarwood Baptist Church.

INVOLUNTARY RESIGNATION

In October 1993, interim department director Tal Davis asked me to assist him with department budget matters, and I agreed to meet with him on Friday, October 22. When I arrived at the Home Mission Board building, Davis told me that a colleague had sent him a copy of my speech in the October 1993 issue of the Georgia *Masonic Messenger* and that he had passed on the newspaper to evangelism section vice president Darrell Robinson the previous day. Davis told me that after Larry Lewis saw the periodical, he called a meeting with the vice presidents, him and, reportedly, the Home Mission Board attorney. It was decided to either ask for my resignation or fire me.

Lewis called Davis and me to his office at 2:00. Lewis said he was requesting my resignation for "gross insubordination" for addressing the

Southeast Masonic Conference. He claimed I had violated an order to "refrain from any and all involvement in the Freemasonry issue."[22] I insisted that no such order was given to me. Insisting that I had been told, Lewis said I would be fired if I did not resign immediately. I requested permission to call my wife before giving an answer. My request was denied.

I reluctantly resigned as requested in a letter to Tal Davis, "Per the request of the administration, I am submitting my resignation as a staff member of the Home Mission Board effective today, October 22, 1993." My professional career as a Baptist was finished. I was given a check (previously prepared) for eleven days of unused vacation and was told I would receive three months' salary as a severance package.

I once saw a cartoon of a haggard man, who looked much like a Southern Baptist Convention employee, walking through the front door of his home. Holding a cardboard box filled with personal items from his office, he greeted his wife with the words "I told the truth and they set me free."

Holly thought the lack of written documentation with restrictions on conduct and association with Masons strange. He wrote:

> In virtually any employment, when a disciplinary action is taken, and when stipulations are made about future conduct, which would result in dismissal if violated, that is documented in writing with all parties witnessing that document. Why the HMB does not have a letter signed by Drs. Lewis, Robinson and Leazer explaining the understanding which they had reached about the restrictions upon Dr. Leazer's activities, is a question Southern Baptists have the right to have answered.[23]

After the meeting in Lewis's office, I remembered a memo I wrote to Ken Carter, associate to Darrell Robinson, on October 3, 1991:

> As I have shared with you previously, I firmly believe that the Freemasonry issue may lead to my dismissal or resignation from the Home Mission Board. I appreciate your reassurance, as well as Darrell's

> [Robinson], but I know that sometimes decisions are taken away from us and made by others. I told Dr. Lewis that the result of this study would be that neither Masons nor anti-Masons would be satisfied with my conclusions. I have had calls promising to work to get me fired if I don't label Masonry a Satanic cult. I received a letter last week promising demonstrations in the streets if my conclusions don't state that Masonic is Satanic. . . . Thank you for letting me share my heart with you at this time. I am concerned that once my report is made public that I might not have an opportunity.

LAWSUIT DIVIDES NORTH CAROLINA CHURCH

The Associated Baptist Press reported in December 1993 that several members of Westport Baptist Church in Lincolnton, North Carolina, had filed suit against the pastor, Mark Cook, and twenty-eight members of the church. The plaintiffs charged that a group of church members substituted a list of deacon nominees without prior notice. The new deacons attempted to change the church's bylaws. The plaintiffs asked the court to declare the deacon election invalid. The defendants' attorney countered that the lawsuit resulted from the pastor's sermons declaring that Freemasonry contradicts biblical teachings. Because some of the plaintiffs were Masons, the press headlined the dispute as one centered on the Freemasonry issue.[24] The suit was later dropped.

In a December 8 letter to 300 Southern Baptists leaders and journalists, Holly, who led a Bible study in Westport Baptist Church, with an optional study on Freemasonry, on the weekend of December 4, defended Cook and accused Masons in the church of attacking the pastor.[25]

HOLLY'S THIRD VOLUME RELEASED

Holly released his third book on the Freemasonry issue within the Southern Baptist Convention in March 1994, sending complementary copies to 1,600 Southern Baptist leaders. This book is a blistering, but unfounded, attack on *A Study of Freemasonry*, Larry Lewis, Darrell Robinson, and me.

Lewis asked Bill Gordon, who had written an excellent critique on Holly's first volume, to write a critique on the third volume in March 1994. Gordon submitted a lengthy critique, which Lewis decided not to release. The critique is not available. If it was done as well as the critique on the first volume, Lewis probably did not want another response from Holly as came after the first critique was released.[26]

Holly, more than any other living person, has been the catalyst in awakening a sleeping giant, the Masonic fraternity. Masons will no longer remain quiet. They are talking. They are holding meetings. They are developing strategies to educate their members and the general public. Most importantly, they are responding to the malicious untruths being spread across the land about their fraternity.

HOME MISSION BOARD REVISITS MASONIC ISSUE

The Home Mission Board directors, at their April 1994 meeting, revisited the Freemasonry issue. A motion condemning the doctrine of universalism (the belief all people will eventually be saved) was passed unanimously. One of the criticisms of Freemasonry adopted in the Board's "Report on Freemasonry" was the alleged teaching of universalism by Freemasonry. The editor of *The Christian Index*, the state paper for Georgia Baptists, removed a statement quoted in the Baptist Press by John Boettjer, editor of the *Scottish Rite Journal*, denying that Freemasonry taught universalism.[27] A statement by James Holly that the vote was "a step in the right direction, but it does not begin to address the problems with Freemasonry," was included in the *Index* story.[28]

A motion to direct the administrative committee to study whether Masons could be appointed as missionaries was defeated on a 30–31 vote after the chairman of the directors broke the tie vote. This issue will certainly be brought up for vote again.

Lewis announced during the Board meeting that all copies of the *Study* had been sold and it would not be reprinted. A rumor circulated around the Home Mission Board building that three boxes of the *Study* remained unsold, and that they were simply removed from the warehouse to a more secure location. Holly repeatedly called for the withdrawal of the *Study* from sale.[29] Undoubtedly, Lewis's announcement that the *Study* would no longer be sold was in response to Holly's request.

Lewis's action demonstrates that Holly's claim that I own the *Study* is baseless fiction.[30] If I had owned the *Study*, I would have sought an outside publisher, just as I had requested before the Home Mission Board published it. Lewis rejected my request. If I had owned the *Study*, I would not have allowed Lewis to make the "radical" changes in the text. While I disagree with the changes Lewis made, he had the authority to make the changes since the *Study* was a Home Mission Board publication. Lewis had the authority to withdraw the *Study* from sale because it was a Home Mission Board publication. My involvement was as an employee of the Home Mission Board, which owns the *Study*.

This chapter is a temporary ending to the anti-Mason crusade within the Southern Baptist Convention to condemn Freemasonry. Former Southern Baptist Joe Barnhart, a philosophy professor at North Texas State University in Denton, Texas, is correct when he says, "Battles do not begin or end because the warriors and generals are tired or vigorous. They go on because social, political, and other forces are at work."[31] While most Southern Baptists want the issue put behind them, a few vocal anti-Masons representing a splinter group within the Convention are committed to carrying on the fight until they achieve victory.

8 James L. Holly's Criticism of A Study of Freemasonry, Part I

I give you a new commandment, that you love one another. Just as I have loved you, you also should love one another. By this everyone will know that you are my disciples, if you have love for one another. (John 13:34–35)

JAMES LARRY HOLLY HAS WRITTEN THREE BOOKS ON FREEMASONRY, EACH OF them titled *The Southern Baptist Convention and Freemasonry*. The first volume, a 57-page booklet, was released in spring 1992 before the Southern Baptist Convention met in Indianapolis in June 1992. This volume was sent to 5,000 Southern Baptist pastors and leaders in anticipation of the resolution Holly planned to introduce at the Convention. A second volume, a 115-page book, was released in 1993. Volumes one and two were placed within the same cover. The third book, with 366 pages, a response to and criticism of *A Study of Freemasonry* published by the Home Mission Board, was released in March 1994 as a separate volume.[1] In the third volume, Holly accuses me of "poor research, faulty attribution, partial quotations, prejudiced opinions, secondary sources, and other violations of scholarly methodology."[2] These charges will be highlighted and used to respond to Holly's criticisms in this and the following chapter.

HOLLY'S GENERAL CRITICISMS

We will begin with a few general criticisms that Holly's makes about the *Study*, before moving to more specific charges. These general criticisms arise because Holly disagrees with the overall development of the material in the *Study*.

Holly, speaking of Bill Gordon's critique of his first volume of his trilogy, *The Southern Baptist Convention and Freemasonry*, writes, "It is obvious that Dr. Gordon does not like *The SBC and Freemasonry*."[3] That Holly does not like *A Study of Freemasonry* has to be the understatement of the century, if not of recorded history. He speaks of the *Study* as "obviously a flawed study,"[4] "inaccurate and unacceptable,"[5] "a prejudiced, non-scholarly, collection of Masonic opinions."[6]

Most of Holly's criticisms of the *Study* arise because it does not take the same approach he would have preferred. It does not make the same points he would have made. It does not quote the same sources he would have quoted. It arrived at a different conclusion than he would have. At one point, Holly asks, "Why does Dr. Leazer quote from *A Bridge to Light* . . . ?"[7] On the same page, he asks, "Why did Dr. Leazer not quote . . . from *A Bridge to Light* . . . ?"[8] Holly asks six times in one paragraph, "Why is it . . . Why are . . . Why wasn't . . . Why was . . . Why doesn't . . . Why didn't . . . ?"[9]

Holly criticizes the Study for using Robert A. Morey's *The Origin and Teachings of Freemasonry* as a source. The *Study* cited Morey's book five times.[10] At one point, Holly argued, "Leazer seemed to use Morey's work as a 'frame work' in which to consider his approach to the study of Freemasonry. Morey's book seemed to provide the framework both for Leazer's and Lewis' hostility to 'anti-Masons.' "[11] Later in his third volume, Holly insists, "More than anyone, Tresner seems to have provided Leazer with his paradigm, with his schema, for organizing his support of the Masonic Lodge."[12] In reality, neither Robert Morey nor Jim Tresner provided the framework, paradigm, or schema for the *Study*.

Holly says in a December 8, 1992, letter to Larry Lewis, "It is my request that the IFW [Interfaith Witness Department] and the HMB [Home Mission Board] redirect their focus from me and my booklet to the Masonic Lodge and their teachings."[13] Yet, Holly repeatedly involved himself in the controversy by writing letters, making phone calls, and sending faxes to Lewis, the Interfaith Witness Department staff, Home Mission Board directors, Convention leaders, the press, and me. He and several men from Mission and Ministry to Men, Inc., met with the department staff, a Baptist Press representative, Larry Lewis and the chairman of the Board of Directors, Brad Allen, in September 1992. Holly wanted to be involved in the study. Holly wrote me, "Of course, your study will be re-inventing the wheel if you ignore the research which has been done by others."[14] Holly wrote Lewis, "Why does Dr. Leazer want to re-invent the wheel? I have sent him a great deal of material."[15] In his second volume, Holly wrote, "If the Interfaith Witness Department of the Home Mission Board needed any help, any encouragement, to take a strong, bold stand against the Lodge, this book provides it."[16]

Yet, I was criticized for "focusing" on Holly's material by Holly, Larry Lewis, and others.

Holly says his fifty-seven-page book was irrelevant for the study; "my booklet is irrelevant to the study being undertaken by the HMB. **Whether my booklet is factual or erroneous is irrelevant**."[17] What kind of scholar would write a book and then not care if it is "factual or erroneous?" If the fifty-seven-page book was "irrelevant," why did Holly send it to thousands of Southern Baptist leaders and to every Southern Baptist pastor in Indiana prior to the Southern Baptist Convention in Indianapolis in 1992? He accuses the Masonic lodge of trying to influence Southern Baptist churches and pastors.[18] Was not Holly trying to influence thousands of Southern Baptist churches and pastors with his mailings? If the fifty-seven-page book was "irrelevant," why did Holly include it with the second volume and release both volumes in one cover? The second volume was released long after Holly began claiming the first volume was "irrelevant." Holly was upset that Interfaith Witness Department staff member Bill Gordon did a critique on his first book. If I had written the book, I would not have wanted it critiqued either.

Holly contends that "Pike is not the issue," yet on the same page he says "what Leazer must deal with is the Masons' attitude toward Pike."[19]

According to Holly, only the 630-page notebook he provided the participants in the September 1992 meeting, was relevant. Why was this notebook relevant and his fifty-seven-page book irrelevant? Holly asks in his third volume why no critique was conducted on the notebook. First, the notebook was written as a "A Report to The Interfaith Witness Department," which I interpreted as an in-house resource. Second, it was not published and sold. I would have asked a staff member to critique the notebook had I known he sent copies to the Home Mission Board's administrative committee, past presidents, and officers of the convention.[20] After sending his notebook to over 100 individuals, he wonders how Jim Tresner received a copy: "Where did Tresner get these materials?"[21] Holly circulated his letters and other writings to dozens of individuals. Tresner could have received a copy from a number of people.

Holly assures his readers that "I know that I am not an Old Testament prophet. I cannot foretell the future. But the voice which I have raised . . . is a prophetic voice."[22] He refers to himself only as "the messenger."[23] The *Holman Bible Dictionary* defines a prophet as "one who speaks for God or Christ."[24] The primary function of the biblical prophet was as one who speaks on God's behalf, not a predictor of the future. Holly believes God wanted him to speak out on Freemasonry.

Holly challenges the readers of his twenty-chapter third volume to read four chapters ("chapters fourteen, seventeen, twenty, and, then, two"), then "If at that time you can remain passive about *A Study Of Freemasonry*, **I have failed, and the loss will be the Kingdom's**."[25] Later, he states his belief that "Dr. Leazer did not serve Dr. Lewis well. Dr. Lewis did not serve the trustees well. The trustees did not serve the Convention well. The Convention is not serving the Kingdom well, . . ."[26] Holly obviously wants to assure his readers of the tremendous burden he believes God has placed on his shoulders. He writes, "I believe that God told me to lay down the issue of Freemasonry [after the June 1993 Southern Baptist Convention in Houston]. Now, I believe that God wants me to write *The SBC and Freemasonry, Volume III*."[27] At one point, he quotes the Lord, whom he says spoke to him while he watched the movie *The Alamo*, complete with "the Lord said" statements.[28] For example, Holly states that "the Lord said, 'There is not a man alive today, who was even conceived when the Alamo fell' " in 1836, over 158 years ago. He also claims the Lord spoke to him during the movie and said, "You cannot live long enough to make it worth while to compromise your convictions."[29]

In his first volume, Holly says Joseph Smith and the Mormon Church received the idea from Masons that God "speaks to men with new and different revelation throughout time." This, of course, is an inane and unsubstantiated charge. It doesn't make sense. Holly goes on to say that "The Bible maintains that . . . God continues to commune with His people in devotions, in prayer and in the Word of God."[30] He says, "The Bible encourages no confidence in any other 'revelation.' "[31] If that is the case, and I agree it is, where did Holly get the ridiculous idea that God speaks verbally to persons in the audience during movies? How authoritative are the alleged words of God in a Hollywood movie?

The conclusions of Holly's third volume are placed at the beginning of his book to influence his readers to a certain conclusion before reading the entire text. The *Study* said,

> Many Masons and their critics begin with conclusions, which they then seek to prove. Larry Kunk points out "the tendency of humans to be limited by their paradigms." A paradigm is a model that a person believes describes the truth about something. As Kunk points out, a person can be misled by his paradigm and make a false conclusion.
>
> Many Masonry critics begin with the paradigm that Freemasonry is an anti-Christian religion. Kunk says, "The reader must look at Masonic writings from the perspective of someone who does not believe that Jesus is the only Son of God." If you make up your mind before you

> take an objective look at Freemasonry, you will probably arrive back at your beginning point because you stay within your paradigm, namely that Freemasonry is an anti-Christian religion.[32]

Holly argues that the Study misquoted Kunk at this point, by eliminating the first eight words of Kunk's sentence.[33] The entire sentence reads, "In order to understand the nature of Freemasonry, the reader must look at Masonic writings from the perspective of someone who does not believe that Jesus is the only Son of God."[34] Holly's argument that the Study was attempting to "distort" Kunk's position is unconvincing.

The original text of the *Study* showed how Ankerberg and Weldon used the same approach as Holly by stating their conclusion before giving any evidence. This paragraph was removed by Lewis during the editing process.

> [In] the first sentence in the chapter entitled "The Plan of Salvation," Ankerberg and Weldon asks, "Did you know that the Masonic Lodge teaches a way of salvation that is not taught in the Bible?" This is an attempt to set a particular paradigm for the reader. The idea that the Lodge teaches a false way of salvation has been programmed in the reader's mind to lead the reader to a particular conclusion.[35]

Having responded to some of Holly's general criticisms of the *Study*, we will examined more specific charges, beginning with the charge of poor research.

POOR RESEARCH

Holly believes Pike "is one of two or three of their [Masonry's] most important writers."[36] He says,

> Far from discrediting Pike or disassociating themselves from Pike, modern Masons are aggressively embracing him and attempting to reinforce his teachings through modernizing the language which he used and providing commentaries so that Pike's teaching can carry the Masonic Lodge into the twenty-first century.[37]

This, of course, is an exaggeration, as is the statement that all Southern Baptists believe in the ordination of women. Some do, but certainly not all and not even most. There are approximately 4,700,000 Masons worldwide with approximately 2,371,000 in the United States. Of these nearly five million Masons, only 495,000 Scottish Rite Masons in the Southern Jurisdiction of the United States recognize Albert Pike as a former Sovereign Grand Commander. Over four million Masons worldwide and nearly two million Masons in the United States do not recognize Pike as an authority, except as a former Sovereign Grand Commander of the Southern Jurisdiction of the Scottish Rite, of which they are not members. To imply that most or all Masons aggressively embrace Albert Pike is an exaggeration and reflects poor research.

In the preface to his second volume, Holly claims there are 1.3 million Southern Baptist Masons. If Holly is correct, approximately 55 percent of all Masons in the United States are Southern Baptists. His figure is highly inflated. He claims in the preface to his second volume that there are 500,000 Southern Baptist Scottish Rite Masons in the Southern Jurisdiction of the United States.[38] Holly dates the preface as January 1993. The Southern Jurisdiction of Scottish Rite Masons says there were 513,589 Scottish Rite Masons in its jurisdiction on December 31, 1992. Holly's unsubstantiated claim of 500,000 Southern Baptist Scottish Rite Masons is highly inflated. In the fourteen states where Southern Baptist churches have the largest number of members, there are only 306,000 Scottish Rite Masons.

Holly attacks the Study's statement that one Scottish Rite Mason estimated fewer than one Mason in 1,000 had read *Morals and Dogma*.[39] That was the estimate of one Mason but it probably was not far off. Ed Decker erroneously believes *Morals and Dogma* is "the most readily available and universally approved doctrinal book of Freemasonry."[40] *Morals and Dogma* is not "universally approved." The Southern Jurisdiction stopped giving copies of *Morals and Dogma* to candidates in 1974. Since 1974, 335,478 Blue Lodge Masons have become Scottish Rite Masons in the Southern Jurisdiction; none of whom were given a copy of *Morals and Dogma*. It is granted that some might have purchased a copy of *Morals and Dogma* from a friend or in a used book store, or borrowed a copy from a library. Ignoring deaths and resignations, probably no more than 160,000 Scottish Rite Masons, those initiated before 1974 and living today, were given a copy of *Morals and Dogma* when initiated. If all of these 160,000 Scottish Rite Masons read *Morals and Dogma*, only 34 out of every 1,000 Masons would have read it. How many would read an 861-page book as difficult to understand as *Morals and Dogma*?

Morals and Dogma is not a "doctrinal book." If it were, why would the Preface state, "Every one is entirely free to reject and dissent from whatsoever herein may seem to him to be untrue or unsound"?[41] That does not sound like a statement which would be found in a doctrinal book.

It is odd that *Morals and Dogma* would be taken out of print if it is the "'Bible' of Freemasonry, as Larry Kunk claims it is often called.[42] It is odd that *Morals and Dogma* would be taken out of print if it is "the handbook for Masons," as Cathy Burns claims.[43]

Holly claims "Pike always refers to Jesus Christ as Jesus of Nazareth. Why?"[44] Even a cursory examination of *Morals and Dogma* proves Holly's claim is erroneous. Pike refers to Christ as "Jesus of Nazareth" at least eight times in *Morals and Dogma*.[45] Yet, he refers to Him as simply "Christ" or as "Jesus Christ" at least sixty-seven times.[46] Pike also refers to Christ as "Him who died upon the cross,"[47] as the "*Good Shepherd*,"[48] as the "Son of God,"[49] as the "Son of man,"[50] as "the Word Incarnate,"[51] as "*Jesus Christ, the Son of God, the Savior*,"[52] as the "WORD of God,"[53] and as "the Only-Begotten."[54] Later, Holly says Pike "admires and reveres" Jesus Christ as a "teacher or reformer."[55] Holly quotes several sentences from pages 310–311 in *Morals and Dogma* in which Pike refers to Christ "Dying thus," without mentioning Christ's resurrection.[56] Pike referred to "The Christ of the Apocalypse, First-born of Creation and of the Resurrection" on page 273 in *Morals and Dogma*. Only three pages prior to Holly's citation, on page 307, Pike says, "The agonies of the garden of Gethsemane and those on the Cross on Calvary preceded the Resurrection and were the means of Redemption."

In the discussion of the 26°, Pike refers to the symbolism of the three sides of the Delta. He states the sides refer to Wisdom or Designing Power, Force or Creating Power, and Harmony or Preserving Power. But, "to the Christian Mason, they represent the Three that bear record in Heaven, the FATHER, the WORD, and the HOLY SPIRIT, which three are ONE."[57] Pike doesn't say a Christian Mason cannot believe in the Trinity; he says they do believe in the Trinity.

Holly cites "an obvious contradiction" in the *Study*.[58] On page 22, the *Study* states that "earlier writers such as Albert Pike and Albert Mackey, have hurt Freemasonry by their zeal to link Freemasonry with antiquity." On page 45, the *Study* says "Mackey repudiated the idea of Masonic descent from 'the Ancient Mysteries.' " These statements do not necessarily contradict each other. Mackey could have changed his position. While "the Ancient Mysteries" are a part of antiquity, not all groups within antiquity are "Ancient Mysteries." The statement on page 22 was a reference to the attempt to trace Masonic roots to King Solomon, the Middle Ages, and other individuals and movements.

Holly says a scholarly study will "examine all sides of a question."[59] The *Study* examined all sides, giving both the Masonic and anti-Masonic positions, and trusting the readers to consider each argument and arrive at the correct conclusion. Holly can hardly claim to have examined all sides; he quotes only Masonic sources that he believes supports his preconceived ideas about Freemasonry.

Ron Carlson claims "that probably only 1 in 10,000 Masons fully understand what they are involved in."[60] If that is true, then 9,999 out of 10,000 Masons must be deceived or ignorant. With 2.5 million Masons in the United States, Carlson would ask us to believe that only 250 Masons in the entire country understand Masonry. It is difficult to respond to such wild accusations, except to say that this kind of claim belongs in a supermarket tabloid.

Holly poses the rhetorical question that every Shriner is "in allegiance with the Islamic faith through the Koran?"[61] He claims the Shrine is "an Islamic order."[62] This is a false charge. The Shrine was organized in New York in 1871. Shrine Temples are found in the United States, Canada, Mexico, and Panama. Shrine clubs are found in seven European countries and in the Philippines. No Shrine Temple or club is found in any Islamic country. This seems strange given Holly's contention that the Shrine is an Islamic order.

Holly asks, "Why does every Shriner swear his oath to the Shrine with his hand on the Koran?" Where did Holly get this idea? A call to any Shrine Temple would reveal that this is absolutely not true.[63] This is another example of Holly's poor research and intentionally misleading questions. A Shriner is asked to use the scripture that is authoritative for him. The Christian uses the Bible; a Shriner from another faith uses his scripture.

A statement in the *Study* reads, "The Lodge tends to follow the lead of the general society, rather than being a leader in racial reconciliation."[64] Holly quotes a statement from *A Bridge to Light* and then says, "This statement, by one of the leaders of a 'general society' of Freemasons, which even Dr. Leazer says 'the Lodge tends to follow.' "[65] Holly later proposes that the general society "is selected from the meaner elements of the culture."[66] Holly would be surprised to learn he is a part of the "general society." The reference to the "general society" in the *Study* was a reference to American society in general, not to any secret group of Freemasons as Holly erroneously believes. Holly brags, "I defy Leazer to show one misapplication or misrepresentation of his words by me!"[67] This is one of many such times.

PARTIAL QUOTATIONS

Partial quotations are often used to change the meaning and intent of the original writer. Several examples of Holly's use of partial quotations will be cited in this section.

Holly discusses the "Royal Secret" taught in the 32°. He claims the Royal Secret, which he also calls the "secret doctrine," "is the Masonic plan of salvation" because it sounds New Age to him. He says, "It is the plan of salvation for the chief agent of the New Age movement, the Masonic Lodge."[68] Nowhere is salvation discussed in the pages cited by Holly in Pike's *Morals and Dogma* or Rex Hutchens's *A Bridge to Light*. Holly's claim is illogical. Most Masons do not receive degrees beyond the 3° or Master Mason degree; only Scottish Rite Masons who receive the 32° learn the teachings of that degree. If the "Royal Secret" "is the Masonic plan of salvation," wouldn't it make sense that all Masons would receive the 32°?

Hutchens clearly states that the Royal Secret "is no secret in the normal sense of the word; that is, it is not something to be hidden from the rest of the world." He goes on to say that the Royal Secret is "hidden only because we do not completely understand it."[69]

Contrary to Holly's erroneous interpretation of Pike, Pike clearly explains that the Royal Secret is "UNIVERSAL EQUILIBRIUM."[70] Pike explains that this equilibrium is between infinite divine wisdom and infinite divine power, infinite divine justice and infinite divine mercy, divine omnipotence and the free will of mankind, authority and individual action and so forth.[71] There is no mention of salvation in the discussion of the Royal Secret by either Pike or Hutchens.

While Holly says the "secret doctrine" of Freemasonry is the Royal Secret or Universal Equilibrium on pages 34–36, he argues five pages later that the "secret doctrine" is that the plan of salvation "is through the Lambskin and its innocence, it is through the good works and the good character of the Mason, that he is to be saved."[72]

Holly quotes *A Study of Freemasonry*:

> Masons insist they use the lambskin apron as an emblem of innocence, a symbol of the purity of life and moral conduct demanded of all Masons. They insist the lambskin does not bring salvation, but rather "the purity of life" it symbolizes brings salvation.[73]

Holly accuses me of using partial quotations to change conclusions in the *Study*. Here Holly omits the sentence in the *Study* that immediately follows the last sentence cited by him, "They [Masons] use the lambskin as a symbol of Christ, who is 'a lamb unblemished and spotless' (1 Pet. 1:19, NASB)."

Holly then changes the quote in the study by saying, "Read carefully Dr. Leazer's own words; he said, 'the lambskin . . . symbolizes . . . the purity of life . . . which bring life.' "[74] He then attacks my soteriology, or doctrine of salvation. The quote clearly states that the argument concerning the lambskin apron is the Masonic position. I stated the Masonic position without giving my position.

Holly quotes Pike as saying, "Deity of the Old Testament is . . . the direct author of evil."[75] An ellipsis (. . .) means the writer intentionally omitted words found in the original source. In this case, Pike's full quote is

> The Deity of the Old Testament is everywhere represented as the direct author of Evil, commissioning evil and lying spirit to men, hardening the heart of Pharaoh, and visiting the iniquity of the individual sinner on the whole people.[76]

Pike's idea is found throughout the Old Testament as people struggled with the source and theological meaning of evil and suffering. Jobs his wife asked, "Shall we receive the good at the hand of God, and not receive the bad" (Job 2:10). In Isaiah 45:6, we read, "I form light and create darkness, I make weal and create woe; I the LORD do all these things." In Amos 3:6, we read, "Shall disaster befall a city unless the LORD has done it?"

Concerning the trinity, Holly says,

> Pike and Masons misunderstand. They take the Christian Trinity to be another example of the polytheism of the pagans. In *Morals and Dogma* Pike said, ". . . whether the Holy Ghost is of the same substance with the Father, or only of a similar substance . . ." is a question beyond the comprehension of man. (*Morals and Dogma*, p. 530) What Christian Mason wishes to affirm the heresy of the Lodge?[77]

The reader receives a completely erroneous understanding of Pike's statement by reading the partial quotation that Holly has lifted out of the middle of Pike's lengthy sentence. To quote Holly, "This pattern is so typical; it is wearisome."[78] The full sentence reads:

> He commands us to love one another, to love our neighbor as ourself; and we dispute and wrangle, and hate and slay each other, because we cannot be of one opinion as to the Essence of His Nature, as to His Attributes; whether He became man born of a woman, and was crucified; whether the Holy Ghost is of the *same* substance with the Father, or only of a *similar* substance; whether a feeble old man is

> God's Viceregent; whether some are elected from all eternity to be saved, and others to be condemned and punished; whether punishment of the wicked after death is to be eternal; whether this doctrine or the other be heresy or truth;—drenching the world with blood, depopulating realms, and turning fertile lands into deserts; until, for religious war, persecution, and bloodshed, the Earth for many a century has rolled round the Sun, a charnel-house, steaming and reeking with human gore, the blood of brother slain by brother for opinion's sake, that has soaked into and polluted all her veins, and made her a horror to her sisters of the Universe.[79]

Read Pike's sentence carefully. Does this sentence sound like a discussion of a Masonic understanding of the doctrine of the trinity? No! Holly's partial quotation of Pike's sentence completely changes the intended meaning of the discussion. Pike is speaking about how differences in interpretations of doctrines have led to centuries of religious wars with brother killing brother in the name of the One who commanded us to love one another.

9 James L. Holly's Criticism of *A Study of Freemasonry*, Part II

Uninspired fallible men make their own opinions tests of orthodoxy, and use their own systems, as Procrustes used his iron bedstead, to stretch and measure the consciences of all others. . . .[1]

We will continue to examine Holly's criticism of *A Study of Freemasonry* in this chapter by examining his charges of faulty attribution, unnamed and secondary sources, prejudiced opinions, and other violations of scholarly methodology.

FAULTY ATTRIBUTION

James Larry Holly accused me of plagiarism in *A Study of Freemasonry*, especially of Jim Tresner's unpublished manuscript, *Perspectives, Responses & Reflections*. "Throughout *A Study of Freemasonry*, we will see Dr. Leazer either quoting Tresner, plagiarizing him or being influenced by him."[2] Holly repeatedly refers to my "friend Jim Tresner" who, Holly claims, gave me an "education in Masonry."[3] Holly's accusations are without foundation. I received far more material and correspondence on Freemasonry from Holly than from Tresner. I actually had little contact with Tresner during the research and writing of the *Study*.

Out of 269 footnotes in the *Study*, Tresner's *Perspectives, Responses & Reflections* was used as a source seven times, six of which are in the section "Introduction to Freemasonry." Holly's material was cited seventeen times in the original manuscript, and four times in the published *Study*. Holly quotes from the "Introduction to Freemasonry" in the *Study*,

> . . . officers of the Blue Lodge include the Worshipful Master (president or chairman), the Senior Warden (first vice president or vice chairman), the Junior Warden (second vice president or vice chairman). . . .[4]

Holly claims this "is a direct quote from Tresner's work" and accuses me of plagiarism.[5] Here's what Tresner writes: "The officers of the local Lodge include the Worshipful Master (president), the Senior Warden (first vice president), the Junior Warden (second vice president)."[6] The statement is similar to Tresner's but it is not "a direct quote." Holly fails to tell his readers that this statement is footnoted as having come from Tresner's manuscript. In other words, Tresner received credit as the source; that is not plagiarism.

Holly is apparently upset that I did not "plagiarize" anti-Masons, for he asks, "Why do we not find language in Dr. Leazer's study which sounds like 'anti-Masons' being plagiarized?"[7] It leaves me wondering if he would have been as upset if I had "plagiarized" anti-Masons.

Holly cites as an example of "dereliction" my "reciting of Masonic propaganda as an unattributed part of his study."[8] He then quotes from *A Study of Freemasonry* to prove his point:

> The psalmist writes, "The eye of the Lord is on those who fear Him" (Ps. 33:18, NASB). Proverbs 15:3 (NASB) states, "The eyes of the Lord [YHWH] are in every place, Watching the evil and the good." This reminds the Mason that his actions do not go unnoticed by God.[9]

The quote in the *Study* continues, "Masonry critics remind us that the All-Seeing Eye was also the Egyptian symbol for Osiris. Some Masons cite this use of the symbol, but others cite the biblical foundation of the All-Seeing Eye. It is uncertain when the All-Seeing Eye became a Masonic symbol."[10]

He claims this quote "is almost a direct quote from page seventy-two of Masonic author Jim Tresner's unpublished manuscript, *Perspectives, Responses & Reflections*."[11] Tresner's full quote reads:

> The anti-Masons also suggest that the "all-seeing eye" used as a Masonic symbol is "really" the eye of the Egyptian God, Osiris. First, of course, Osiris is not associated in Egyptian religion with an eye. Horus is associated with the symbol, as is Ra. Horus represented the concept of the triumph of right in the world, and Ra was the Egyptian name for the one God, of Whom all other gods were merely aspects or

manifestations. See Budge or any standard work on ancient Egyptian theology.

In Masonry, the all-seeing eye is used as a symbol for God, reminding us that He sees every act and knows every thought. It is not, in Masonry, associated with any Egyptian deity.[12]

Tresner did not cite either of the biblical references included in the *Study*. My statement in *A Study of Freemasonry* is hardly "almost a direct quote" from Jim Tresner's manuscript. Rather, since I was not using Tresner's manuscript, there was no reason to cite it as a source.

Holly again accuses me of plagiarism because of my quotes from *The Murrow Masonic Monitor* and two books giving the Scottish Rite rituals. He charges my quotes were "taken from Tresner's work."[13] The quotes in question, allegedly from Tresner's manuscript, consists almost exclusively of quotations from other Masonic sources. Tresner and I quoted the same sources. However, Tresner does not provide source documentation for the quotes. Source documentation is provided in the *Study*. The quotes in the *Study* were taken from the original sources as indicated in the footnotes in the *Study*.[14]

In a somewhat baffling attack, Holly claims the *Study* quoted Sovereign Grand Commander C. Fred Kleinknecht "without attribution."[15] At question is the statement: "*A Bridge to Light*, by Rex R. Hutchens, was published in 1988 to replace *Morals and Dogma* and to encourage Scottish Rite Masons 'to investigate more fully the profound teachings of the Rite and learn how to apply them in their daily lives.'"[16] The quote is footnoted as coming from *A Bridge to Light*; the following sentence in the *Study* states that "*A Bridge to Light* is recommended by C. Fred Kleinknecht."

Holly insists *A Bridge to Light* is not intended to replace *Morals and Dogma* and questions a statement in the *Study* that states it is to replace *Morals and Dogma*. He asks, "Who told him [Leazer] this? Upon what basis does he make such a speculative statement?"[17] First of all, C. Fred Kleinknecht, in the foreword to *A Bridge to Light*, says that many people do not have the education and intelligence to understand *Morals and Dogma*.[18] Second, *Morals and Dogma* has not been given to Scottish Rite Masons since 1974. Third, they are not being printed; the only copies available are those that might be found in some libraries and used book stores. The Supreme Council, 33°, Southern Jurisdiction, U.S.A., has a few copies which may be purchased. It would seem that if *A Bridge to Light* is not intended to replace *Morals and Dogma* that *Morals and Dogma* would still be in print and available for those Scottish Rite

Masons who study *A Bridge to Light*. This is the basis on which I made the statement.

UNNAMED AND SECONDARY SOURCES

Holly criticizes me for quoting "unnamed" sources in the study, yet he repeatedly cites "unnamed" sources in his three volumes and sees no problem with this. I am reminded here of Jesus's teaching on judging others:

> Do not judge, so that you may not be judged. For with the judgment you make you will be judged, and the measure you give will be the measure you get. Why do you see the speck in your neighbor's eye, but do not notice the log in your own eye? Or how can you say to your neighbor, 'Let me take the speck out of your eye, while the log is in your own eye?" You hypocrite, first take the log out of your own eye, and then you will see clearly to take the speck out of your neighbor's eye (Matt. 7:1–5).

Holly quotes an unnamed "pastor" and "another church staff member."[19] He quotes from "one edition of a Masonic Bible, which has since been burned by its owner."[20] He quotes an unnamed "African pastor" in a letter to the Home Mission Board directors on April 10, 1992.

Holly also mentions an unnamed Roman Catholic physician who sent the department director three large notebooks of material condemning Freemasonry.[21] My crime was that I did not accept without criticism materials by James Holly, John Ankerberg, John Weldon, Larry Kunk, Jack Chick, Texe Marrs, Ed Decker, Pat Robertson, the unnamed Roman Catholic physician, and others.

Holly criticizes the *Study* for using Robert Morey's *The Origins and Teachings of Freemasonry* as a secondary source.[22] Morey's book was cited five times out of 269 footnotes in the study, while Holly quotes Morey at least nineteen times in his book,[23] noting that he finds much in Morey's book "which is valuable."[24] Is Holly using a different or double standard? Is it wrong when the *Study* cites Morey and acceptable when Holly quotes him?

He criticizes the *Study* for citing John Ankerberg and John Weldon's quote from *Coil's Masonic Encyclopedia*:

> Freemasonry has a religious service to commit the body of a deceased brother to the dust whence it came and to speed the liberated

> spirit back to the Great Source of Light. Many Freemasons make this flight with no other guarantee of a safe landing than their belief in the religion of Freemasonry.[25]

Holly expresses his doubt that either Ankerberg, Weldon, or I examined the quote in *Coil's Masonic Encyclopedia*. I cannot speak for Ankerberg or Weldon, although I would guess that they examined the text in the original. I can assure my readers that I examined the original to be certain that Ankerberg and Weldon quoted it correctly, which they did.

I take issue with Holly's interpretation that "***Coil's Encyclopedia* endorses**" the belief that Masons believe they can go to heaven through the Lodge. That is an unjustified and unsupportable interpretation. Coil stated a fact that "many Freemasons make this flight with no other guarantee of a safe landing than their belief in the religion of Freemasonry;" he did not give his endorsement. The *Study* reminded readers that "**Freemasonry does not save anyone.**"[26]

John J. Robinson responds to the anti-Masons' criticism of the Masonic funeral services by reminding his readers that the service is in addition to the religious service. He compares the Masonic funeral services to military funeral services where a squad of soldiers fire a volley into the air to honor their fallen comrade. Law enforcement officers, many of whom do not know their dead officers, cover their badges with black tape and attend the funeral services.[27]

PREJUDICED OPINIONS

Holly criticizes the *Study* for using the term *anti-Mason* because it is "offensive."[28] Holly uses the term "anti-Masonic" in the Spring 1992 preface to his first volume of *The Southern Baptist Convention and Freemasonry*, a year before the *Study* was published. At another place, he says the term is "a pejorative term at best, and overtly derogatory at worst."[29] Then, admitting there is no "better shorthand term," he uses the term throughout his third volume. Perhaps Holly believes he can use the term without being "offensive" by always putting quote marks around it. If he believes the term *anti-Mason* is "offensive," why would Holly's statement "Let every Mason be shown to be a liar"[30] not also be offensive? Is not Holly's statement offensive that Freemasonry "is the avowed enemy of Jesus Christ and of Christianity" to millions of Christian Masons who faithfully serve Christ in their churches and daily lives?[31] Is not Holly's statement offensive that "Freemasonry is one of the allies of the Devil"[32] or that every Mason has "betrayed the Lord Jesus Christ?"[33]

He states that "Mission and Ministry to Men, Inc., is not an anti-Masonic ministry organization" in a letter to the Home Mission Board directors on April 10, 1992, as well as in the preface to his first volume and in the "Conclusion and Recommendations" in his second volume. However, all of his letters attacking Freemasonry were written on Mission and Ministry to Men, Inc., letterhead. His three volumes on the Southern Baptist Convention and Freemasonry were published by Mission and Ministry to Men, Inc. It is difficult for an objective person to believe Holly's disclaimer that his ministry is not anti-Masonic. An anti-Mason is defined as a person who is opposed to Freemasonry; Holly's letters, books, and testimony clearly show he is an anti-Mason.

Holly criticizes Larry Lewis and Richard Land, executive director of the Southern Baptist Christian Life Commission, for signing a nonbinding document with a group of evangelical and Roman Catholic leaders in March 1994. The document, "Evangelicals and Catholics Together: The Christian Mission in the Third Millennium," states that "Evangelicals and Catholics are brothers and sisters in Christ." Holly asks, "How could they imagine they were not 'signing it for the SBC,' when their only identity in its signing was as SBC agency heads?"[34] Following the same logic, how can anyone imagine Mission and Ministry to Men, Inc., is not an anti-Masonic organization?

Holly charges that the *Study* makes only positive statements about Freemasonry. He claims, "Dr. Leazer finds it absolutely impossible to make a negative statement about anything Masonic."[35] That is a patently untrue charge as even a cursory reading of the *Study* shows. Perhaps Holly's attempt to have the *Study* withdrawn arose from his concern that readers would check if his charges were true. Negative statements about Freemasonry are often placed in bold print in the *Study*. Among these statements are: **"Worshipful Master is an archaic title. Masons would do well to replace this title with some other title. Many Christians feel this practice violates the biblical admonition to call no man master."**[36] **"It cannot be denied that some of the religions studied in these degrees are pagan and that their teachings are totally incompatible with Christianity."**[37] **"To compare scripture to a square and compass[es], even symbolically, is an affront to the faith."**[38]

Holly apparently does not find the negative statements harsh enough. He refers to one of the statements listed above:

> Finally, it is stated: '. . . their teachings are totally incompatible with Christianity.' **However, it is only so stated because in Dr. Leazer's own words, 'It cannot be denied.** . . .' Would he deny it, if he could? One is left to wonder.[39]

The term *incompatible* is apparently not harsh enough for Holly. "Incompatible" is defined as being not compatible or not able to exist in harmony or agreement, incongruous, conflicting, and discordant. "Incompatible" is a harsh word. Holly says:

> "Inappropriate" may be a correct term for Dr. Leazer's conduct of this study, as Dr. Lewis pointed out in the *Florida Baptist Witness*, but it is hardly adequate to express the revulsion any believer, and particularly a Christian leader, ought to have to this obvious violation of the Word of God. It seems that Dr. Lewis has also adopted Dr. Leazer's habit of understatement to attempt to conceal the sin of belonging to the Masonic Lodge.[40]

In his second volume, Holly asks, "Can anyone, anywhere, walk into a Masonic Lodge and attend all of its meetings? The answer is obviously 'No, they can not.' "[41] Masons are often criticized for holding "secret meetings." Someone else might ask, "Can anyone, anywhere, attend all Southern Baptist Convention meetings?" The answer is, "No, they cannot." Of course, Southern Baptists don't hold "secret meetings." They hold "executive sessions." For example, five armed Nashville, Tennessee, policemen guarded the door while the Southern Baptist Convention executive committee met behind closed doors and voted to fire respected *Baptist Press* director Alvin C. Shackleford and news editor Dan Martin in July 1990.[42] The Home Mission Board directors removed press, staff, and guests and met in executive session in August 1986 to dismiss a presidential search committee, which the fundamentalist-controlled board believed was too moderate.[43] When Southwestern Baptist Theological Seminary trustees fired long time president Russell Dilday in March 1994, they went into executive session, excusing press, faculty, and students during the seventy-five-minute closed-door session.[44] Top leaders of the Southern Baptist Convention's fundamentalist movement held a private meeting in Atlanta, Georgia, in April 1994. It was a secret meeting in that the meeting was not announced and only a few select fundamentalist leaders were invited to the closed-door meeting.[45] Every organization holds confidential, closed, or secret meetings. To single out Masons for doing what many other organizations routinely do is like the pot calling the skillet black.

Holly cites four of Albert Mackey's twenty-five "Landmarks of Freemasonry," which Mackey enumerated in 1858. Holly points out that "Twenty-one Grand Lodges in the United States have either formally adopted Mackey's Landmarks or they accept them by custom."[46] Holly is correct. Thirteen Grand

Lodges have formally adopted Mackey's Landmarks; eight others accept them by custom. Thirty-nine Grand Lodges do not use Mackey's Landmarks. One of Mackey's Landmarks, which Holly cites, states **"That Freemasonry is a secret society, in possession of secrets that cannot be divulged."**[47] Holly misleads his readers because nowhere in this Landmark, the twenty-third, does Mackey state "That Freemasonry is a secret society, in possession of secrets that cannot be divulged." Mackey refers to Freemasonry as "a secret association" and refers to "its secret character."[48] To imply that an organization is evil or sinister because it has "secrets" is a questionable posture at best. To say "they" have "secrets," while "we" have "things which are of a confidental nature," is a trivial word game.

Landmarks have been used to mark boundaries for centuries. In Deuteronomy 27:19, we read, "Cursed be anyone who moves a neighbor's boundary marker." Mackey enumerated his Landmarks in 1858, four years after J. M. Pendleton published a tract titled "An Old Landmark Reset," and with J. R. Graves began the Landmark Movement within the Southern Baptist Convention.

Secrecy within Freemasonry is a figment of the anti-Masons' imagination and gnostic conspiratorial witchhunting. Gnostics, from the Greek *gnosis*, or knowledge, refers to those who believe they have discovered some secret knowledge that no one else knows. Even Holly admits Masonic oaths "can be found in easily accessible publications."[49] Still, anti-Masons insist they have discovered some Masonic secret that no one else in the world has discovered. Actually, the only "secrets" remaining in Freemasonry today relate to the ways Masons recognize each other. Even these "secrets" are known by thousands of non-Masons. Secrecy in Freemasonry is a tradition or a wish rather than fact or present reality.

Holly cites a misleading article that appeared in *The Orlando Sentinel* in June 1986 in his effort to discredit the Shrine. He quotes a statement that only 1 percent of money received by the Shrine from its 175 circuses in 1984 was contributed to charity. Holly states that the remainder was used by the Shrine for the operation of its 191 temples.[50] It is difficult to know whether Holly simply failed to check the reliability of the claims set forth in the article in his haste to find another condemnation of Freemasonry, or whether he used it knowing it was inaccurate.

There are two Shrine corporations: the Iowa or fraternal corporation and the Colorado corporation, which operates the Shriners hospitals. The two corporations are generally referred to as the Iowa and Colorado corporations because of the state in which each was incorporated. The Shrine conducts more than 1,800 fund-raising activities annually under strict guidelines detailing policies and procedures for Shrine fund-raising. Some fund-raisers are strictly for the benefit of the temples; others benefit the Shriners hospitals. Persons contributing to Shrine fund-raisers may have been or may be confused concerning the purpose of the fund-raiser; the purpose is clearly stated on tickets and promotional advertisements today.

The Iowa or fraternal corporation sponsors Shrine circuses as well as other fund-raising activities where the net proceeds benefit the sponsoring temple. A statement of purpose is always included on all fund-raising promotional materials and admission tickets. For fraternal fund-raisers, the statement reads: Proceeds are for the benefit of ______________ temple. Payments are not deductible as charitable contributions. The temple may disburse proceeds as it desires.

The Colorado corporation sponsors charitable fund-raisers. **One hundred percent** of the net proceeds from charitable fund-raisers must be given to the Shriners hospitals. For charitable fund-raisers, such as the East/West Shrine College All Star Football Game, established in 1925, promotional material and tickets include the following statement: Proceeds are for the benefit of Shriners hospitals for crippled children.

The Colorado corporation operates 19 orthopedic hospitals and three burn centers. Three of the orthopedic hospitals have established spinal cord injury rehabilitation centers. They are the only spinal cord injury rehabilitation units in the nation designed for children and adolescents. The Shrine has spent more than $2.25 billion for the operation of its hospitals and more than $511 million on construction costs. The Shrine hospitals' 1993 operating budget was $336 million, up from $306 million in 1992. Of the 1993 operating budget, $46 million was spent on construction and equipment and nearly $20 million on research on such childhood diseases as scoliosis, brittle bone disease, juvenile rheumatoid arthritis, and spina bifida. The Shriners Hospitals budget for 1994 totaled nearly $394 million.[51]

Children are accepted as patients up to age 18 if, in the opinion of the hospital's chief of staff, there is a reasonable possibility that treatment will benefit the child and if treatment at another facility would place a financial burden on the child's family or guardian. Contrary to Holly's claim that charity is shown "only [to] those who are 'ever such as we are', i.e., Masons and their families,"[52] Shrine hospitals are open to all children regardless of their race, religion, or relationship to a Shriner. There is never a charge to the patient, parent, or third party for any service or treatment received. Insurance payments are not accepted even if the patient has insurance. The entire cost of operating the hospitals is received from a five-dollar annual fee assessed each

Shriner and from charitable fund-raisers, interest from its endowment, gifts, wills, and trusts. Interested individuals may call the Shrine general offices in Tampa, Florida at (813) 281–0300 and ask for literature or their Internal Revenue Service charitable statement.

Headquarters for both corporations is located in Tampa, Florida, in a building owned by the Colorado corporation. To prevent any hint of impropriety, the Iowa corporation pays rent to the Colorado corporation for office space used as well for computer, accounting, and other services provided.

Holly says the Shrine opened its first hospital in 1922 in an effort to improve its "playboys and jesters" image.[53] While Holly's charge is made by others, it is a gross insult to the thousands of Shriners and other volunteers who have donated countless millions of hours transporting patients long distances to hospitals or playing with children born without arms or legs. Would the 450,000 patients who have received specialized care at Shrine hospitals agree with Holly? Would Tony Volpentest agree with Holly? Tony was born without hands and feet. But with prostheses received at a Shrine hospital, he set three world records at the 1992 Paralympics in Barcelona, Spain. His time of 11.63 seconds in the 100-meter dash was less than two seconds off the world record set by the fastest Olympic sprinter.

One phone call to the Shrine headquarters in Tampa would have shown that *The Orlando Sentinel* article on the Shrine was misleading and inaccurate.

OTHER VIOLATIONS OF SCHOLARLY METHODOLOGY

Holly criticizes the *Study* was stating that Ezra A. Cook and his father-in-law, Jonathan Blanchard, were anti-Masons and then citing a book published by Ezra A. Cook Publications, Inc.[54] The *Study* quoted *Look to the East: A Ritual of the First Three Degrees of Masonry*, edited by Ralph P. Lester, to support the Masonic teaching that Hiram Abif's "raising" was for reburial in another grave and not a resurrection.[55] Ezra A. Cook was an anti-Mason but that doesn't require that a publishing house that bears his name is also anti-Mason. Ezra A. Cook Publications, Inc., is a business that sells books, both pro-Mason and anti-Mason, because there is a market.

According to Holly, the Study "pounces upon" an error in John Ankerberg and John Weldon's *The Secret Teachings of the Masonic Lodge*, "innocent as it is," by pointing out that Jonathan Blanchard was never a "former Sovereign Grand Commander and a 33rd Degree Mason," as Ankerberg and Weldon claim.[56] Ankerberg and Weldon cite Jonathan Blanchard as author of *Scotch Rite Masonry Illustrated: The Complete Ritual of the Ancient and Accepted*

Scottish Rite, refering to Blanchard and quoting this book more than fifty times. Although Ankerberg and Weldon name Blanchard as author of *Scotch Rite Masonry Illustrated*, the author of the book is not given in the book; the author is not known. Holly excuses Ankerberg's "mistake" as "a small enough crime."[57] To quote Holly concerning the Study, "That is not scholarship."[58] Is Holly's bias showing? Holly also quotes from *Scotch Rite Masonry Illustrated* in his first volume.[59]

The important point made in the *Study* was that *Scotch Rite Masonry Illustrated* "was actually an exposure of Cerneauism, a 'clandestine' (illegitimate) pseudo-Masonic organization of the 1800's."[60] As such, it should not have been used by Ankerberg, Weldon and Holly as a reliable Masonic source.

Cerneauism took its name from Joseph Cerneau, who formed an irregular or clandestine organization beginning in 1807 in the midst of confusion as Scottish Rite Freemasonry organized in the United States. Cerneauism dissolved as an organized Masonic group by 1920.

James Holly mentions the statement in the *Study* that Baptists in Charleston, South Carolina, in 1798 "advised that the matter of Southern Baptist membership in Freemasonry 'be left with the judgment of the individual.' "[61] Holly asks, "Why wouldn't Dr. Leazer give Southern Baptists the opportunity to know that the opinion of the Charleston Association was not unanimous?"[62] The *Study* didn't say it was unanimous, but Holly offers no documentation it wasn't. Instead, he points out that the Southern Baptist Convention was not formed until 1845 and so there could not have been any "Southern Baptists" in Charleston in 1798. While the Southern Baptist Convention was not in existence in 1798, there were Baptists in Charleston, South Carolina, since at least as early as 1696.[63]

Holly refers to a letter I wrote to him on August 3, 1992, in which I said, "I find it difficult to believe they [conservative Southern Baptist pastors and laypeople who are Masons] all have been deceived by Satan or have bowed their knees to him."[64] Because of this letter, Holly concluded I had already made up my mind about Freemasonry "before the assignment ever came to the HMB." That, of course, is not true. I was still conducting research, and the testimonies of these men would form only a small part of my research. Holly will remember that the Home Mission Board received his resolution against Freemasonry in June 1991, so the assignment had already been given to the Board.

At one point, Holly complained to Larry Lewis that Lewis had released a letter from him "without discussing it with me."[65] At the same time, Holly did not think it inappropriate to release personal letters I wrote to Craig Branch, director of the Birmingham office of Watchman Fellowship, Inc., and to D. L. Talbert of Chattanooga "without discussing it with me."

Holly reports that he asked me after our September 1992 meeting, "Do you understand that there is a serious problem for Christians with the Masonic Lodge?" He states that I responded without hesitation, "Yes, I do."[66] Holly states, "Anyone listening to those tape recordings [made of the meeting] would draw the conclusion that Dr. Leazer and the IFW [Interfaith Witness Department staff] were in agreement with the presentation which we made to them."[67] Holly is correct about my response, but I had not yet made up my mind concerning Freemasonry. Holly and his associates from Mission and Ministry to Men, Inc., made an impressive presentation. However, subsequent research showed serious flaws in Holly's claims about Freemasonry, and the *Study* reflected that research.

Holly refers to an alleged conversation I had with Ron Sutherland of Atlanta, Georgia, a friend of Holly who was present at the September 1992 meeting. According to Sutherland, I told him on two occasions (March 1992 and March 1993) that "**Masonry is an abomination.**"[68] In response, I do not recall making that statement. The Interfaith Witness Department staff will testify that "abomination" is not a word I typically use, although Holly uses the word on at least three occasions in *The Southern Baptist Convention and Freemasonry, Volume III.*[69] I doubt I would have made this statement in March 1992 and am certain I would not have made it after my research in March 1993, as Holly and Sutherland claim. **In my research I did not find Freemasonry to be an abomination.**

Holly rejects as "not true" the statement in the *Study* that "Christian Masons affirm that Jesus Christ is 'the way, and the truth, and the life; no one comes to the Father, but through Me' (John 14:6, NASB)."[70] He does not qualify his charge that the statement is "not true"; therefore, it is an absolute statement. Would Holly say that Southern Baptist Masons George W. Truett, B. H. Carroll, L. R. Scarborough, William W. Hamilton, Louie D. Newton, John T. Christian, and hundreds of thousands of other Christian Masons have denied or are denying that Jesus Christ is "the way, and the truth, and the life; no one comes to the Father, but through Me." His absolute statement makes it appear he is.

Throughout his third volume, Holly claims to know the personal motivations of individuals who differ with him. He says, "From the beginning, Dr. Leazer seemed to see his role as the defender of the Lodge."[71] He accuses me of making up my mind about Masonry "many years ago."[72] In a letter to Holly on October 28, 1993, Larry Lewis said he absolutely rejected Holly's charges that the *Study* and "Report" "were developed under supervision of Masons."[73] I had little contact with Masons during the research and writing of the *Study*, except when asking to borrow books or to ask specific questions. I am not aware of any contact Lewis might have had with Masons.

Holly wonders why former Board of Directors chairman Ron Phillips, Larry Lewis, and an unnamed director "allowed such a high-handed and illegal motion to be voted upon?"[74] He charges the motion to adopt the Home Mission Board "Report on Freemasonry" was "high-handed and illegal" because there was no reasonable time allowed for discussion. Holly conveniently forgets to tell his readers that a lengthy discussion was had by the directors during the previous evening. Holly believes the Home Mission Board should ask forgiveness for not carrying out its assigned task: "There is no need for groveling; simply, a Christian confession will do. Whereupon, the convention will say, 'of course, we forgive you.' Whereupon, the Lord Jesus Christ will say, 'well done, thou good and faithful servant!' "[75]

He criticizes the actions of chairman of the Board of Directors Brad Allen[76] and the "Conservatives [who] now run the SBC" for doing the same thing as the moderates were accused of doing before the takeover.[77] He indicates he will pray for the Southern Baptist Convention and ask God not to reject the Convention because of its "Laodicean spirit."[78] He compares the "self-imposed ignorance" of "many Southern Baptist ministers" to that of "non-hero" Albert Speer, "Chief Architect of the Third Reich and then the Munitions Minister for Adolf Hitler."[79]

Holly states his opinion that "many men who occupy leadership positions not only in the Southern Baptist churches, but also in the Baptist General Convention of Texas" believe in universalism and reincarnation.[80] I do not know of any Southern Baptist in any leadership position who believes in either universalism or reincarnation. Why doesn't Holly name one? This is just another example of the anonymous accusations easy to believe and difficult to counter, that run rampant in the Convention.

While arguing earlier in his books that Freemasonry is a religion, he changes his approach when he compares Freemasonry with homosexuality: **"It doesn't make any difference if Freemasonry is or is not a religion. Freemasonry is still incompatible with Christianity.** Homosexuality is not a religion, but it is incompatible with Christianity."[81] Holly continues his crude comparisons, "There is no hope of winning Masons by joining the Lodge, any more than there is hope of winning prostitutes by frequenting brothels."[82] He continues:

> Should a Southern Baptist join the Communist party in order to be a witness? Should a Southern Baptist join a 'sex-swapping' club in

> order to be a witness? Who is going to witness to all of the nudists? Surely, the Home Mission Board will soon appoint a practicing nudist as missionary to those unprotected people![83]

Continuous Witnessing Training is a Southern Baptist evangelism program. Holly accuses the *Study* of "suggesting that membership in the Masonic Lodge can be a Continuous Witness Training Program."[84] The *Study* does not mention Continuous Witnessing Training. Holly asks another absurd question: "Would the HMB encourage the 'flirty fishing' techniques of David Moses' [*sic*] Children of God."[85] "Flirty fishing" is the practice of Moses David's Children of God to use sex to attract donors or members; it has allegedly been discontinued.

Holly says he never asked for or demanded that I be fired from the Home Mission Board.[86] He never asked or demanded that I be fired, but he repeatedly called for my removal as head of the study on Freemasonry. My removal from the study on February 22, 1993, followed another call by Holly for my removal from the study. He wrote that the Home Mission Board directors should "ask Dr. Leazer to resign."[87] After learning that Bill Gordon was writing a critique on his first volume, Holly wrote to Gordon and mentioned that he [Holly] "wrote the syllabus which ultimately resulted in [Baptist Sunday School Board president] Lloyd Elder's resignation."[88] My staff and I felt tremendous pressure from Holly throughout the research and writing of the *Study*.

Holly repeatedly blames Masons in Southern Baptist churches for the lack of revival within our denomination. "Until they are dislodged from the church, the Lodge will continue to disrupt God's plan and desire to revive His people."[89] "There are many hindrances to revival in the Southern Baptist Convention. Freemasonry is only one of them. It is, however, not only one of the most obvious, it may be the key one."[90] "Few things will promote revival among us as a strong stand for the glory of the Lord through rejecting the leavening influence of the occultism of the Lodge."[91] Holly knows Southern Baptists desire revival and attempts to win their approval by using an argument unsupported by good evidence.

Following Holly's theory, it would appear that churches and denominations that have condemned Freemasonry or expelled Masons from membership should have experienced tremendous revival. The Lutheran Church–Missouri Synod condemned Freemasonry in 1980, and for many years previously. According to the 1980 *Handbook of Denominations*, the Lutheran Church–Missouri Synod had 2.9 million members.[92] By 1992, the Lutheran Church–Missouri Synod's membership has **fallen** to 2.6 million.[93] That denomination did not experience revival because they condemned Freemasonry, and neither has any other denomination that has condemned Freemasonry. The American Roman Catholic Church has experienced the highest percentage of growth in recent years, but this is due primarily to immigration from Latin American and Caribbean countries, not revival.

Charles Z. Burchett, pastor of the First Baptist Church of Kirbyville, Texas, has worked with James Holly to condemn Freemasonry since Burchett introduced the 1985 resolution "Free-masonry [*sic*] Not Compatible with Baptist Faith and Message, Bold Mission Thrust, or Cooperative Program." According to the 1983 Texas Baptist Annual, First Baptist Church of Kirbyville reported 35 baptisms, a resident membership of 473 persons, total income of $167,005 and Cooperative Program offerings of $15,334. Nine years later, according to the 1992 Texas Baptist Annual, the First Baptist Church of Kirbyville, with Burchett still serving as the pastor, reported 2 baptisms, 216 resident members, total income of $70,290 and Cooperative Program offerings of $840. Burchett accompanied Holly to the September 1992 meeting with the Interfaith Witness Department staff to hear Holly's criticisms of Freemasonry. Statistics would suggest that Burchett's church has not experienced revival since he took a stand against Freemasonry at least as early as 1985. Holly's claim that the lack of a Southern Baptist condemnation of Freemasonry is preventing revival is simply a smoke screen to hide his true motive and is without foundation.

Bill Gordon, in his critique of Holly's *The Southern Baptist Convention and Freemasonry, Volume I*, says Holly's "assertions overstate the problem of Freemasonry in the Convention, reveal an ignorance of the history of revivalism in America, and underestimate the power of Almighty God!"[94] Holly shows a weakness of faith in God.

10 Other Criticisms by James L. Holly

Every man must give an account of himself to God, and therefore every man ought to be at liberty to serve God in that way that he can best reconcile it to his conscience. . . . It would be sinful for a man to surrender that to man, which is to be kept sacred for God.[1]

In this chapter, we will examine James Holly's criticisms of Freemasonry's attitudes toward African-American Masons and my address to the Southeast Masonic Conference in August 1993.

ATTITUDES TOWARD AFRICAN-AMERICANS

Holly writes, "While it is difficult to document, it appears that the Ku Klux Klan was founded by Freemasons and was financed by Masons. . . . If records were available to be examined, it might be seen that the majority of Klan members even today would be found to be Masons."[2] This is a slight rewording of the statement Holly and Burchett made in the manuscript provided to the Home Mission Board's Interfaith Witness Department staff at their September 1992 meeting: "While it is difficult to document, the Ku Klux Klan was founded by Freemasons and supported by Masons. If records were available to be examined it is certain that today the majority of Klan members would be found to be Masons."[3] It appears Holly became less certain of his position on this point between September 1992 and January 1993 when he wrote the preface to his book. It is questionable scholarship, to say the least, to qualify a charge with "While it is difficult to document" and "If records were available to be examined, it might be seen."

The Ku Klux Klan appealed to the fears of many white Protestant Americans.[4] Sometime Methodist preacher William J. Simmons of Atlanta, Georgia, revived the Ku Klux Klan in 1915 and served as its first Imperial Wizard. Modeled after an earlier Ku Klux Klan that arose in the South during Reconstruction, Simmons's anti-Catholic, anti-Semitic, anti-Black prejudice found many followers among fundamentalist Protestant churches throughout the nation. Simmons's Klan appealed to the many Protestant fears of eventual Roman Catholic domination over Protestantism. Many Protestant ministers, and certainly some Masons, became Klan chaplains, organizers, or members.[5]

Historian William W. Sweet points out that the Ku Klux Klan and fundamentalism arose in the same period in the 1920s and that "students of society have recognized in the Ku Klux Klan and Fundamentalism identical types of reactionism."[6]

A 1994 Vatican statement found that fundamentalists are marked by prejudices, including racism. The 130-page document released by the Pontifical Biblical Commission of the Roman Catholic Church in March 1994 criticized the fundamentalist approach to the Bible, saying,

> Its relying upon a noncritical reading of certain texts of the Bible serves to reinforce political ideas and social attitudes that are marked by prejudices—racism, for example—quite contrary to the Christian gospel.[7]

The Southern Baptist Convention was formed because Baptists in the northern states contended that Baptists in the southern states who were slaveowners were unworthy to be missionaries. Baptists in the South, therefore, separated from Baptists in the North to form the Southern Baptist Convention in 1845 so slaveowners who wanted to serve as missionaries could do so.

Rhetoric was heated in the years prior to 1845. Richard Fuller of Beaufort, South Carolina, whose arguments were published in *Domestic Slavery as a Scriptural Institution* in 1845, argued that slavery existed throughout the Old and New Testaments of the Bible, and that the inspired writers never once attacked it as sinful.[8]

R. B. C. Howell, who served as second president of the Southern Baptist Convention from 1851 to 1859, argued that "slavery is legitimate, benevolent, and scriptural."[9] He put his outrage in an editorial in *The Baptist,* now the Tennessee Baptist Convention's *Baptist and Reflector*, after a Baptist missionary in Burma sent ten dollars to aid in the escape of runaway slaves: "If we send money to him, we, thereby, indirectly contribute the means by which our own slaves are kidnapped and dragged off! Brethren, will you do this? We know you will not."[10] Howell's mother-in-law owned slaves that his wife inherited when his mother-in-law died in 1859. Howell, pastor of the First Baptist Church of Nashville, Tennessee, along with three other Nashville ministers, was thrown into prison as Confederate sympathizers in 1862. A Knights Templar Mason in his church persuaded the military governor, Andrew Johnson, to release the 61-year-old pastor.

Improvement in race relations is a recent development within the Southern Baptist Convention. W. A. Criswell's words in 1956 reflected the attitude of a majority of Southern Baptists until recent years.

> It is better for them to be over there in their way, in their church, with their preacher, carrying on as they like to do, and then I'm over hear [*sic*] with my flock and my kind and we are carrying on like we want to do; and everything is just fine. Who said it wasn't fine? I'll tell you who said it wasn't fine. It's some of those two-by scantling, good-for-nothing fellows who are trying to upset all of the things that we love as good old Southern people as good old Southern Baptists. They are not our kind, I say.[11]

Southern Baptists across the South sharply criticized the Southern Baptist Theological Seminary in Louisville, Kentucky, for inviting Martin Luther King to speak to the student body in 1961.[12]

The first black Baptist to join a Southern Baptist church in Georgia was Sam Oni, a Ghanian student who enrolled as the first black student at Mercer University in Macon, Georgia, in 1963. Oni joined Vineville Baptist Church as a college freshman after he was refused admittance to another Southern Baptist church because of his race. He speaks of himself as "a victim of cross racism" and of his "faith-shattering experience" in America.[13] Southern Baptists were willing to send missionaries to Africa to witness to Africans, but were slow to allow their converts to worship in Southern Baptist churches.

The first African-American staff member of the Home Mission Board, Roland T. Smith, came to the Board in 1942 as director of Negro Work. However, he "had an office in his home rather than at the Board because social codes of the day restricted Negroes from actually working in the Home Mission Board building."[14] When African-American Emmanuel McCall joined the Home Mission Board in 1968, the Home Mission Board received telephone calls and letters protesting the election.

It was not until 1968, the year that he was elected president of the Southern Baptist Convention and four years after the passage of the Civil Rights Bill, that Criswell had a change of heart:

> To separate by coercion the body of Christ on the basis of skin pigmentation was unthinkable, unchristian, and unacceptable to God. . . . This burden of heart I told the deacons. It was a long meeting, but the most Spirit-filled session I ever attended in my life. We wept together; we prayed together; we prostrated our very souls before the Lord. And the two hundred men voted unanimously to declare publicly that our church is a church of the open door. Anybody, everybody can come and be welcomed in the name of our living Lord.[15]

At the Southern Baptist Convention in 1968, two months after Martin Luther King, Jr., was assassinated, the messengers passed a resolution "to personally accept every Christian as brother beloved in the Lord and welcome to the fellowship of faith and worship every person irrespective of race or class."[16] But in spite of Criswell's change of heart and the 1968 resolution, Southern Baptist attitudes toward African-Americans have been slow to change. Southern Baptists have not been leaders in racial reconciliation.

None of the eighty-nine Home Mission Board trustees in 1989–1990 were African-Americans. Fourteen of the trustees were women. Three African-Americans were Home Mission Board trustees in 1993–1994. Sixteen of the trustees were women, including one of the three African-Americans.

The February–March 1994 issue of *SBC LIFE*, a new, full-color promotional newsmagazine published by the SBC Executive Committee, listed seventy individuals who supported the missions program of the Convention. One women was pictured among the seventy. Sixty-nine were white men. No African-Americans were included.

A "Declaration of Repentence," urging the Southern Baptist Convention to reject racism and "publicly repent and apologize to all persons of African descent for condoning and perpetuating individual and systemic racism in our lifetime," was not considered by the Convention at its 1994 meeting in Orlando. The Baptist Press reported the Race Reconciliation Task Force spent too much time in prayer and missed their time to present the document to the Convention.[17]

The 1993 Home Mission Board Report on Freemasonry criticized the fraternity because "most lodges (although not all) [refuse] to admit for membership African-Americans." There is racial intolerance within American Freemasonry; it reflects racism found throughout American society.

Prince Hall, along with fourteen other African-Americans, were initiated into Freemasonry in 1775 and formed a lodge in Boston. However, the Grand

Lodge of England did not issue a warrant until 1784. Previously, an African-American Lodge in Fredericksburg, Virginia (now Fredericksburg Lodge No.4), received a charter from the Grand Lodge of Scotland in 1758. Records indicate it had been in existence since at least as early as 1752.[18]

Holly charges that the term *clandestine* is a "racist designation."[19] Two terms are used within Freemasonry to describe lodges: regular and clandestine or irregular. The terms recognized and unrecognized lodges are also used by Masons. A regular Masonic lodge is one recognized by a Grand Lodge. A regular Mason is a member of a recognized lodge. Regular Masonic lodges may include African-American members. About twenty Grand Lodges recognized by the Grand Lodge of North Carolina have African-American members.[20] The Grand Lodge of North Carolina recognizes Grand Lodges in Africa, India, Asia, South America, and Europe where Blacks are members. The Black members of these Grand Lodges are "regular" or "recognized."

A clandestine Masonic group is a group without a warrant, dispensation, or charter from a Grand Lodge not recognized by another, particular Grand Lodge. The term *clandestine* has nothing to do with race, except that clandestine lodges in the United States generally have African-American members. The term *clandestine* cannot be equated with race. The Grand Lodge of Iowa, for example, does not recognize the National Grand Lodge of Greece or the Grand Orient of Italy; they are considered clandestine by the Grand Lodge of Iowa.[21] Among the Grand Lodges not recognized by the Grand Lodge of Mississippi are Finland, Luxembourg, Norway, the Netherlands, Sweden, Switzerland, Uruguay, and Venezuela; they are considered clandestine by the Grand Lodge of Mississippi.[22]

The issue of mutual recognition is discussed in many Masonic meetings. The number of African-American Grand Lodges in a locality is a significant problem. One source listed 185 African-American Grand Lodges in the United States, including Prince Hall Grand Lodges.[23] Another researcher found five African-American Grand Lodges in Detroit; nine African-American Grand Lodges in New Orleans; and sixteen African-American Grand Lodges in New York City. While the Prince Hall Grand Lodge is best known, it has only 10,000 members in New York. A lesser known African-American Grand Lodge, the Enoch Grand Lodge, has 100,000 members. These African-American Grand Lodges do not recognize one another, making recognition by regular Grand Lodges even more difficult. Prince Hall Freemasonry has fourty-two Grand Lodges with over 500,000 members worldwide.[24] Prince Hall Grand Lodges, like all other Grand Lodges, are sovereign and individually decide which Grand Lodges will be recognized.

Grand Lodges have regularly approached Prince Hall Grand Lodges for dialogue. The Grand Lodge of California voted to conditionally recognize the Prince Hall Grand Lodge in that state in 1994. Other Grand Lodges are in dialogue with Prince Hall Grand Lodges. Most of the Grand Lodges which have no current dialogue with Prince Hall Grand Lodges are in states where Southern Baptists are strongest.

Prince Hall Grand Lodges often reject dialogue because they do not want to lose identity by being absorbed into the much larger Grand Lodges. For example, there are 90,000 Masons in the Grand Lodge of New York, but only 10,000 Prince Hall Masons in New York. If Prince Hall Masons were united with the Grand Lodge, they would be overwhelmed and lose both their identity and the opportunity for leadership roles, much as has been the case in the Southern Baptist Convention.

Another stumbling block is the American Masonic innovation called exclusive jurisdiction. The original purpose of exclusive jurisdiction was to avoid squabbling among Grand Lodges as the country grew. Exclusive jurisdiction is the position that only one Grand Lodge can be legitimate in a state. Exclusive jurisdiction, along with questions concerning the formation of Prince Hall Grand Lodges, appear to be two major stumbling blocks that are slowly being removed.

Holly erroneously states that

> It is public knowledge that no Black can join a regular Lodge of Freemasons in America. Therefore, they formed their own lodge, called Prince Hall Lodges, which have no interchange with the Masonic Lodges to which 1.3 million Southern Baptists belong.[25]

Here again Holly exaggerates the number of Southern Baptist Masons. Holly is simply wrong about his claim that no African-American can join a regular Masonic lodge. Alpha Lodge 116 in Newark, New Jersey, is the best known regular lodge with African-American members.[26] This lodge is presumably all African-American, but no racial lists are maintained. Although most Grand Lodges do not recognize Prince Hall Masonry, twenty-one Grand Lodges had African-American members in 1992.[27]

Nine Grand Lodges recognize Prince Hall Grand Lodges as legitimate. They are: Colorado, Connecticut, Idaho, Minnesota, Nebraska, North Dakota, Washington, Wisconsin, and Wyoming. Three Canadian Grand Lodges recognize Prince Hall Grand Lodges: New Brunswick, Quebec, and Prince Edward Island. It is hoped that accepting African-Americans as members in regular lodges and recognizing Prince Hall Freemasonry will continue to accelerate in American Grand Lodges.

To add a brief post-script to this section, Holly attacked Masonic researcher S. Brent Morris, claiming Morris's "integrity has been questioned by Black Freemasons."[28] Holly's insinuation is absolutely inexcusable. Morris is one of a few whites who have been made an honorary Fellows of the Phylaxis Society, the research society of Prince Hall Freemasonry, having himself been made a Fellow on March 6, 1988.[29] Concerning the Holly attack on Morris, Joseph A. Walkes, Jr., 33°, a Prince Hall Mason and editor of *The News Quarterly*, wrote, Holly "is saying that Prince Hall Freemasonry has attacked Dr. S. Brent Morris (because of my preface of the Pike/Klan article) but that is not true. We made Morris a Fellow of the Phylaxis Society, so Dr. Holly doesn't know what he is talking about."[30]

KEYNOTE ADDRESS TO THE SOUTHEAST MASONIC CONFERENCE

After the June 1993 Southern Baptist Convention in Houston adopted the "Report on Freemasonry," I was invited to speak at the Southeast Masonic Conference in Atlanta, Georgia on August 6, 1993, to interpret the results of the investigation and the Convention vote in Houston concerning Freemasonry. I felt Southern Baptists owed Masons an explanation and agreed to speak to the conference. The address was subsequently printed in the October 1993 issue of the *Masonic Messenger* of the Grand Lodge of Georgia. The speech resulted in a request for my resignation from the staff of the Home Mission Board.

Holly refers to the speech several times in the third volume of his trilogy, *The Southern Baptist Convention and Freemasonry*. He asks, "**Why would a Christian employee of the HMB, no longer the head of the IFW [Interfaith Witness Department], but still an employee of the HMB at the time of his August 1993 speech to the Southeast Masonic Conference, encourage the Masonic Lodge to renew, but not reform?**"[31] Holly obviously never read the speech carefully.

Holly quotes me as saying, "There are a number of positive steps you can take immediately. . . . Your very survival as a fraternity depends upon it. . . . I find that The Masonic Renewal Committee of North America is on target. . . ."[32] Holly deliberately misleads his readers by using ellipses to change the meaning of my speech.

My words without Holly's ellipses follow. Words omitted by Holly are struck out. As the reader can see, I repeatedly call for change within the fraternity.

> There are a number of positive steps you can take immediately. ~~I would recommend that you lay everything on the table. Nothing, no ritual, no teaching, no practice, should be off limits. Look at literally everything.~~ Your very survival as a fraternity depends upon it. ~~You may decide that many or most of your ritual, teaching and practices cannot or should not be changed, but I would implore you to take a close look at them. Any organization has to change to survive.~~[33]

I then said, "I find that The Masonic Renewal Committee of North America is on target," as Holly states, but I also said in the same paragraph that "I disagree with the statement that 'The ritual need not change.'"[34]

Continuing, I asked, "I believe you would eliminate much of the anti-Mason sentiment if you would discontinue the public Masonic funeral service. Could you find some other way to honor your deceased brother?"[35]

I said, "As a non-Mason, I believe there are Masonic teachings that should be changed or eliminated. . . . I believe the oaths and penalties could be revised without loss of meaning. Worshipful Master is an archaic title. Can some other title be used?"[36] I believe it is absolutely essential that the fraternity change.

Robert Ringer, author of *Million Dollar Habits*, says one of the main roadblocks to making things happen is resistance to change. He writes, "Homeostasis, the tendency to cling to the status quo, or to existing conditions, and avoid change is a common human trait. Unfortunately," Ringer says, "it is also a self-defeating and self-destructive habit."[37] Life is always changing. New, faster, and larger planes replace older, smaller, and slower planes. Clothing styles come and go. New drugs to fight illness are found; old diseases disappear. Lawmakers pass new laws that replace other laws. Your weight changes as you age. Ringer concludes, "If change is inevitable"—and he argues convincingly it is—"[then] why not assign it a positive rather than a negative value?"[38]

How can Holly claim I "encourage[d] the Masonic Lodge to renew, but not reform?" He can't. In spite of Holly's general misinterpretation of Masonic teachings, he raises some legitimate criticisms, as did the *Study*, that Masons need to address.

Holly quotes from my speech:

> I know many of you feel relief that the Southern Baptist Convention did not condemn Freemasonry, but you should not be satisfied with the report adopted by the Convention. **You cannot agree with the eight**

> **points found in the report.** I hope you will respond clearly and quickly to each of these points.[39]

Then he says,

> Leazer also recommends that the Masonic Lodge **take action against the SBC** in overturning even the compromising report which has been adopted. It is unconscionable for an employee of the SBC to **encourage hostile action** toward the Convention.[40]

Where in my speech do I recommend that the Masonic Lodge "take action against the SBC" or "encourage hostile action toward the Convention?" Not one place.

In the speech I referred to an article in the August 1993 issue of *The Scottish Rite Journal* in which J. Walter Carpenter, a Home Mission Board director and editor of the independent *Southern Baptist Watchman*, cautioned that Masons must be aware of the criticisms of the report and give them close attention and action.[41] Carpenter is quoted in the *Journal* that "The ball is in your court, and I hope at long last you will do something with it."[42] This was the immediate context for my remarks.

I also said, "Booklets explaining Freemasonry, such as the excellent 'Conscience and the Craft' by Jim Tresner, would be helpful to give to pastors and other church leaders."[43] Does that sound like "hostile action toward the Convention?"

Holly quotes me as saying, "I understand the Masonic position that each writer speaks only for himself, but I think you are sometimes your own worst enemy when you recommend certain books to your readers. . . ."[44]

He then asks, "Why is Dr. Leazer willing to allow the Masonic Lodge to avoid all responsibility for their writers, when in *A Study of Freemasonry* the Masons tell him what books and publications are authoritative?"[45] I am calling Masons to take responsibility for the books they recommend to their readers. Holly's ellipses omit the continuation of the quote. It continues, "I support the right of every Mason to write any book he wishes, but I question the wisdom of these books being recommended to fellow Masons. Every Mason has a right to write books, but not all such books are profitable to read."[46] I am calling Masons to be responsible readers.

Holly charges that "The idea that no Mason speaks for anyone but himself came directly from pages 16–19 of Jim Tresner's *Perspective, Responses & Reflections*."[47] Actually, this idea is common knowledge among Masons.

Holly quotes me as saying, "Education is one of the keys in responding to charges leveled by the anti-Masons. This education can never end. It is the life blood of Freemasonry. . . ."[48] Then he makes an unbelievable charge that education "is the foundation statement of 'secular humanism.'" He refers to Deuteronomy 32:46–47, where "Moses declares that the Word of God is the life of God's people." Is Holly saying that the only legitimate knowledge is that which is found in the Bible? Is not education worthwhile that teaches an individual mathematics, science, medicine, engineering, geology, literature, and so forth? Why does the Home Mission Board require its staff to attend a prescribed number of seminars about the Home Mission Board mission and policies? Education is the lifeblood of any organization. I am certain Holly reads about new advances in medicine. That is education.

Holly quotes my statement that "My study does not agree with the conclusions in the Home Mission Board report."[49] I also said that "Anti-Masons will use the first part of the summary adopted in Houston, 'in light of the fact that many tenets and teachings of Freemasonry are not compatible with Christianity and Southern Baptist doctrine' to their advantage." This prediction has proven true. In a March 21, 1994, letter to the Home Mission Board directors and staff, Holly asked that the board of directors "emphasize the cautions given in the 'Recommendation' to the Convention that 'many tenets and teachings of Freemasonry are incompatible with Christianity.' " He repeated this call in a similar letter on April 1, 1994: "Let the world know that the SBC will stand for truth regardless of the cost and regardless of the consequences by emphasizing the statement 'many tenets and teachings of Freemasonry are incompatible with Christianity,' which essentially establishes that Freemasonry is incompatible with Christianity."

My research did not justify an absolute statement that "in light of the fact that many tenets and teachings of Freemasonry are not compatible with Christianity and Southern Baptist doctrine." The *Study* called for a statement such as "in light of the fact that **some believe** many tenets and teachings of Freemasonry are not compatible with Christianity and Southern Baptist doctrine. . . ." I did not agree with the conclusions in the "Report" because it does not reflect the research and conclusions in the *Study*. As I said in the August 6, 1993, speech, "It does not reflect my conclusions as a non-Mason and I feel certain it does not reflect yours."[50]

11 Responding To Specific Attacks On Freemasonry, Part I

"Even if one accepts the strongest case against the Masons, they do not represent anything near the danger as, for example, the New Age movement."[1]

THE CLAIM THAT FREEMASONRY IS A RELIGION

Anti-Masons repeatedly claim that Freemasonry is a religion.[2] Because of this claim, the subject, "Is Freemasonry a Religion or a Fraternity," was addressed in the *Study*. This approach infuriated James Holly: "The HMB and Dr. Leazer were assigned the responsibility of determining if Freemasonry and Christianity are compatible, **yet he spends most of his time trying to prove that Freemasonry is not a religion.** No one asked the question 'Is Freemasonry a religion?' "[3] In response, only 7 out of 71 pages of the *Study*, only 7½ pages out of 81 pages in the original manuscript are devoted to this issue. That is hardly "most" of the *Study*.

Holly continues to refer to the question of whether Freemasonry is a religion throughout his third volume. "This reflected Dr. Leazer's lack of understanding of the 1992 SBC motion, for it did not address the question as to whether Freemasonry is a religion or not."[4] "Whether Freemasonry is a religion or not is irrelevant. . . ."[5] "If Dr. Leazer is answering the question 'Is Freemasonry a religion?' he, in fact, is answering a question which no one has asked. Whether Freemasonry is a religion or not is irrelevant. . . ."[6]

Holly raised the "Freemasonry is a religion" issue in his first volume when he charged that "The parallels between the ancient mystery religions and Freemasonry are obvious."[7] In his third volume, he states, "This is the religion of Freemasonry; it is not compatible with biblical Christianity."[8]

John Ankerberg and John Weldon claim that "Freemasonry is a religion."[9] This position is the primary reason Ankerberg and Weldon condemn

Freemasonry. William Schnoebelen asks, "Can Masonry Really Be a Religion?"[10] Concluding it is a religion, he writes, "In the next few chapters, we will see if the religion of Freemasonry is somehow compatible with or opposed to true Bible-based Christianity."[11] Anti-Mason E. M. Storms writes, "Masonry is more than a social club, school of geometry, or an humanitarian fellowship. It is a religious movement whose god is not the God of the Christian."[12] Anti-Masons attempt to prove that Freemasonry is a religion so it can be condemned as unbiblical or anti-Christian. While anti-masons claim Freemasonry is a false religion, most Masons are adamant that their fraternity is not a religion. A discussion of whether Freemasonry is a religion, as was done in the *Study*, was entirely appropriate.

The *Study* found that while most Masons insist Freemasonry is not a religion, there are obviously religious teachings within the fraternity. Holly insists that "it doesn't make any difference what 'Masons insist.' "[13] Freemasonry is not indifferent to religion. Religious teachings within Freemasonry include the requirement to profess a belief in God and to pray for His guidance before any significant undertaking. Masons are told to place duty to God above all other relationships. Unfortunately, this does not always happen, as it does not always happen with the church membership. The *Study* concluded that "some Masonic writers and rituals exacerbate this controversy by comparing Freemasonry to obviously pagan religions."[14] This problem is exacerbated by other Masons who explain their opinions poorly and by anti-Masons who read into Masonic writings teachings not intended by the writers.

The *Study* found that Masons may make Freemasonry their religion. In response, Holly asked, **"How can men make something 'their religion', which Dr. Leazer and the Lodge says is not a religion, i.e., the Masonic Lodge?**[15] People make many things their religions. It is a matter of opinion and definition. Some people have a religious experience while gazing at the Grand Tetons in Wyoming or the Great Barrier Reef off the eastern coast of Australia. United Methodist Bishop Carl Sanders was quoted in the *Study* as saying, "You can make a god out of anything—your business, your labor union, your civic club, your Lodge and even your Church."[16]

Thomas Hager, Grand Master of Masons in Tennessee, stated "the official position of the Grand Lodge, Free and Accepted Masons of Tennessee, on the subject of Freemasonry and Religion" in an April 22, 1994, letter to Baptist Press and a July 11, 1994, letter to the Associated Press. Hager said, "Freemasonry is not a religion, nor is it a substitute for religion." Individual Masons may believe that Freemasonry is a religion, but that is not the official position of the Grand Lodge of Tennessee. The Grand Lodge of any state is the highest authority in Freemasonry.

Masonic writers have been inconsistent about the relationship between Freemasonry and religion. In *Mackey's Revised Encyclopedia* we read that Freemasonry

> has no pretension to assume a place among the religions of the world as a sectarian "system of faith and worship," in the sense in which we distinguish Christianity from Judaism, or Judaism from Mohammedanism. In this meaning of the word [religion] we do not and cannot speak of the Masonic religion, nor say of a man that he is not a Christian, but a Freemason. . . . Freemasonry is not Christianity, nor a substitute for it. It is not intended to supersede it nor any other form of worship or system of faith. It does not meddle with sectarian creeds or doctrines, but teaches fundamental religious truth not enough to do away with the necessity of the Christian scheme of salvation.[17]

Yet, Henry W. Coil said, "Mackey called Freemasonry religion; Pike dissented."[18] The argument made in the original manuscript of the *Study* was that some Masons believe Freemasonry is a religion while other Masons do not believe Freemasonry is a religion. That is the most one can conclude. We must constantly ask, "What does the individual mean by his use of the term *religion*?" The facts simply do not permit the conclusion that Freemasonry is a religion, as Holly, Ankerberg, Decker, and other anti-Masons insist.

J. Walter Carpenter, Home Mission Board director and editor of the independent *Southern Baptist Watchman*, stated that "the overwhelming majority of Masons belong to the organization because it is benevolent and fraternal, not because they put any stock in these writings or regard the organization as a religious entity."[19]

At one time, Albert Pike could write that "every Masonic Lodge is a temple of religion; and its teachings are instruction in religion."[20] At another time, Pike could write, "Masonry is not a religion. He who makes of it a religious belief, falsifies and denaturalizes it."[21]

Holly gives his interpretation of Pike's statement that Freemasonry is a religion, "It means that, to Pike, Masonry is the original understanding of God which came through nature, and that any attempt to add man's religious edifice to it, corrupts the 'nature faith.' "[22] Pike said nothing about "nature faith." He used the term *denaturalizes* in the sense of the real intent of Freemasonry. In other words, those who make it a religious belief change the real intent and innate qualities of Freemasonry, i.e., that "falsifies and denaturalizes it." Pike explains that "those who have attempted to direct it toward useless vengeance, political ends, and Jesuitism have merely perverted it to purposes foreign to its pure spirit and real nature."[23]

Pike then explains his understanding of the real intent and innate qualities, the natural and genuine, if you will, of Freemasonry. He says they are:

> love;
> truth;
> justice;
> generosity;
> goodness;
> morality;
> living a true, just, affectionate, self-faithful life;
> loyal obedience to God's law;
> being true to one's mind, conscience, heart, and soul;
> denying oneself for the sake of a brother;
> unimpeachable in business;
> patriotism;
> and loving one's enemies.[24]

Pike says these qualities found in Freemasonry are "the cardinal tenets of the old primitive faith, which underlie and are the foundation of all religions."[25] This is "blasphemy" in Holly's eyes. Pike doesn't say that **"all religions blossomed"** from Freemasonry, as Holly charges,[26] but that these ethical qualities are found in all religions, as well as within Freemasonry. These ethical qualities may not all be taught or practiced equally well in all of the religions or within any particular faith, but they are present in the teachings of all religions. Christianity does not lose its uniqueness when faced with similar ethical teachings in other faiths; Christianity's uniqueness is found in the person and work of Jesus Christ.

In this same discussion, Pike also says, "For there is a religion of toil,"[27] and "There is also a religion of society."[28] Pike is not saying that toil is a religion or that society is a religion. He is using the term *religion* in a much broader sense than one typically thinks when a person uses the phrase *the Christian religion.* Pike is using the term to mean the general awareness that people have of a Supreme Being and of doing what is pleasing to him in our toil and in our relationship with each other and the general society.

USE OF THE TERM WORSHIPFUL MASTER

Thou shalt worship thy father and thy mother, that thou be long lived upon earth. (Exodus 20:12)[29]

The Home Mission Board "Report on Freemasonry"[30] states that the use of terms such as *Worshipful Master* is incompatible with Christianity or Southern Baptist doctrine. The writer of the "Report" failed to understand the Masonic usage of the term. Fundamentalists tend to believe the only definition or usage a term can have is the one they give it. The New World Dictionary states that *worshipful* can mean "worthy of being worshiped," but the term can also be used to mean "honorable; respected; used as a title of respect for magistrates, certain lodge officials, etc."[31] Masons use the term to mean honorable or respected. Coil explains that the term "has no necessary religious or sacred implication but usually means only honorable, respectable, or venerable."[32] A Masonic Bible answers the question, "What is the significance of this term [*worshipful*] applied to the Lodge and to the Master? Answer. The Old English meaning of 'worship' and 'worshipful' is retained; the idea is that of honorable, one to be reverenced, a venerable institution or person."[33]

The Old English term for greatness of character, honor or dignity was *weorthscipe*. English Reformer John Wycliffe (1324–1384) is credited with producing the first complete version of the Bible in the English language, although much of the work was probably done by his associates. His translation of Exodus 20:12 reads, "Thou shalt worship thy father and thy mother, that thou be long lived upon earth."[34] It is obvious that Wycliffe's term *worship* did not refer to the divinity of one's parents, but was a term meaning "to honor." The term *worship* has a different meaning today than it did to Wycliffe and others living in fourteenth-century England. Masons use the term today as did Wycliffe.

Mackey says the term's usage can be traced to the early English practice of referring to certain officials as "your worship." Mackey states that the Gilds of London began to refer to themselves as "Worshipful," such as "the Worshipful Company of Grocers."[35] In Canada, England and certain other nations, it is customary to speak of judges and mayors as "your worship." The mayor of London is referred to as "Worshipful Lord Mayor." The term *worshipful* may be archaic; but when its usage is understand, it is not offensive or sacrilegious.

One of the two houses of the British Parliament is called the House of Lords. The New Testament teaches that Jesus is Lord. Is it offensive or sacrilegious to call these British politicans "Lords?"

The *Study*[36] pointed out that the term *Reverend* is used only once in the Bible (Psalm 111:9, KJV) where it is used of God's name, "holy and reverend is his name." Yet, it is common for Christians to refer to their priests and ministers as "Reverend." Christians are not identifying their priests' and ministers' names with God's name.

THE GREAT ARCHITECT OF THE UNIVERSE

In a somewhat puzzling statement, Holly writes, "Once again, in his discussion of the Masonic name for God, Dr. Leazer follows the party line. Quoting a Masonic source, he copies their reliance upon John Calvin's designation of God as an 'Architect' to justify the Lodge's naming of Him as GAOU [*sic*]."[37] John Calvin (1509–1564) was a preeminent Reformed theologian who is considered the father of Presbyterianism today. The *Study* quoted Calvin's *Commentary* upon the Book of Psalms:

> David shows how it is [in Psalm 19] that the heavens proclaim to us the glory of God, namely by openly bearing testimony that they have not been put together by chance, but were wonderfully created by the supreme Architect. . . . As soon as we acknowledge God to be the supreme Architect, who has erected the beauteous fabric of the universe, our minds must necessarily be ravished with wonder at his infinite goodness, wisdom, and power.[38]

The Study also quotes Calvin's *Institutes of the Christian Religion*: "Hence God was pleased that a history of the creation should exist a history on which the faith of the Church might lean without seeking another God than Him whom Moses set forth as the Creator and Architect of the world."[39] "The former is exemplified when we consider how great the Architect must be who framed and ordered the multitude of the starry host so admirably."[40]

The Masonic source cited in the *Study*, which Holly refers to, but doesn't quote, is from Professor Wallace McLeod:

> Actually this phrase [the Great Architect of the Universe] entered Freemasonry by way of the first *Book of Constitutions*, printed in 1723. The compiler was Rev. Dr. James Anderson, a graduate of Aberdeen

intends them to mean; symbols can mean different things to different people."[54] The sentence was edited out by Larry Lewis.

Holly argues there is a remarkable distinction between signs and symbols.[55] There can be a distinction between signs and symbols, but writers often use the words interchangeably. As an example of the interchangeability of the words, the *Holman Bible Dictionary*, when discussing the rainbow, states, "The Mesopotamian Epic of Gilgamesh, another ancient flood account, does not include the **sign** of the rainbow. The rainbow and its beauty became a **symbol** of the majesty and beauty of God."[56]

Dictionaries use words such as *token*, *pledge*, *sign*, *emblem*, and *object* used to represent something abstract when defining *symbol.* A. Berkeley Mickelsen states,

> A symbol is a sign which suggests meaning rather than stating it. For example, God established the rainbow as a sign, pledge, or symbol *('oth)* that he would not bring another flood to destroy mankind. This particular symbol, like many others, requires explanation.[57]

Mickelsen continues by giving the characteristics of symbols:

(1) The symbol itself is a literal object. . . .
(2) The symbol is used to convey some lesson or truth. . . .
(3) The connection between the literal object and the lesson it teaches becomes clearer when we learn what the one who used the symbol meant to convey by it.[58]

Each Advent season many Christian congregations use Chrismons in their Advent celebrations. Chrismons are historically significant symbols of the Christian faith that are placed on Christmas trees as ornaments, to remind members of what the season means. The Greek Cross (+) can remind them of Christ or of an addition sign as in 2 + 2 = 4. The fish can remind them of Christ or of the bass they caught last summer in their grandparent's farm pond. The Easter lily can remind them of the resurrection or of a visit to a botanical garden with their parents. A butterfly can remind them of eternal life or of the insect that lighted on their hand in the butterfly exhibit at Calloway Gardens in Georgia. When we talk with our children about the symbolic meaning of the Chrismons, we explain what meaning they convey. The question that must be used: how does the one using the symbol intend that it be used.

Holly, who believes the All-Seeing Eye is an occultic symbol, says, "for a Christian to take an occultic symbol, i.e., the All-Seeing Eye, and try to make it a symbol for the One true, doesn't change the nature of what it was to begin with."[59] Mickelsen says, "Only the man who is wise in his own judgment (ct. Rom. 12:6) has all the answers on symbols."[60]

The *Holman Bible Dictionary* says of God's eye(s),

> God's eye or eyes is a frequent picture of God's providential care. God guides with His eye (Ps. 32:8), that is, gives counsel while offering His watchcare. Deliverance from death and famine result from God's watchful eye (Ps. 33:18–19). The image of God's eye(s) ranging throughout the earth (2 Chron. 16:9; Prov. 15:3; Jer. 16:7) symbolizes God's knowledge of all human activity and His control over it. Apocalyptic pictures involving numerous eyes (Ezek. 1:18; 10:12; Rev. 4:6), likewise, reassure of God's awareness of His people's plight wherever they might be.[61]

The *Study* pointed out that a number of symbols used by Christians began as pagan symbols or because of pagan beliefs. The bridal veil was introduced to protect the bride from an evil spell that might be placed on her by a spurned suitor. Only after the bride was protected by the sacrament of marriage could the veil be raised. The Christmas tree and Easter eggs were originally pagan symbols. The evergreen tree was a symbol of immortality since it did not lose its color or needles in the winter; eggs have long been symbols of fertility. As the original manuscript of the *Study* and Mickelsen state, a symbol means what the user intends it to mean. For Masons, the All-Seeing Eye symbolizes the fact that God knows and sees all of our thoughts, words, and actions, even those hidden from the eyes of others.

THE LEO TAXIL HOAX

In his first volume, Holly repeats the Taxil Hoax popular among anti-Masons. As the *Study* explains, the Taxil Hoax concerns a speech allegedly given by Albert Pike on July 14, 1889.[62] Holly quotes from this hoax.

> **Masonic Religion should be, by all of us initiates of the higher degrees, maintained in the purity of the Luciferian Doctrine. . . . Yes, Lucifer is God,** and unfortunately Adonay is also god. . . . **but Lucifer, God of Light and God of Good,** is struggling for humanity against Adonay, the God of Darkness and Evil."[63]

This hoax is repeated by J. Edward Decker, Jack Harris, Gary H. Kah, William Schnoebelen, Pat Robertson, Cathy Burns, Muhammad Safwat al-

Saqqa Amini, Sa'di Abu Habib, and other anti-Masons.[64] C. Fred Kleinknecht, Sovereign Grand Commander of the Southern Jurisdiction of the Scottish Rite, wrote to Robertson explaining that the alleged speech was a hoax; saying, "If we must disagree let us base our disagreements upon truth."[65] Robertson didn't respond. It speaks volumes about the desire of an individual to report the truth when an error is pointed out to him and he chooses to ignore or reject the truth.

> *Be careful that you are not persuaded to believe a particular story simply because you wish it to be true.*[66]

As the *Study* found, Wesley P. Walters reported the alleged speech was taken from a French publication of Abel Clarin De la Rive titled *The Woman and Child in Universal Masonry (La Femme et L'Enfant dans la Franc-Maconnerie Universelle*, Paris: Delhomme et Briquet, 1894). The *Study* states,

> The hoax was created by Gabriel Antoine Jogand-Pages, who was both an anti-Mason and an anti-Catholic, in an attempt to embarrass both groups. Raised in a Jesuit school, Jogand-Pages hated the Roman Catholic Church. Using the name Leo Taxil, he attacked the Pope in his publication *The Secret Loves of Pius IX*. He also joined the Masonic Lodge but was soon expelled. Taxil began to write about alleged immoralities and orgies in the Lodge, during which the forged statements of Albert Pike first appeared. He also fabricated a Diana Vaughan, who claimed she was a daughter of a Satanist in Louisville, Kentucky, who was associated with Albert Pike. Taxil admitted his hoax in January 1897.[67]

Holly admitted in his first volume that the alleged statement came from a questionable source,[68] but he still used it. What kind of scholarship is that? It reminds me of a question asked of a politician, "Why do you make false statements about your opponents?" The sad answer: "Because people believe them."

Holly explains when he became aware of the Leo Taxil hoax and then passes it off as irrelevant.

> I became aware of the potentially fraudulent nature of this quote when the printer of *The SBC and Freemasonry, Vol. I,* which also

> printed Robert Morey's book, *The Origins and Teachings of Freemasonry*, sent me a copy. Unfortunately for the Masonic Lodge, and for Dr. Leazer's defense of them, the refutation of this quotation does nothing to rehabilitate the writings of Albert Pike."[69]

It is surprising Holly did not discover the truth about this hoax before he published his first volume in 1992. His excuse that "There is no conclusive evidence either way"[70] questions his objectivity. Reviewer William E. "Bill" Gordon, Jr., says "The evidence that the passage he cites is a hoax is very conclusive!"[71] Morey's book was published in 1990 and Walters' article in October 1989. Art deHoyos and Brent Morris list at least twenty accounts about Taxel's hoax that were published prior to Holly's first volume.[72] Holly said he used the hoax because **"it was believable."**[73] In other words, Holly used the hoax because it fit his preconceived idea that Freemasonry is Satanic. Ed Decker said he also used the alleged statement "because **it fits in quite well** with other writings of Albert Pike, which are known to be authentic," while admitting that at least one Masonic writer had questioned whether Pike had actually given the speech.[74] Cathy Burns merely cites Decker as documentation for the alleged statement.[75]

> *[Rumors are] told to you by someone that you trust—a member of your church or a neighbor—and they tell you a story that sounds plausible, and you wouldn't think they're lying to you. They're probably not, they're just passing on what they've heard. The thing just gets passed on and on until it's accepted as fact.*
>
> *When people are in a situation of uncertainty, people begin to cast about for information to fill the void. If a story comes along that seems plausible within their frame of reference, it is accepted.*[76]

The *Study* made the observation that

> Many Masonry critics believe almost anything, especially the most sensational stories, that shows Freemasonry in an unfavorable light. They repeat stories they hear without checking facts, and ignore any evidence contrary to their beliefs. An untruth repeated until it becomes common knowledge does not cause it to become true.[77]

Holly continued defending his citing of the bogus Pike statement by arguing the refutation "does nothing for the Luciferian sentiments of Albert Pike, as those beliefs are documented elsewhere for all to read."[78] But he doesn't give a single quote for "all to read." As Holly stated, "accusation without documentation . . . is hardly a scholarly approach."[79]

Pike refers to Lucifer six times, the Devil eight times, and Satan twenty-two times in *Morals and Dogma*. After examining each of the thirty-six times Lucifer, the Devil, or Satan is used, there is no evidence that Pike was Luciferian or that he believed Lucifer was God. For the majority of the times Lucifer, the Devil, or Satan were cited, they were references to how an individual or religion, such as Gnosticism or the Manichaeans, used the names.

Holly cites Walter Leslie Wilmshurst's (1867–1939) allegorical interpretation of Matthew 2:15, "'Out of Egypt have I called My son' is, in one of its many senses, a biblical allusion to this passing on of the catholic Mysteries from Egypt to new and virgin regions, for their enlightenment,"[80] in his attempt to demonstrate that the god of Freemasonry is Lucifer. Wilmshurst is a minor, relatively unknown Masonic writer who is cited by anti-Masons more than Masons.

Both Holly and Bill Gordon refer to Wilmshurst's statement as blasphemous.[81] Wilmshurst's allegorical interpretation cannot be reconciled with the Hosea 11:1 prophecy fulfilled in Jesus' return with his family from Egypt to Israel after Herod's death, "When Israel was a child, I loved him, and out of Egypt I called my son."

Gordon found that Wilmshurst's statement, while revealing a decided pagan bias, "does not indicate that Lucifer is the god of the Lodge as Holly had promised to prove 'from the mouth of Masons themselves.' "[82] Holly attempts to equate Freemasonry with the Egyptian mystery religions. Gordon concludes that "is a valid observation of Wilmshurst's book."[83] Holly then asserts that the "purpose of mystery religions in the ancient world was the establishing of Luciferian worship among men."[84] Gordon concludes that "Holly presents no evidence that the Egyptian mystery religions consciously worshiped Lucifer as a god."[85]

In his response to Gordon's critique, Holly reminds Gordon that he "must face the fact that even the Roman Catholic Church has identified the god of the Lodge as Lucifer."[86] Holly refers the reader to a statement by Roman Catholic Robert I. Bradley, which he quotes twice in his second volume on pages 19 and 95:

> **The goal of Masonry is the overthrow and replacement of the Christian religious and political order with a new order based on naturalism. . . .** Freemasonry in its modern mode is "modernity" in

> the deepest (i.e., the philosophical and religious) sense of that term. It is, in a word, "Counterfeit Catholicism." For its "God" is the "Counterfeit God": The one who would be as God, the one who is the prince of this world, the one who is the Father of lies.[87]

Elsewhere, it has been shown that the Roman Catholic Church has been opposed to Freemasonry since 1738, but especially since the loss of the Italian Papal States in 1870. Italian patriot and Mason Giuseppe Garibaldi led in the unification of the Papal States into the nation of Italy, leaving the Roman Catholic Church with only the 109-acre Vatican City. This led to the infamous encyclical *Humanum Genus* in 1884 in which Pope Leo XIII condemned Freemasonry as a "wicked force" and a "contagious disease" because Freemasons:

(1) call for religious liberty;
(2) call for separation of [the Roman Catholic] Church and state;
(3) call for education of children by laymen rather than the [Roman Catholic] Church;
(4) believe people have the right to make their own laws and elect their own government.[88]

It appears from a reading of *Humanum Genus* that the Catholic Church is opposed to Freemasonry for political, rather than theological, reasons.

It is interesting that Holly cited a Roman Catholic Jesuit priest for support of his position, while the Roman Catholic Church has taken an especially strong stand against fundamentalism. The Pontifical Biblical Commission, in an unusually harsh 130-page document, concluded that "Fundamentalism actually invites people to a kind of intellectual suicide."[89]

The points of condemnation cited by Pope Leo XIII are the identical causes for which Baptists have fought for and died for the past 385 years.

Jose Maria Cardinal Caro y Rodriquez, Archbishop of Santiago, Chile, wrote, "What is the God whom the new and universal religion of Masonry adores? Is it God, the Supreme Architect of the Universe, as they have called him? Is it Nature with which many identify that God? Is it Man in whom that identity is realized with greatest perfection? Is it the Sun as the most perfect symbol of the power of nature? Is it Satan, whom the Masons hold to be the good God? Yes, it is all of that."[90] The Archbishop outlines his opposition to Freemasonry when he claims Masons were behind the removal of the crucifix and images from public schools "as if we were not in a Catholic country," a reference to Chile. He charges that Masons were behind the organization of

Boy Scouts "with the concealed purpose of alienating the children from the [Catholic] Church." Furthermore, he states that Masons are behind the effort to replace the Catechism and the influence of Catholic parents with "teachers of a lay morality, without religion."[91] The Archbishop charges that Freemasonry favors and helps Protestantism, which he defines as "a rebellion against the authority established in His Church by Our Lord Jesus Christ, expressly contained in the Bible, and indirectly and logically it is a rebellion against the same authority of Our Lord Jesus Christ."[92]

The Archbishop and Holly have nothing in common theologically. They both have found Freemasonry a convenient whipping boy to explain why things are not as they would wish.

12 Responding to Specific Attacks on Freemasonry, Part II

Some minds are like concrete—thoroughly mixed up and permanently set.[1]

THE DEITY AS FATHER

Masons are criticized for their affirmation of the Fatherhood of God. Ankerberg and Weldon say, "This doctrine of universal fatherhood of God is not biblical. Scripture is clear that only those who receive and believe in Jesus Christ have a proper standing with God and are His true sons."[2]

The *Holman Bible Dictionary*, published by the Southern Baptist Sunday School Board's Holman Bible Publishers, states that God is known in the Bible "as Father in three separate senses that must not be confused."

> (1) He is Father of Jesus Christ in a unique sense—by incarnation (Matt. 11:25–27, Mark 14:36; Rom. 8:15; Gal. 4:6; 2 Pet. 1:17);
> (2) He is Father of believers—by adoption or redemption (Matt. 5:43–48; Luke 11:2, 13; Gal. 3:26);
> (3) He is Father of all persons—by creation (Ps. 68:5; Isa. 64:8; Mal. 2:10; Matt. 5:45; 1 Pet. 1:17).[3]

Isaiah 64:8 says, "Yet O LORD, you are our Father; we are the clay, and you are our potter; we are all the work of your hand."

Malachi 2:10 says, "Have we not all one father? Has not one God created us? Why then are we faithless to one another, profaning the covenant of our ancestors?"

First Peter 1:17 says, "If you invoke as Father the one who judges all people impartially according to their deeds, live in reverent fear during the time of your exile."

Eric C. Rust, writing in the *Mercer Dictionary of the Bible*, says that "throughout the Letters and the rest of the NT, God is described as father of all mankind."[4] "The Baptist Faith and Message," a statement of faith adopted by the Southern Baptist Convention in 1963, speaks of God as "fatherly in His attitude toward all men."

The concept of deity as Father is also found outside the biblical canon. It is a common belief found throughout history in the writings of poets and other scriptures. Homer, who wrote *The Iliad* by 550 B.C., speaks of Jove (or Jupiter), the Olympian Lord of Thunder, as "Father Jove."[5] Plato (c.428 B.C.–c.348 B.C.) speaks of God as "the father and maker of all this universe."[6] The Creator is spoken of as "Father" in the Hindu scripture Brihad-Aranyaka Upanishad, which was written prior to 300 B.C.[7]

The hymns of the ancient Babylonians spoke of their deity as "Father of the Land." The Canaanites spoke of El as the "all-father" or "father of the gods."[8]

The Canaanites used the name *El Elyon*, or simply *Elyon*, for the highest god of the Canaanite pantheon. Melchizedek is spoken of as "priest of God Most High" [El Elyon] (Gen. 14:18). Abram (Abraham) identified Yahweh with El Elyon: "I have sworn to the LORD [Yahweh], God Most High [El Elyon], maker of heaven and earth" (Gen. 14:22). Elyon is used as a synonym for Yahweh in Deuteronomy 32:8–9.

The Bible speaks of God revealing Himself as a unique God of all nations: "There is none like you, O Lord; you are great, and your name is great in might. Who would not fear you, O King of the nations?" (Jeremiah 10:6–7). The Psalmist spoke of God's name as majestic or glorious in all the earth: "O Lord, our Sovereign, how majestic is your name in all the earth! You have set your glory above the heavens" (Psalm 8:1). Genesis 1–11 testifies that men, other than Israelites, may know God. Conservative Christians contend this self-revelation of God is only partial, for there is no unfolding of redemptive love and grace. Any man may know of God as Creator. He may know of His power and majesty, but be ignorant of His redemptive love and grace.

The Bible speaks of mankind as made in the image of God (Genesis 1:26), with the capacity to respond to God and live in fellowship with Him. Since we are made in His image, it is natural that all cultures have similar yearnings to worship Him. Darrell W. Robinson writes, "Humankind is incurably religious. In every person is a God-shaped void."[9] The Bible speaks of God's self-revelation in nature, a doctrine called natural or general revelation: "The heavens are telling the glory of God; and the firmament proclaims his handiwork" (Psalm 19:1). God placed within each person a conscience that leads a person to know right from wrong. Various cultures have stories about a moral fall, a messianic or hero figure, stories of gods who come to earth to rescue mankind and gods who die and rise again. However, it is the Christian contention that the understanding of God in these cultures is distorted to different degrees. In other words, though natural or general revelation leads mankind to an awareness of God's existence, it is only a partial understanding of God. Redemptive love and saving grace are fully revealed and available only through God's Son.

Many conservative and most fundamentalist Christians insist that the deity worshiped in religions other than the Judeo-Christian faiths cannot be the God revealed in the Bible. Other conservative Christian theologians argue that the God worshiped by Muslims, Hindus, and adherents of other faiths is the God who reveals Himself in the Bible, but that the understanding of God in Islam, Hinduism, and other faiths is incomplete and corrupted by mankind's sin. To these theologians, God perfectly revealed Himself in the person and work of Jesus Christ.

THE CLAIM THAT FREEMASONRY TEACHES RESURRECTION IN ITS RITUAL: THE HIRAM ABIF LEGEND

Holly has repeatedly shown he eagerly distorts Masonic writings. For example, he quotes Rex Hutchens's *A Bridge to Light*, in an effort to prove that Albert Pike taught the doctrine of the resurrection.[10] Hutchens is, in turn, quoting *Morals and Dogma*, a fact Holly does not mention. Holly omits five words in Pike's statement found in Hutchens's *A Bridge to Light* and adds "(the 25th Degree)" in his volume. Holly cites the quote as:

> This degree . . .teaches the necessity of reformation as well as repentance, as a means of obtaining mercy and forgives, **(the 25th Degree) is also devoted to an explanation of the symbols of Masonry; and especially to those which are connected with the ancient and universal legend, of which that of Khir-Om Abi [Hiram Abif] is but a variation; that legend which representing a murder or a death, and a restoration to life,** by a drama in which figure Osiris, Isis and Horus, . . . and many other representative of the active and passive Powers of Nature, taught the Initiates in the Mysteries that the rule of

> Evil and Darkness is but temporary, and that of Light and Good will be eternal.[11]

Then Holly exclaims, "Here *A Bridge to Light* affirms the death, burial and resurrection motif of the Master Mason ritual."[12] It is obvious that Holly has failed to grasp Pike's teaching in this degree. Holly claims this paragraph affirms the "resurrection motif of the Master Mason ritual." But Pike uses the word *restoration,* not *resurrection*. The word *resurrection* is not used in the degree. Pike explains his use of *restoration:*

> No doubt the decay of vegetation and the falling of the leaves, emblems of dissolution and evidence of the action of that Power that changes Life into Death, in order to bring Life again out of Death, were regarded as signs of that Death that seemed coming upon all Nature; **as the springing of leaves and buds and flowers in the spring was a sign of restoration to life.**[13]

Pike says the teaching in this degree "is both philosophical and moral," words that Holly omits in his quote from *A Bridge to Light*. Pike explains his use of the word *restoration* by citing the cycles of nature as evidence that "Evil and Darkness," in which mankind is implicated, is "temporary." "Light and Good" will eventually triumph over "Evil and Darkness," just as new life comes forth in the spring.

As is his custom, Pike quotes or refers to a number of philosophers and theologians to illustrate his teaching, while admitting that "we smile at these notions of the ancients; but we must learn to look through these material images and allegories, to the ideas, struggling for utterance, the great speechless thoughts which they envelop."[14]

Holly takes issue with the discussion of the raising of Hiram Abif, which he says was a resurrection, in the *Study*. Holly quotes the *Study*:

> The legend of Hiram Abif in the ritual for the Master Mason's degree is criticized by Masonry critics. According to I Kings 7:13-47, Hiram Abif was a bronze worker in Solomon's Temple. . . . The ritual for the Master Mason's degree says that three workers in the Temple attempted to learn the secret Master's Word from Hiram. When he refused to reveal it, they killed Hiram and buried his body secretly. The body was discovered after King Solomon ordered a search for it. Only the strong grip of a Master Mason' by King Solomon could raise Hiram's body from the grave.[15]

Holly claims I quoted a "single source" to prove my argument that the raising of Hiram Abif was not a resurrection, but merely done to rebury him in another grave. Careful reading of the *Study* clearly shows that I did not quote a "single source," but three sources. I quoted anti-Mason William Schnoebelen who wrote, "After a lot of ritualized fussing around, Solomon takes the decomposing right hand of Hiram Abif by the 'Strong Grip of the Lion's Paw,' the Master Mason grip, and hauls his carcass out of the ground, **apparently resurrecting him (although this is never clear).**"[16] I also quoted Albert Mackey, "Quoting the Masonic *Book of Constitutions*, Mackey writes, '. . . after some time allowed to the Craft to vent their sorrow, ordered his obsequies to be performed with solemnity and decency, and **buried him in the Lodge near the Temple—according to the ancient usages among Masons—and long mourned his loss.**"[17] Why would anyone rebury a person who had been resurrected from the dead? From *Look to the East: A Ritual of the First Three Degrees of Masonry,* I quote the phrase **"carried it [Hiram Abif's body] to the Temple, and buried it in due form."**[18] Coil says that after the discovery of Hiram Abif's body, Solomon "order'd him to be taken up and decently buried, and the 15 Fellow-Crafts with white Gloves and Aprons should attend his Funeral."[19] Why would anyone attend the funeral of a person who had been resurrected from the dead?

Holly argues that since Hiram Abif's body was "raised" from the grave, "the clear implication is resurrection."[20] The word *raised* could imply resurrection; language is an inexact science. A body is "lowered" into a grave. The antonym of "lower" is "raise." If a body is in a grave (buried), it must be lifted/raised out of the grave. The idea in the Hiram Abif legend is removal of the body from one grave to place it in another grave, not resurrection. Today, if a murderer kills and buries his victim, it is customary to search for the body and, if found, to remove it from the temporary grave to a permanent one. Plain statements by numerous Masonic sources show that Hiram Abif's body was merely moved from one grave to another. Morris and deHoyos give six examples from anti-Masonic books that support the Masonic teaching that Hiram Abif was reburied.[21]

Although Masons do not teach that Hiram Abif was resurrected from the dead, Pike saw his murder, burial, and raising as "symbols, both of the death, burial, and resurrection of the Redeemer; and of the death and burial in sins of the natural man, and his being raised again to a new life, or born again, by the direct action of the Redeemer."[22] Pike continues by explaining that the Redeemer is Christ.[23] Pike says in this discussion that morality or good works and philosophy or education cannot raise an individual to new life. Only the "strong grip" of "the Lion of the House of Judah," who is Christ, can raise a person to a new life.

HIRAM ABIF'S NAME

Holly asks, "Why does Dr. Leazer adopt the Masonic name for Hiram? The Bible calls him 'Hiram of Tyre.' Masons called him 'Hiram Abif.' Leazer adopts the Masonic vocabulary without explanation."[24] First, any Bible dictionary shows that there were two Hirams associated with the building of the Temple. One was Hiram, King of Tyre, who was the son of Abibaal ("my father is Baal"). The second was Hiram Abi, referred to as Huram Abi or Huram-abi in some translations.[25] The Hebrew Scriptures refer to him as "Huram his master craftsman."[26] Hiram Abi was from Tyre and had a widowed Jewish mother. In Hebrew, "ab" means "father;" "abi" means "my father" as in Abibaal, meaning "my father is Baal;" and "abiv" means "his father." The *New American Standard Exhaustive Concordance of the Bible* says the name can also be spelled "Churam."[27] Martin Luther translated the name as "Huram Abif" in 2 Chronicles 2:13 and 4:16.[28] There is no support in the Bible for the Masonic Hiram Abif legend, but one can look back as far as Martin Luther to find a non-Masonic use of the name *Hiram* or *Huram Abif.*

THE CLAIM THAT FREEMASONRY TEACHES UNIVERSALISM

Holly charges that the so-called secret doctrine of Freemasonry is universalism.[29] He attempts to prove his argument by quoting the final sentence of Pike's discussion of the 26.

> While all these faiths assert their claims to the exclusive possession of the Truth, Masonry inculcates its own doctrine, and no more: . . . That God is ONE; that His Thought uttered in His WORD, created the Universe, and preserves it by those Eternal Laws which are the expression of that Thought: that the Soul of Man, breathed into him by God, is immortal as His Thoughts are; that he is free to do evil or to choose good, responsible for his acts and punishable for his sins: that all evil and wrong and suffering are but temporary, the discords of one great Harmony, and that in His good time they will lead by infinite modulations to the great, harmonic final chord and cadence of Truth, Love, Peace, and Happiness, that will ring forever and ever under the Arches of Heaven, among all the Stars and Worlds, and in all souls of men and Angels.[30]

Holly claims this sentence proves that Pike teaches universalism. He writes, "Universalism was never more clearly stated. No one will perish in eternal flames of Hell."[31] Holly completely missed the intent of Pike's discussion. Universalism and hell are not discussed in the 26.

Pike's passage speaks of man as "responsible for his acts and punishable for his sins." Elsewhere, Pike speaks of "The agonies of the garden of Gethsemane and those on the Cross on Calvary preceded the Resurrection and were the means of Redemption."[32] Those are not the words of a universalist. Pike writes as a layman, as a poet and a philosopher, not a biblical theologian. He does not give the critical attention to the nuances of his statements as do trained biblical theologians. And so he has left himself open to attack by others.

Pike speaks of "Harmony" in the statement quoted above. He uses the term to mean "equilibrium," as in the final resolution of the justice and mercy of God in light of the fact that men have chosen to do evil.[33] Pike also speaks of "Harmony" in connection with "HOPE, for the final triumph of Good over Evil, and for Perfect Harmony as the final result of all the concords and discords of the Universe."[34] While "Harmony" could arguably be seen as relating to eschatology or the doctrine of last things, any argument that it refers to universalism is not justified. The Christian hope of the Second Coming of Christ does not require, does not justify, a belief in universalism. Neither does Pike's hope of a future "Harmony."

The doctrine of universalism can be understood in two ways. First, universalism can speak of the biblical teaching that God's purposes were not limited to Israel, but were extended to all mankind. This is clearly seen in Yahweh's blessing to Isaac: "I will make your offspring as numerous as the stars of heaven, and will give to your offspring all these lands; and all the nations of the earth shall gain blessing for themselves through your offspring (Gen. 26:3)."[35] This was emphasized in Christ's Great Commission: "Go therefore and make disciples of all nations . . . (Matt. 28:10)."

Second, universalism can speak of the teaching that all moral creatures, even the devil himself, will share in the grace of God's salvation ultimately. This position is also known as "Apocatasasis," or universal salvation. In other words, everyone will be saved. This view has been held by certain Christians through the centuries, including Origen (185–254)[36] and Gregory of Nyssa (330–395).[37] Although condemned as a heretical doctrine by the fifth ecumenical council, the Second Council of Constantinople, in 553, it continued to be held by some Christians, including some Anabaptists. It was held by German theologian Friedrich Schleiermacher (1768–1834), whose influence extends today to many liberal Christian theologians. Universalism or the doctrine of universal salvation, however, is rejected by conservative Christians today.

During the April 1994 Board of Directors meeting, eleven Home Mission Board directors, who erroneously referred to themselves as "trustees," a term also used by Holly throughout his third book, signed a "Clarification of Recommendation of 1993 HMB Freemasonry Report to SBC." The "Clarification" expressed concern that Christians who are Masons lend "credibility to the false doctrine of universalism" allegedly "spread . . . by a group numbering 4,000,000 [*sic*] in the United States."[38]

No action was taken on the "Clarification" after the Home Mission Board directors adopted a statement condemning universalism at the March 1994 meeting in Atlanta[39] to clarify the statement that "the heresy of universalism (the belief all people will eventually be saved), which permeates the writings of many Masonic authors, which is a doctrine inconsistent with New Testament teaching."[40] The "Report" cites *Morals and Dogma*, page 847, as documentation for this criticism. However, there is nothing on page 847 which remotely suggests that Pike believed in universalism. Pike does say that poets dream that hell will become useless and that Good alone will be triumphant and reign in Eternity. He refers to the Persian belief that Ahriman and his followers will be reconciled with God, and that evil will end. But Pike doesn't say he believes this or that Masons must believe what the poets or Persians believe. Why the "Report" cites *Morals and Dogma*, page 847, is unclear and puzzling. It is obvious that the writer of the six-page "Report on Freemasonry" did not read, (or if he did, misunderstood), page 847.

Ankerberg and Weldon refer to the Study's quote from *Coil's Masonic Encyclopedia:* "Many Freemasons make this flight with no other guarantee of a safe landing than their belief in the religion of Freemasonry."[41] Ankerberg and Weldon interpret this statement as a confession by Coil that Masonry is a religion and that many Masons believe they are guaranteed salvation through their faith in Freemasonry.[42] The *Study* quickly pointed out that this interpretation is neither biblical nor Masonic. As Ankerberg and Weldon point out, Coil continues, "If that is a false hope, the fraternity should abandon funeral services and devote its attention to activities where it is sure of its ground and its authority."[43] It is a false hope. I recommended in my speech to the Southeast Masonic Conference in August 1993 that Masons drop the funeral service. The United Grand Lodge of England has no Masonic funeral service.[44]

A few Masonic authors believe in universalism; more Masonic authors reject the belief in universalism; most don't write about universalism and don't express a position for or against it. I have heard many Baptist evangelists bemoan the fact that many Southern Baptist have adopted an incipient universalism and that they don't really believe in the lostness of mankind. Who would condemn all Southern Baptists because some believe in universalism? That is what anti-Masons and the Home Mission Board's "Report on Freemasonry" do with their absolute statements about Freemasonry and universalism.

SALVATION

The *Study* quotes from the Monitor of the Grand Lodge of Texas concerning salvation. It quotes a portion of a prayer offered by the Worshipful Master before a candidate is "raised" to the Master Mason degree. The quoted conclusion is "Yet, O Lord! have compassion on the children of Thy creation; administer them comfort in time of trouble, and **save them with an everlasting salvation!**"[45] Holly agrees that the prayers admit "that salvation come from God, but it," he says, "does not address the conditions under which that salvation is given."[46] Perhaps the conditions are not given, but it is clear that the everlasting salvation comes from God. Since Freemasonry is not a religion, and does not think of itself as a religion, it does not make pronouncements on the specifics of salvation any more than the U.S. Congress or the Boy Scouts of America.

The *Study* quotes other statements from prayers in the *Monitor* of the Grand Lodge of Texas to which Holly alludes, but does not quote. They are,

> O Almighty and Eternal God! There is not number of Thy days or of Thy mercies. Thou hast sent us into this world to serve Thee, but we wander far from Thee in the path of error.
>
> We place you [the deceased Mason] in the arms of our Heavenly Father, who grants his love and protection to those who put their trust in him.
>
> Because of an unshaken faith in the merits of the Lion of the Tribe of Judah, we shall gain admission into the celestial Lodge above where the Supreme Architect of the Universe presides.[47]

Even Holly admits "Each statement suggests the possibility of reliance upon faith for salvation."[48] The statements are more than a "possibility;" they state that through an unshaken faith in the Lion of the Tribe of Judah, who is Jesus Christ, we gain admission to heaven.

In his second volume, Holly refers to a portion of a funeral service in *Masonic Burial Services* by Robert Macoy.[49] Holly erroneously claims this proves Masons are "welcomed into heaven, not by the Blood of Jesus, but by his Masonic membership." An extensive quote is provided by Holly to prove his argument:

> Almighty and Heavenly Father—infinite in wisdom, mercy and goodness—extend to us the riches of Thy everlasting grace. Thou alone are a refuge and help in trouble and affliction. In this bereavement we look to thee for support and consolation. May we believe that death hath no power over a faithful and righteous soul! May we believe that, though the dust returneth to the dust as it was, the spirit goeth unto thyself. As we mourn the departure of a brother beloved from the circle of our Fraternity, may we trust he hath entered into a higher brotherhood, to engage in nobler duties and in heavenly work, to find rest from earthly labor, and refreshment from earthly care. . . .
>
> . . . we should so regulate our lives by the line of rectitude and truth, that in the evening of our days we may be found worthy to be called from labor to refreshment, **and duly prepared for a translation from the terrestrial to the celestial Lodge, to join the Fraternity of the spirits of just men made perfect.**
>
> . . . And having faithfully discharged the great duties which we owe to God, to our neighbor, and ourselves; when at last it shall please the Grand Master of the universe to summon us into his eternal presence, may the trestle-board of our whole lives pass such inspection that it may be given unto each of us to 'eat of the hidden manna,' and to receive the 'white stone with a new name' that will insure perpetual and unspeakable happiness at his right hand.[50]

Holly steps into the twilight zone by concluding that "The white stone refers to the possibility of being 'black-balled' in the Lodge."[51] The statement ". . . it may be given unto each of us to 'eat of the hidden manna,' and to receive the 'white stone with a new name'" has nothing to do with being blackballed, or rejected for membership in "the Lodge" or by God. Rather, the statement is from Christ's words in Revelation 2:17: "To everyone who conquers I will give some of the hidden manna, and I will give a white stone, and on the white stone is written a new name that no one knows except the one who receives it." The phrase "from the terrestrial to the celestial Lodge," which Holly quotes but does not comment on, is from 1 Corinthians 15:40 (KJV): "There are also celestial [heavenly] bodies, and bodies terrestrial [earthly]: but the glory of the celestial is one, and the glory of the terrestrial is another."

Holly quotes a portion of the annual address of the Grand Master of the Grand Lodge of Texas in 1961:

> . . . My brethren, if you could read the letters that I receive from these Brethren who have arrived at the very time of life when they could enjoy the happy reflections consequent upon a well spent life, and could die in the hope of a glorious immortality; and you and I are guilty of letting them go suspended.[52]

Then, directing his emotional appeal to his readers to win their agreement to his conclusion, which is unsupported by good evidence and logic, Holly says, **"This has to be the ultimate debtor's prison eternity in hell because you failed to pay your Masonic dues and died out of fellowship with the Masonic Lodge."**[53] The Grand Master's statement says nothing about "eternity in hell." He is simply referring to the distress a lifelong Mason feels, if in his old age he is no longer able to pay his annual dues. The Grand Master says Masons should feel guilty about that. Holly commits a logical fallacy known as *argumentum ad populum*, making an emotional appeal to the gallery.

LIGHT IN FREEMASONRY

The Home Mission Board's "Report on Freemasonry" criticizes Freemasonry for the "prevalent use of the term 'light,' which some may understand as a reference to salvation rather than knowledge or truth." Many anti-Masons believe the term *light* refers to an alleged salvation available through Freemasonry. As any dictionary indicates, there are many definitions of light. The term does not always refer to Jesus Christ or salvation. The definition is determined by the person using the term, not by the interpreter. The motto of the *Baltimore Sun* is "Light for all." Would anyone argue that the *Baltimore Sun* is teaching salvation in its pages. No, it uses "light" in the sense of knowledge or information, just as do Masons. The motto of Yale University is "LUX," a Latin word for "light." The list could go on.

Holly quotes *Morals and Dogma,*

> According to the Kabalah, as according to the doctrines of Zoroaster, everything that exists has emanated from a source of infinite

> light. . . . The world was His Revelation, God revealed, and subsisted only in Him. . . . You see, my brother, what is the meaning of Masonic "light."[54]

Holly's second ellipses (. . .) eliminated an unbelievable 44 lines of text and 460 words. In the pages immediately prior to the reference to Masonic "light," Pike discusses the Phoenicians, Hinduism, Philo the Jew, the Egyptians, the Persians, Strabo, Aristotle, Porphyry, Apollonius of Tyana, the New Platonists, Pythagoras, the Kabalah, and Marcion, and quotes John 1:1, 3–5, and John 8:12.[55]

Pike explains the meaning of Masonic "light" following the last sentence quoted by Holly.

> You see why the EAST of the Lodge, where the initial letter of the Name of the Deity overhangs the Master, is the place of Light. Light, as contradistinguished from darkness, is Good, as contradistinguished from Evil: and it is that Light, the true knowledge of Deity, the Eternal Good, for which Masons in all ages have sought.[56]

Pike here associates "Light" with the "Good" found in a true knowledge of God. Elsewhere, he says "Light" "is the apt symbol of truth and knowledge."[57]

Coil gives his definition of Light:

> Light is everywhere the symbol of intelligence, information, knowledge, and truth and is opposed to darkness, which symbolizes ignorance and evil. So, in the ceremonies, the candidate is said to be brought from darkness to light.[58]

Holly says "the Word of God does not place a high premium upon the mind of man in order to discover truth."[59] He cites I Corinthians 2 as support for his argument. The Apostle Paul tells the Corinthians about God's wisdom and that he came with a simple message about Jesus Christ. Paul said he spoke clearly what he had learned about God. Holly, although speaking disparagingly against public education, obviously places a great emphasis on education as he regularly refers to books in his library.

The New Testament is filled with references to using our minds for the glory of God. Christ taught that we are to love God with "all" our mind, as well as with heart and soul (Matt. 22:37). The Apostle Paul taught that we are to think about things true, honorable, just, pure, pleasing, commendable, and worthy of praise (Phil. 4:8). He told the Colossians to set their minds on Christ (Col. 3:2). The New Testament also tells us that minds can be corrupted (Col. 1:21), but God created our minds to use. Education is not evil, unless used for evil purposes. It is a sad commentary on humanity that too many people stop learning at age 40 and die at age 70. Not to use God's gift of our mind is to make us no more than animals.

Read Pike's words in *Morals and Dogma:*

> Reason must, for these, cooperate and coincide with Faith, or they remain still in the darkness of doubt,—most miserable of all conditions of the human mind."[60]

> Exalt and magnify Faith as we will, and say that it begins where Reason ends, it must, after all, have a foundation, either in Reason, Analogy, the Consciousness, or human testimony.[61]

> What we call Reason, that is, our imperfect human reason, not only may, but assuredly will, lead us away from the Truth in regard to things invisible and especially those of the Infinite, if we determine to believe nothing but that which it can demonstrate or not to believe that which it can by its processes of logic prove to be contradictory, unreasonable, or absurd.[62]

STUDY OF PHILOSOPHY IS A WORTHWHILE DISCIPLINE

Pike wrote *Morals and Dogma* in the shadow of liberal Protestant theologian Friedrich Schleiermacher (1768–1834) and in an optimistic period of history when it was believed mankind could usher in a period of peace and harmony prior to Christ's second coming. *Morals and Dogma* reflects that optimism. This view, known as postmillennialism, was popular among many Christians, including early Southern Baptist leaders such as B. H. Carroll. Postmillennialism lost its popularity after World War I. The opposite eschatalogical theory, known as premillennialism, is widely held today. Premillennialists reject any hint of the optimistic view of mankind held a century ago. Therefore, Pike's optimistic view of mankind is rejected by many premillennial, conservative Christians.

Repeatedly, Pike and other Masonic writers, insist that it is not the prerogative of Freemasonry to affirm or deny specific doctrinal positions held by different faiths. That is the prerogative of each faith. Freemasonry is a fraternity, not a religion. Pike writes that it is "beyond our jurisdiction" to tell a Muslim that the Prophet Muhammad is unessential, to tell a Hebrew that the Messiah came two thousand years ago, or to tell a Christian what to believe about Jesus Christ.[63] But nowhere does Pike tell a Christian he cannot believe that Jesus Christ is the one true Savior. Reflecting the optimism of his day, Pike states that "Evil will ultimately be dethroned," but that the explanation for the existence of evil "is beyond the domain of Masonry to decide."[64]

Theodicy is "the defence of the justice and righteousness of God in the face of the fact of evil."[65] Theodicy comes from two Greek words for God and justice. Theodicy is a difficult problem for Christians who believe that God is infinitely good and all-powerful and yet evil exists. Theologians have identified two streams of thought concerning theodicy. One is named after Irenaeus (130–202), bishop of Lyons, who is considered the Church's first systematic theologian. Irenaeus saw Adam and Eve as children in the Garden of Eden and the fall as an understandable part of moral development and growth. The Irenaean stream of thought, also called the eschatological approach because it looked to the future rather than to the beginning of human history, tended to be more optimistic about mankind and was popular in the eighteenth and nineteenth centuries. It placed more emphasis on the grace of God than on the sinfulness of man. The Irenaean position held that man has the potential for perfection, but, in reality, Christ was the only perfect Man who ever lived. Friedrich Schleiermacher (1768–1834) was an exponent of what could be called an Irenaean understanding of theodicy. The Irenaean stream fit well with the optimism and postmillennial eschatology of the late nineteenth century. Pike only mentioned Irenaeus four times in *Morals and Dogma,*[66] none in reference to Irenaeus' theory of evil. However, that Pike was influenced by this kind of optimism, given the period in which he lived, is a valid conclusion.

Opposed to the Irenaean stream is the Augustinian type of theodicy. Augustine (354–430) emphasized the fall of Adam and Eve in the Garden of Eden as a fall into fatal sin. Subsequently, all mankind has been born into a state of guilt and condemnation. Eternal torment in hell is the lot of all mankind unless God, by His grace, brings it to repentance and eternal life. Augustine put more emphasis on the fall and original sin than did Irenaeus. The Augustinian explanation of evil has been the most popular understanding of theodicy in both Catholic and Protestant churches through the centuries.

Certainly, Pike does not speak of the uniqueness of Christ or the Christian faith, but *Morals and Dogma* is not a Christian theology book. Morals and Dogma gives philosophical, moral, and religious ideas that different individuals and faiths have struggled with for the past 2,500 years. For example, Pike, in his lecture on the 26, mentions the Basilideans; Irenaeus; Tertullian; Clemens, bishop of Alexandria; Origen; Archelaus, bishop of Cascara in Mesopotamia; Cyril, bishop of Jerusalem; Basil, bishop of Caesarea; Gregory, bishop of Constantinople; Ambrose, archbishop of Milan; Augustine, bishop of Hippo; Chrysostom, bishop of Constantinople; Cyril, bishop of Alexandria; Theodoret, bishop of Cyropolis; Minucius Felix, a lawyer of Rome; Maximus Taurinus; Egyptian, Chaldean, and Persian gods; Plutarch; Plato; Philo; Aurelius; Hindu deities; Etruscans; Buddhists; Chinese Sabaeans; the Kabalah; Simon Magus; Bardesanes; Basilides; the Gospel of John; the Valentinians and other Gnostics; the Ophites; Tatian; the Elxaites; Noetus; Paul of Samosata; Arius; Manes; the Priscilianists; the Mandaites; and so forth.[67] In this lecture, Pike illustrates the great diversity of beliefs proposed by these different faiths and their exponents. He also refers to "the Son of God, Who died upon the cross to redeem mankind."[68] One must understand that Pike does not intend to give a recitation on Christian doctrine, but an exposition on religious ideas held by a diverse group of thinkers over a period of 2,500 years.

In the preface to *Morals and Dogma*, we find that readers are "entirely free to reject and dissent from whatsoever herein may seem to him to be untrue or unsound."[69] Pike wrote,

> What is truth to me is not truth to another. The same arguments and evidence that convince one mind make no impression on another. This difference is in men at their birth. No man is entitled positively to assert that he is right, where other men equally intelligent and equally well informed, hold directly the opposite opinion. Each thinks it impossible for the other to be sincere, and each, as to that, is equally in error.[70]

That people disagree about art, politics, economic theory, raising their children, movies, football teams, food, weather, and so forth is a fact of life. Although I may like one baseball team, my neighbor is free to differ with me. We can attempt to convince each other of our respective positions.

Pike's statement allows debate, dialogue, and discussion of one's position in an effort to convince another person to accept and adopt the position as his or her own. A Christian, whose belief about the person and work of Christ is not the same as a non-Christian's belief, may attempt by word and deed to convince the non-Christian to accept the Christian faith. The non-Christian is free to reject the argument if it is not convincing to him. Pike strongly believed that neither individual has the right to persecute the other because they hold different beliefs.[71]

The study of philosophy is a legitimate and worthwhile intellectual discipline. In philosophy, a person studies the development of ethical, political, religious, esthetic, metaphysical, and epistemological thought in Greek, Roman, Chinese, Hindu, and other "pagan" systems as well as within the Christian faith. To study Leibniz's theory of monads or Kant's *Critique of Pure Reason* does not require that we must accept any of their ideas.

Baptist writers have found support for biblical teachings in pagan religions and philosophies. William Cooke Boone, in a "Study Course Book" for the Baptist Sunday School Board, wrote this:

> Tacitus, a Roman writer, speaks of the time when "Men were as yet without any evil passions and passed their lives without any reproach and crimes." The Egyptians looked back to the time of their god, Ra, as a time of purity and perfection. There is a similar tradition in India and among the Persians and Greeks. The Tree of Life is seen on many Assyrian sculptures and bas reliefs."[72]

Boone, who pastored Southern Baptist churches in several states, continued his argument by referring to the Babylonians, Zoroastrians, the people of Tibet, and "an Egyptian goddess . . . shown piercing a serpent's head."[73]

While a student at Southwestern Baptist Theological Seminary, I took a course on the Christian faith and Greek philosophy under Russ Bush, now academic dean at Southeastern Baptist Theological Seminary. No one can charge Bush with being a liberal or neo-orthodox. In the course, we studied the Platonists and Pythagoreans and learned that they were the only Greek schools of philosophy who shared the Christian concern about life after death.[74] We examined the influence of Greek ideas on early Christian theology. We learned the limits of philosophy when set beside what God has revealed about Himself and His world.

Pike, even with his emphasis on education, knowledge, and truth, acknowledged there are limits to man's knowledge. "We but hide our ignorance in a cloud of words;—and the words too often are mere combinations of sounds without any meanings."[75]

One of my Bibles, with the square and compasses on the cover, has extensive reference aids to assist the reader in understanding the Bible. In it, one reads:

> But His love is best revealed in the gift of His Son. In the Cross of Christ we find His plan for the redemption of a sin-cursed world. The

> Bible teaches there is no other way than this given under Heaven among men whereby we must be saved. From whatever point of view we regard this Book, we can say of it as David once said of Goliath's sword, "There is none like it. Give it to me."[76]

This Masonic Altar Bible includes "Instructions for Personal Soul-Winning." The instructions include a section on "the Essential Requisites for Personal Soul-Winning." They are "A zeal for the salvation of the lost," "The leadership of the Holy Spirit," "Faith in the sufficiency of Christ to save to the uttermost," and "Sympathy, tactfulness, perseverance."[77] We learn from this source, as well as others, that "Masons believe in an eternal heaven for the redeemed of the Lord."[78]

Freemasonry is like any other human organization. Members come with various faith commitments. Most Masons are Christians; many are members of other faiths. Masons accept men from different faiths as friends, fellow citizens, brothers, and individuals for whom God loves and cares.

CONCLUSION

I come with mixed emotions. I began teaching Sunday school classes when I was 18 years old, a student at the Naval Academy. I have been a Baptist since I was a child. My religious heritage means a lot to me. Rosalynn and I have been in a quandary, not knowing what to do. But I want to assure you that in the CBF, my wife and I have found a home.[1]

JAMES L. HOLLY ASKS IN HIS THIRD VOLUME, "ARE WE NOW ALLIED WITH THE Masonic Lodge?"[2] The answer is "No!" Although Holly and some Masons may believe we have, the Southern Baptist Convention has not aligned itself with Freemasonry. That was never the design or intent of the *Study*. In its conclusion, the original manuscript submitted to Larry Lewis stated, **"The Interfaith Witness Department reaffirms its position taken in 1986; Freemasonry is NOT a religion."**[3] The final sentence in the original manuscript was **"We, therefore, with no hesitation, recommend the following: that the Southern Baptist Convention take a position neither for nor against Freemasonry and its related branches, and that membership in Freemasonry be left with the judgment of the individual."**[4] Both sentences were deleted by Lewis. Part of this recommendation came from the decision by Charleston, South Carolina, Baptists in 1798 that membership in Freemasonry "be left with the judgment of the individual."[5] Nowhere in "A Report on Freemasonry" is found any hint that the Southern Baptist Convention has allied itself with Freemasonry. The vote at the 1993 Southern Baptist Convention did not align the Convention with Freemasonry; rather, messengers voted not to condemn the fraternity.

Holly asks, "Have Southern Baptists abandoned the Word of God and made 'individual conscience' the supreme rule of faith?"[6] The answer is again "No!" The preface to "The Baptist Faith and Message," a statement of faith adopted by the Southern Baptist Convention in 1963, states:

> Baptists emphasize the soul's competence before God, freedom in religion, and the priesthood of the believer. However, this emphasis

> should not be interpreted to mean that there is an absence of certain definite doctrines that Baptists believe, cherish, and with which they have been and are now closely identified.

"The Baptist Faith and Message" also states that "God alone is Lord of the conscience." Any freedom carries with it responsibility. Freedom of religion or conscience is no different. Ultimately, each person is responsible to God for what he believes and does, not to his fellow man.

Holly asks, "Can we allow the assertion that Southern Baptists have blessed the Masonic Lodge to go unchallenged?"[7] The Southern Baptist Convention has not blessed the Masonic Lodge. Anyone who believes the Convention has blessed Freemasonry is wrong and doesn't understand the polity of the Convention.

Holly asks, "Have we instead given Masons a loaded gun with which to press their attack against pastors who wish to see their churches unfettered from the shackles of the occult?"[8] First, I reject Holly's identification of Freemasonry with the occult. That is simply not true. A few Masons may be occultists, but not all or even most, just as a few Southern Baptists may be universalists, but not all or even most. Every church is still free to determine who may be members; they can refuse membership or leadership roles to Masons if they wish. Masons, who are refused membership or leadership roles, should find a church where they can serve God as He leads.

THE FUTURE OF THE SOUTHERN BAPTIST CONVENTION

The Southern Baptist Convention faces an uncertain future. The Freemasonry issue has taken on a life of its own; it will continue to haunt the Southern Baptist Convention for years. Many Southern Baptists are demoralized after fifteen years of constant infighting between moderates and fundamentalists. Moderate Southern Baptists have lost the struggle to regain any leadership role in the convention. Moderate Southern Baptists cannot expect to be named to positions of influence within the convention for many years.

Perhaps the greatest threat to the Southern Baptist Convention is financial. Offerings to the Convention through the Cooperative Program appear to have plateaued or declined since a record offering of $140,710,282 was received in 1989–1990. The offering had fallen to $136,589,730 by 1992–1993, forcing staff and program cuts throughout the Convention. It is too soon to know whether this drop is a temporary reaction to the controversy. Fundamentalist churches, who have typically been less supportive of the Cooperative Program, could easily make up the shortfall.

There are a number of reasons for the reduced offerings since 1990. Certainly, many Southern Baptists have begun sending their missions offerings, normally sent through the Cooperative Program, to the Cooperative Baptist Fellowship, headquartered in Atlanta, Georgia. Moderate churches have traditionally been the strongest supporters of the Cooperative Program and other mission offerings. Some Southern Baptists, disgusted with the feud of the past fifteen years, have simply reduced or stopped contributing to the Cooperative Program. Fundamentalist churches, often mega-churches with huge, expensive programs of their own, have failed to make up the loss of revenue from other churches.

Moderate Baptist state conventions may allow churches more flexibility to designate around traditional Cooperative Program channels to other mission causes. The Cooperative Missions Giving Study Committee of the Baptist General Convention of Texas announced in April 1994 it is considering a recommendation to focus on Texas Baptist causes and to allow individual churches to decide how their mission funds would be distributed beyond Texas. The new agreement, which would require approval at the annual meeting of Texas Baptists, is seen as an effort to allow churches to express their will and wishes concerning changes in the direction of the Southern Baptist Convention.

If the Southern Baptist Convention takes an anti-Masonic stance, as a number of leaders are committed to doing, individual Southern Baptist Masons will have to make a tough decision. Some will resign from the Masonic lodge to retain membership in their local churches. Some will remain quiet and not draw attention to their fraternal membership. Others will move their church memberships to Southern Baptist churches that ignore the position of the Southern Baptist Convention. Some will designate their mission offerings around the Cooperative Program to the moderate Cooperative Baptist Fellowship. Some will join non–Southern Baptist churches.

If the Southern Baptist Convention takes an anti-Masonic stance, several possibilities are seen. Some churches will simply ignore the Convention's stance, as each church is autonomous. Other churches will refuse to allow Masons to hold leadership in the church, whether as Sunday School teacher, deacon, or pastor. Southern Baptist seminaries will be pressured to include Freemasonry in their courses on heretical religious groups. The Southern Baptist Convention mission boards will be pressured to reject for missionary appointment any person who is a Mason. A motion to study whether to appoint

Masons as missionaries failed after the outgoing Home Mission Board chairman broke the tie vote and voted against the motion in April 1994. Convention literature will reflect an anti-Masonic stance.

In the third volume on Freemasonry, Holly says the "**right choice is**" to "urge all Southern Baptists to refrain from participation or membership in 'the Masonic Lodge.'"[9] That is the goal of Holly's personal vendetta against the fraternity.

Southern Baptist New Testament theologian Jack McGorman, in a discussion of Galatians 5:15, illustrated the danger of Christians fighting one another with this ditty:

> There was once two cats from Kilkenny.
> Each thought there was one cat too many,
> So they fought and they fit,
> They scratched and they bit.
> Until except for the nails
> And the tips of their tails,
> Instead of two cats,
> There weren't any.[10]

Southern Baptists, whether Masons or not, can be certain that the Freemasonry issue will continue to haunt the denomination for many years. If the Southern Baptist Convention adopts an anti-Masonic position, the issue will begin to tear apart local churches as they debate how to respond to the decision of the Convention. The end result would be devastating to churches, families, individuals, and the Kingdom of God. There are not enough Christians on the face of God's earth for us to keep on "killing" each other.

APPENDIX

NUMEROUS DELETIONS, ADDITIONS, AND CHANGES WERE MADE IN THE STUDY on Freemasonry after it was submitted to Larry L. Lewis, president of the Home Mission Board, on January 22, 1993. Many of the significant deletions, additions, and changes in the study have been noted earlier in this book. Other significant deletions, additions and changes in the study before its release to the general public in March 1993 are as follows.

SIGNIFICANT DELETIONS

A significant portion of the introductory section was deleted from the original manuscipt. The following material was deleted.

> On 17 September 1992, five staff members of the Interfaith Witness Department; Larry L. Lewis, president of the Home Mission Board; Darrell W. Robinson, vice president, Evangelism Section of the Home Mission Board; and Brad Allen, chairman of the Evangelism Committee of the Board of Directors of the Home Mission Board; met with James L. Holly, Charles Z. Burchett, and two staff from Holly's ministry to discuss their concerns about the study assigned to the department. Holly and Burchett presented a 649-page report, entitled *Freemasonry and The Southern Baptist Convention*. Each of the thirteen sections was discussed during the meeting. The department staff found the meeting and the report most helpful. The five department staff members were Tal Davis, Jimmy Furr, William E. Gordon, Jr., Kenneth James, and Gary Leazer. None of the staff members of the Interfaith Witness Department is or ever has been a Mason.

At the beginning of the study, a number of questions were submitted to Masonic leaders for response. Those questions are found in Appendix A at the end of this report. No meeting was held with Masons like the meeting with Holly and Burchett. These questions and books by Masonic critics, such as Holly, Ankerberg, and Rongstad, were used as the staff began research on the assignment. Numerous other sources were used as the research progressed.

The department director received over 2,000 letters from concerned Southern Baptists and other Christians between July 1 and December 31, 1992. Each letter was read and taken seriously, although because of the volume of mail not all writers received a personal response. They were most appreciated.

In a letter to the directors of the Home Mission Board and others, including the director of the Interfaith Witness Department, James L. Holly suggested that the issue should be resolved after asking the question, "What would we do if we were not afraid?" In the letter, Holly says;

> God does not require fruitfulness of His children; He only requires faithfulness. If we are faithful to God and are failures in the sight of man, that is good; if we are faithful and are successful in the sight of man, that is good. All the success in the world will not make up for all of our unfaithfulness to God.

This is wise counsel and was followed completely. This report was bathed in prayer and research and written to be fair and objective, as far as is humanly possible.[1]

This testimony from a Southern Baptist pastor was deleted.

One Southern Baptist pastor, who is not a Mason, wrote, "For two years while I was in seminary, I received an Eastern Star scholarship. It seems unlikely that Satan would fund the education of his enemy, and I assure you, I am his enemy.[2]

The following paragraphs were deleted from the section on the difficulty in reaching objective conclusions about Freemasonry.

Stories about Freemasonry are invented for a number of reasons. Perhaps someone was promoted over an individual. If that person was a Mason, hurt feelings can result because of a belief the Mason was promoted because of his lodge membership. Of course, unjust promotions or rewards, perceived or real, can happen for a number of reasons in schools, businesses and even in religious organizations. People have been promoted because they were related to the supervisor; belonged to the same political party, country club, church or lodge; were of the same gender or race; or for a thousand other reasons. It is not right, but we are humans. All humans are sinners and it is basic human nature to discriminate for selfish reasons.[3]

As an example of the desire of Masons to cooperate with this study, Richard S. Sagar, building manager of the Atlanta Masonic Temple, wrote,

> This letter is to invite you to make full use of this library, with no strings attached, as much as you wish for any research you need. Our building is normally open from about 8:00 A.M. to late evening, Mondays through Fridays. The usage of the library will be entirely at your convenience; however I recommend day time use for peace and quietness. I promise that as far as I am concerned, no undue pressures or obligations will be put on you. I am also available to try to answer any questions you may have, and will make every effort to see that they are factual and impartial.[4]

7) Tens of thousands of faithful, conservative Christians belong to Freemasonry and do not believe there is any conflict between Christianity and Freemasonry.

Robert A. Morey points out that most Masons in the United States are members of Christian churches and that many pastors and deacons are Masons. He asks, "Can anyone seriously think that such 33rd degree Masons as Senator Jesse Helms, the Christian champion of conservative politics, is a worshipper of Lucifer?"[5]

In the discussion of A. Ralph Epperson's misinterpretation of Albert Mackey's reference to the direction north, the concluding statement was deleted; "A person can disagree with Mackey's reasoning, but he should not misrepresent it as does Epperson."[6]

In the section on salvation and afterlife, Larry Kunk's charge that "All Masons are guilty of practicing witchcraft," and thus, that no Mason can inherit the kingdom of God, was removed.[7]

A lengthy discussion on the relation between faith and works was deleted.

The relation between faith and works has divided Christians for centuries. The Bible clearly teaches that "For by grace you have been saved through faith; and that

> not of yourselves, it is the gift of God; not as a result of works, that no one should boast" (Eph. 2:8–9). But Paul continues, "For we are His workmanship, created in Christ Jesus for good works, which God prepared beforehand, that we should walk in them" (Eph. 2:10). James tells us
>
> > What use is it, my brethren, if a man says he has faith, but he has no works? Can that faith save him? . . . Even so faith, if it has not works, is dead, being by itself. But someone may well say, "You have faith, and I have works; show me your faith without the works, and I will show you my faith by my works (James 2: 14, 17–18).
>
> E. Y. Mullins reminds us, "Genuine faith is never thought of by the New Testament writers as having no relation to works. True faith is a

working faith. . . . Works do not save, but saving faith may be recognized by the fact that it is a working faith."[8]

As has been noted, the entire section on "Conspiracy Theories Concerning Freemasonry" was deleted from the original manuscript. Most of this material has been included in chapter 5.

Significant quotes from Pope Leo XIII's 1884 encyclical *Humanum Genus*, the strongest papal condemnation of Freemasonry. Of the following, only the highlighted material was retained. The manuscript reported that the Pope attacked because Freemasons

1) **call for religious liberty.** "It [teaching religious truth] being the special duty of the Catholic Church, and her duty only, to keep the doctrines received from God and the authority of teaching with all heavenly means necessary to salvation and preserve them integrally incorrupt." "It is a fact that the sect leaves to members full liberty of thinking about God whatever they like."

2) **call for separation of [the Roman Catholic] Church and state.** "So law and government are wrested from the wholesome and divine virtue of the Catholic Church and they want, therefore, by all means to rule States independent of the institutions and doctrines of the Church." Freemasons, referred to as Sectarians, "say openly . . . that the very spiritual power of the Pope ought to be taken away, and the divine instruction of the Roman Pontificate ought to disappear from the world."

3) **call for the education of children by laymen.** "In the instructions and education of children, they do not leave to the ministers of the Church any part either in directing or watching them. In many places they have gone so far that children's education is all in the hands of laymen."

4) **believe people have the right to make their own laws and elect their own government.** "Hence [the Freemasons believe] the people are sovereign; those who rule have no authority but by the commission and concession of the people; so that they can be deposed, willing or

> unwilling, according to the wishes of the people. The origin of all rights and civil duties is in the people or in the State, which is ruled according to the new principles of liberty."
>
> Roman Catholic writer Paul A. Fisher, referring to the *Humanum Genus*, concluded that "the Papal catalogue of criminal activity by Freemasons was awesome and frightening."[9]

It is difficult for this Baptist to see what is wicked, criminal, or frightening about these Masonic teachings.

A list of organizations found "objectionable" by the Lutheran Church Missouri Synod was deleted. The list of "objectionable" organizations included the Awana Youth Association, an independent missions organization for youth that is popular in fundamentalist Southern Baptist churches.[10]

After a discussion of sixteen deceased Southern Baptist leaders who were Masons, including George W. Truett, B. H. Carroll, and L. R. Scarborough, the original manuscript asked,

> Can anyone believe that these great men of God "have allowed Satan to blind them?" Holly states, "The spirit-filled believer who is in daily fellowship with Christ cannot be in fellowship with the Masonic Lodge. Therefore it is the contention of this presentation that no Freemason should be elected to a leadership role in a Southern Baptist Church [*sic*]." Can anyone say that George W. Truett (or any other of the men mentioned above) was not spirit-filled or that he bowed in worship of Satan, even ignorantly? Were these men members of two religions: Christianity and Freemasonry? They were if Freemasonry is a religion.[11]

This paragraph was deleted by Larry Lewis.

Much of the contents of the "Conclusion and Recommendation" in the original manuscript was deleted or changed. Some of this material has already been included in this book. The following paragraph was deleted.

Freemasonry is not opposed to the Christian church. A number of Southern Baptist churches had their beginnings in Masonic halls. Masons have been instrumental in enabling Southern Baptist missionaries and Baptist churches to secure government approval to minister in many Central and South American countries. As has been shown, some of the past leaders in the Southern Baptist Convention were Masons. Many of the most faithful, conservative, soul-winning Southern Baptists are Masons. We can also point to individual Masons who are not faithful, soul-winning Southern Baptists; but we can also point to Southern Baptists who are not faithful to the Church because of football games, hunting, shopping trips, or laziness.[12]

The ditty by Jack Gorman cited in the conclusion to this book was removed from the original manuscript. Immediately following this ditty, the original manuscript referred to the Old Testament story of David and Saul.

David's attitude after Saul's death is a valuable lesson for us as we decide this issue. Though Saul had threatened to kill David, David honored Saul with a lament (2 Samuel 1:17–27) and publicly thanked the valiant men of Jabesh-gilead for risking their lives to give Saul and his sons a proper burial (2 Samuel 2:5–7). David's attitude teaches us we do not need to tear another person down in order to build ourselves up. To do so does not please God. Masons are not the enemy of the church; approximately one half million Masons are members of Southern Baptist churches. Certainly, there are Southern Baptist Masons who support their lodge more than their church, but let's deal with that problem. Certainly, there are Masons who are not Christians, but the overwhelming majority are. Certainly, not all Masons are as conservative as Southern Baptists, but all believers belong to Christ.

There are not enough Christians on the face of God's earth for us to keep on "killing" each other. Let's stop this madness.

Our heart's desire is that we find God's leadership in resolving this difficult and divisive issue tearing apart our beloved denomination. We have taken this assignment seriously and with God's help and the prayers and support of His people have conducted a fair and balanced study. We began with no conclusions in mind except to try to find the truth. We have found the charges that Freemasonry is a false, Satanic religion with its own plan of salvation apart from faith in Jesus Christ to be without foundation.[13]

The final sentence in the conclusion to the original manuscript was deleted. It read:

> **We, therefore, with no hesitation, recommend the following: that the Southern Baptist Convention take a position neither for nor against Freemasonry and its related branches, and that membership in Freemasonry be left with the judgment of the individual.**[14]

Even though the staff of the Interfaith Witness Department had been studying Freemasonry since 1985, and constantly since 1991, we were told we could not make a recommendation.

SIGNIFICANT CHANGES

A number of significant changes were made in the original manuscript, often simply to remove the names of anti-Masons or to change sentences deemed "pro-Mason."

> The Masonic Lodge, like many Christian churches, has been slow to respond to the acceptance of blacks into its membership. The Lodge, like many Christian churches, tends to follow the lead of the general society, rather than being a leader in racial reconciliation. Fortunately, racial reconciliation is slowly occurring, although not quickly enough, in both the Lodge and the Church.
>
> Holly and Burchett write, "While it is difficult to document, the Ku Klux Klan was founded by Freemasons and supported by Masons. If records were available to be examined it is certain that today the majority of Klan members would be found to be Masons." Stating a Masonic position, Jim Tresner writes, "membership in the KKK is sufficient cause in many states, including Oklahoma, to deny a man membership in Masonry." Tresner says he has personal knowledge of

"men [who] have been denied membership to Masonry on the basis of KKK membership." Holly and Burchett commit a logical fallacy called *Argumentum ad Ignorantium* or argument from ignorance in their argument concerning Freemasonry and the Ku Klux Klan. This fallacy holds that a conclusion must be true since it cannot be or has not been proven false. A popular example of this fallacy states that "Unicorns must be real since it cannot be proven they do not exist." Holly also commits this fallacy in *The Southern Baptist Convention and Freemasonry* when he writes, "One edition of a Masonic Bible, which has since been burned by its owner, states: . . ." Ghost sources must not be used in scholarly research.[15]

These paragraphs were edited and changed to read as follows in the published study,

Some critics claim the Ku Klux Klan (KKK) was founded by Freemasons and supported by Masons. Stating a Masonic position, Jim Tresner writes, "Membership in the KKK is sufficient cause in many states, including Oklahoma, to deny a man membership in Masonry." Tresner says he has personal knowledge of "men [who] have been denied membership in Masonry on the basis of KKK membership."

The Masonic Lodge has been slow to respond to the acceptance of blacks into its membership. The Lodge tends to follow the lead of the general society, rather than being a leader in racial reconciliation. However, racial reconciliation is slowing occurring in the Lodge.[16]

Masons must decide if this title [Worshipful Master] is so essential to Masonic tradition that it cannot be replaced with titles such as president or chairman.[17]

This statement was changed to read:

Masons would do well to replace this title with some other title. Many Christians feel this practices violates the biblical admonition to call no man master.[18]

In the discussion on the Masonic ritual (section 7), the original study quoted William T. Still and commented,

> William T. Still states, "The following details of the initiation oaths of the first three degrees of Masonry are closely-guarded Masonic secrets. In fact, every Mason must swear to kill any fellow Mason who reveals them."[19] Southern Baptist leaders B. H. Carroll, George W. Truett, and L. R. Scarborough were Masons. Does anyone really believe they would have promised to kill anyone for revealing Masonic "secrets," especially since they were already public knowledge? Still makes this clearly false claim for the emotional impact it must surely have on his readers because there is not truth whatsoever in his statement.[20]

References to Carroll, Truett, and Scarborough were deleted, along with the question. The words *Masons insist* was added to the last sentence, to read "Masons insist Still makes . . . ;"[21] Actually, people other than Masons also insist "Still makes this clearly false claim for the emotional impact."

Again, in the section on the ritual, "Grand Lodges could lessen attacks by Masonic critics if they would revise, eliminate or begin referring to the penalties as the traditional, symbolic penalties",[22] was changed to read, **"Even if symbolic, these penalties are very offensive to many Christians. Grand Lodges should either revise or eliminate the oaths and penalties."**[23]

The sentence "That the Christian takes the obligation on the Bible in God's name is a point of contention for Masonic critics",[24] was changed to read, **"That the Christian Mason takes the obligations by swearing on the Bible in God's name is a point of contention for many non-Mason Christians."**[25]

Repeatedly, references to anti-Masons were changed to draw attention away from individuals such as Holly, Ankerberg, and Weldon. For example, references to Ankerberg and Weldon[26] were regularly changed to "Critics."[27]

The statement "**Symbols mean what the user intends them to mean; symbols can mean different things to different people**",[28] was changed to read, "Symbols can mean different things to different people."[29]

In the section on God, the simple sentence "The name Bul is found in the Old Testament," was changed to read "Masons point out that the name Bul is found in the Old Testament."[30] Masons are not alone in pointing out this fact; any good dictionary of the Bible does the same thing.[31] The sentence was changed to imply something sinister in what the Masons say.

Holly cites W. L. Wilmshurst's allegorical interpretation in *The Meaning of Masonry* of "Out of Egypt did I call my Son" (Matt. 2:15), which Wilmshurst sees as "a biblical allusion to this passing on of the catholic Mysteries from Egypt." William E. Gordon, reviewing Holly's first volume, writes,

> Wilmshurst's statement, while blasphemous, does not indicate that Lucifer is the god of the Lodge as Holly has promised to prove 'from the mouth of Masons themselves.' Nowhere does Wilmshurst state that Lucifer is the god of Freemasonry. . . . What Wilmshurst does is to teach his pagan concept of religion under the guise of revealing the deeper symbolism of Masonry. His book does deserve criticism, but Holly fails to offer an effective critique because of his obsession with proving that the god of the Lodge is Lucifer.

The final sentence, with its reference to Holly, was removed from the published edition.[32]

Two pages were deleted from the original manuscript at the conclusion of the section on God. Most of this material came from William E. Gordon's review of Holly's first volume. Holly was upset that Gordon's critique was being used in the study. Gordon's critique found that while Holly states that "EN SOPH is the god to the Lodge," Holly provides no documentation.[33] Holly quotes Albert Mackey, "The Kaballah was first taught by God to a select company of angels, who formed a theosophical school in Paradise. After the fall the angels most graciously communicated this heavenly doctrine to the disobedient child of earth."[34] Holly interprets this statement as referring to the fall of Lucifer and his legions of angels. Gordon states:

> First, the quote cited by Mackey does not state that the fall referred to was the fall of the angels. The context rather indicates that this fall is the fall of humanity and not the fall of the angels. Second, Mackey neither states that he is giving the Masonic view on this subject nor does he claim to be giving his personal view. Instead, he clearly states that he is presenting the position of Jewish scholars concerning the Kabbala.[35]

Gordon is right on target when he states that Holly misinterprets (whether intentionally or by carelessness only Holly can say) Mackey. While Mackey was giving the view of some Jewish scholars, Holly attempts to mislead his readers that Mackey's statements are Masonic teachings.

Holly claims that Simon ben Jochai, who appears in the thirtieth degree of Scottish Rite Masonry, "Is Lucifer himself or one of his demons."[36] The original manuscript stated that Gordon found Holly's identification of Simon ben Jochai with Lucifer "puzzling." Gordon concluded:

> Simon ben Jochai (Yohai) was a famous Jewish Talmudist. . . . The citation quoted by Holly is a continuation of Mackey's quote of Ginsburg and is offered by Mackey only to provide a Jewish understanding of the Kabbala. Its usage by Mackey does not indicate that the being in the coffin in the 30th degree is Lucifer. The most it indicates is that some Kabbalistic Jews apply Isaiah 14:16 to Simon ben Jochai (Yohai).[37]

A paragraph stating that Masons interpret the 30° symbolically was deleted. In the last paragraph in the section on God in the original manuscript, Larry Kunk's reference to 2 Corinthians 6:14 is cited: "Do not be mismatched with unbelievers. For what partnership is there between righteousness and lawlessness? Or what fellowship is there between light and darkness." Kunk applies this passage to the Masonic lodge since Muslims, Buddhists, Jews, and others are found in lodges around the world. The original manuscript pointed out that

> "Non-Christians are found in social and business clubs where Christians join and participate with others as equals, even though Christians do not accept the faiths of their non-Christian associates." The original manuscript then pointed out that Southern Baptists had joined with Catholics, Jews, Christian Scientists, Mormons, Unitarian-Universalists, and other faiths in a agreement to share a single channel on the Vision Interfaith Satellite Network. Jack Johnson, president of the Southern Baptist Radio and Television Commission, who said the agreement "could bring better understanding between faiths and a tremendous influence for good in communities all over the nation." This paragraph was deleted because a number of Southern Baptists disapproved of any agreement to work with other faiths, and the Southern Baptist belief that one agency (the Home Mission Board) should not criticize a decision of another agency (the Radio and Television Commission).[38]

❧ ❧

In the original manuscript, the opening paragraph in section eleven on salvation and future life stated:

> The first sentence in the chapter entitled "The Plan of Salvation," Ankerberg and Weldon ask, "Did you know that the Masonic Lodge teaches a way of salvation that is not taught in the Bible?" This is an attempt to set a particular paradigm for the reader. The idea that the Lodge teaches a false way of salvation has been programmed in the reader's mind to lead the reader to a particular conclusion.[39]

These sentences were replaced by the single sentence "Many critics believe Freemasonry teaches a false path of salvation."[40]

❧ ❧

The sentence "Many critics falsely interpret 'from darkness to light' as 'from lostness to salvation' because they begin with the assumption that Freemasonry is a religion and that it teaches salvation" was changed to "Many critics falsely interpret 'from darkness to light' as 'from lostness to salvation.'"

❧ ❧

In the conclusion of the original manuscript, the following paragraph was changed.

> It was not found that Freemasonry teaches an occultic or any other plan of salvation. While some Masons may believe that Freemasonry will save them, this is not Masonic teaching. A belief among many church members is that faithful church attendance, tithing, or not committing certain sins will enable them to enter heaven. This is not biblical teaching and the church cannot be said to hold that teaching because some of its members do.[41]

This paragraph was radically changed to read "While a few Masons may believe that Freemasonry will save them, the overwhelming majority insist this is not Masonic teaching."[42]

SIGNIFICANT ADDITIONS

This paragraph was added in the section on whether Freemasonry is a religion or a fraternity,

> **Many Christians are also offended when Masons refer to their buildings as mosques or shrines. . . . While the symbolic connection with Solomon's Temple is held, Masons would reduce criticism if they referred to their buildings simply as "halls" or "lodges."**[43]

A sentence (the first) and the words *Masons insist* and *They insist* were added to the discussion on the use of the lambskin apron,

> Many Christians are concerned about the use of the lambskin apron because they believe it signifies works salvation and that a Mason believes he has already achieved a pure life essential to salvation. Masons insist they use the lambskin apron as an emblem of innocence, a symbol of the purity of life and moral conduct demanded of all Masons. They insist the lambskin does not bring salvation, but rather "the purity of life" it symbolizes brings salvation.[44]

The first (added) sentence, as written, in this paragraph implies that "Many Christians" believe the lambskin apron "signifies works salvation." Masons do not believe the lambskin apron "signifies works salvation."

In the discussion of Masonic passwords, the following sentence was added to the Study: **"The use of words such as Shaddai and Abaddon are especially offensive to many Christians."**[45]

NOTES

INTRODUCTION

1. James C. Hefley, *The Conservative Resurgence in the Southern Baptist Convention* (Hannibal, Missouri: Hannibal Books, 1991), p. 32.

CHAPTER ONE

1. Quoted in Henry C. Vedder, *A Short History of the Baptists* (Valley Forge: Judson Press, 1907), p. 202.

2. Smyth & Helwys is the name of the moderate Baptist publishing house in Macon, Georgia.

3. Vedder, *A Short History of the Baptists*, pp. 262–63.

4. H. Shelton Smith, Robert T. Handy, and Lefferts A. Loetscher, *American Christianity*, Vol. I (New York: Charles Scribner's Sons, 1960), pp. 167–70.

5. Sydney E. Ahlstrom, *A Religious History of the American People* (New Haven: Yale University Press, 1971), p. 169.

6. See discussion in Robert A. Baker, *The Southern Baptist Convention and Its People* (Nashville: Broadman Press, 1974), pp. 33–34.

7. Ibid, p. 65.

8. Robert A. Baker, *A Baptist Source Book* (Nashville: Broadman Press, 1966), pp. 33–34.

9. Baker, *The Southern Baptist Convention and Its People*, p. 66.

10. Ibid, p. 67.

11. From *A Declaration of Rights*, adopted by the Virginia Convention of 1776, section sixteen, quoted in Baker, *A Baptist Source Book*, pp. 34–35. The statement was originally written by Baptist George Mason. James Madison amended the statement to substitute "free exercise of religion" for "toleration."

12. Quoted by Zaqueu Moreira de Oliveira, "Richard Furman, Father of the Southern Baptist Convention," in *The Lord's Free People in a Free Land*, William R. Estep, ed. (Fort Worth: Faculty of the School of Theology, Southwestern Baptist Theological Seminary, 1976), p. 92.

13. Robert G. Torbet, A History of Baptists (Valley Forge: The Judson Press, 1963), p. 276.

14. Quoted by Moreira de Oliveira, "Richard Furman," in *The Lord's Free People in a Free Land,* p. 91.

15. Baker, *The Southern Baptist Convention and Its People: 1607–1972,* p. 159.

16. Joe W. Burton, *Road to Augusta* (Nashville: Broadman Press, 1976), p. 171.

17. Helen Turner, *Fundamentalism and the Southern Baptist Convention: The Crystallization of a Millennialist Vision* (Unpublished dissertation, University of Virginia), p. 430.

18. George W. Cornell, "At issue: Christian and Mason," *Daily News-Sun* (Sun City, Arizona), April 23, 1993, pp. B1–B2.

19. William C. Boone, *What We Believe* (Nashville: Convention Press, 1936), pp. 70–71.

20. Michael J. Clingenpeel, "Don't Mess With the Annuity Board," *Religious Herald,* March 3, 1994, p. 4.

21. John J. Robinson, "Masons, Slavery and Coca-Cola," *The Scottish Rite Journal,* March 1993, p. 31.

22. Dan Martin, "Smith Says 'New Peace' Is His Contribution," *Baptist Standard,* May 12, 1982, p. 4.

23. Turner, *Fundamentalism in the Southern Baptist Convention,* p. 419.

24. *Annual of the Southern Baptist Convention* (Nashville: Executive Committee of the Southern Baptist Convention, 1981), p. 56.

25. *Annual of the Southern Baptist Convention* (Nashville: Executive Committee, Southern Baptist Convention, 1982), p. 58.

26. Francis A. Shaeffer, *The Great Evangelical Disaster* (Westchester, Ill.: Crossway Books, 1984), p. 116.

27. Ibid, p. 133.

28. Albert Pike, *Morals and Dogma* (Washington, D.C.: The Supreme Council of the Thirty-Third Degree for the Southern Jurisdiction of the United States, 1963), p. 24.

29. Ibid, p. 547. Italicized in the original.

30. Ibid, p. 273.

31. Ibid, p. 307.

32. Presnall H. Wood, "The White House and SBC Resolutions?" *Baptist Standard,* July 21, 1982, p. 6.

33. Tom Teepen, "Southern Baptists Embrace Civil Religion," *The Atlanta Constitution,* June 7, 1991, p. A14.

34. "Religious Liberty," Baptist Faith and Message (Nashville: The Sunday School Board of the Southern Baptist Convention, 1963), p. 19.

35. Advertisement in the *Religious Herald,* January 13, 1994, p. 10.

36. "Quayle signs books, courts votes," *Word & Way,* June 23, 1994, p. 16.

37. "Diversity of Speakers, Subjects Marks Pastor's Conference" [*sic*], *Florida Baptist Witness,* June 23, 1994, p. 10.

38. Torbet, *A History of Baptists,* p. 520. Emphasis is found in the original quote by Torbet.

39. Ibid, pp. 520–21.

40. Albert Pike, *A Reply of Freemasonry in Behalf of Humanity to The Encyclical Letter* "Humanum Genus" *of the Pope Leo XIII* (Washington, D.C.: The Supreme Council, 33°, of the Southern Jurisdiction of the Scottish Rite of Freemasonry, 1964), pp. 5–21.

41. Pike, p. 42. Pike was referring to the opening paragraph of *Humanum Genus* where Pope Leo XIII contrasted "the Kingdom of God on earth" and "the kingdom of Satan."

CHAPTER TWO

1. Edward J. Carnell quoted in Lloyd J. Averill, *Religious Right, Religious Wrong* (New York: Pilgrim Press, 1989), p. 52.

2. George M. Marsden in Norman J. Cohen, ed., *The Fundamentalist Phenomenon: A View from Within; A Response from Without* (Grand Rapids: William B. Eerdmans Publishing Company, 1990), p. 22.

3. Turner, *Fundamentalism in the Southern Baptist Convention, p. 7.*

4. Quoted in Turner, *Fundamentalism in the Southern Baptist Convention,* p. 70.

5. Ibid, p. 47, commenting on Nancy Ammerman, *Bible Believers: Fundamentalism in the Modern World* (New Brunswick: Rutgers University Press, 1987), p. 8.

6. Cathy Lynn Grossman, "Extremists' Actions Tarnish Fundamentalists' Image," *USA Today,* March 25, 1993, p. 8D.

7. "Religious Identity: How Christians See Themselves," *USA Today,* March 25, 1993, p. 8D.

8. "Selection from the Book of Moses," *The Pearl of Great Price* (Salt Lake City: The Church of Jesus Christ of Latter-day Saints, 1982), p. 1 (Moses 1:1).

9. Averill, *Religious Right, Religious Wrong,* pp. 23–24.

10. Anti-Masons attempt to identify Freemasonry with the New Age Movement of the last twenty-five years because of the name *The New Age Magazine,* which was introduced in 1903. The name of *The New Age Magazine* was changed to *The Scottish Rite Journal* in 1990 because of the growing popularity of the New Age Movement and one of its magazines, *New Age Journal.* [The Home Mission Board's *A Study of Freemasonry* stated (p. 9) that the *New Age Journal* includes a disclaimer in every issue: "The publisher of *NEW AGE JOURNAL* has no affiliation with any fraternal organization."]

11. A. A. Hodge and Benjamin B. Warfield, "Inspiration," in *The Presbyterian Review,* 2 (April 1881), quoted in Averill, *Religious Right, Religious Wrong,* pp. 25–26.

12. Kendell H. Easley, Adult Bible Study, January–March 1994 (Nashville: Baptist Sunday School Board, 1993), p. 18.

13. James T. Draper, Jr., *The Church Christ Approves* (Nashville: Broadman Press, 1974), p. 42.

14. Ibid, p. 43.

15. Holly was referring to Queen Esther's statement in the Old Testament Book of Esther 4:16.

16. Turner, *Fundamentalism in the Southern Baptist Convention*, p. 13.

17. Draper, *The Church Christ Approves*, p. 38.

18. Ibid, pp. 40–41.

19. Ibid, p. 41.

20. Ibid.

21. James L. Holly, *The Southern Baptist Convention and Freemasonry:* Volume III (Beaumont, Texas: Mission and Ministry to Men, Inc., 1994), p. 1. Emphasis added.

22. Turner, *Fundamentalism in the Southern Baptist Convention*, p. 305.

23. "Official HMB Fact Sheet," December 31, 1992.

24. "Snellville Conference Prompts Cancellation of BSSB Event," *The Christian Index*, January 13, 1994, p. 4.

25. Advertisement in *The Christian Index*, January 13, 1994, p. 9.

26. Boone, *What We Believe*, p. 73.

27. Quoted in Averill, *Religious Right, Religious Wrong*, p. 113.

28. Tim Nicholas, "W. A. Criswell Counsels Pastors in 2-Hour Session," *Religious Herald*, January 13, 1994, p. 16.

29. Averill, *Religious Right, Religious Wrong*, p. 51.

30. *Baptist Standard*, April 7, 1956, quoted in Joe Barnhart, *The Southern Baptist Holy War* (Austin: Texas Monthly Press, Inc., 1986), p. 72.

31. Draper, *The Church Christ Approves*, p. 40.

32. Quoted in Averill, *Religious Right, Religious Wrong*, p. 52.

33. For an excellent discussion of changing dispensational views, see Craig A. Blaising, "Contemporary Dispensationalism," *Southwestern Journal of Theology*, Vol. 36, No. 2 (Spring 1994), pp. 5–13.

34. Paul Boyer, *When Time Shall Be No More: Prophecy Belief in Modern American Culture* (Cambridge: The Belknap Press of Harvard University Press, 1992), p. 98.

35. Turner, *Fundamentalism in the Southern Baptist Convention*, p. 263.

36. James L. Holly, *The Southern Baptist Convention and Freemasonry, Vol. I* (Beaumont, Texas: Mission and Ministry to Men, Inc., 1992), p. 29. Bold print found in original text.

37. Lloyd Averill, *Religious Right, Religious Wrong*, p. 45.

38. Stephen Arterburn and Jack Felton, *Toxic Faith: Understanding and Overcoming Religious Addiction* (Nashville: Thomas Nelson, Publishers, 1991), p. 29. This outstanding book has been reprinted under the title *Faith That Hurts, Faith That Heals: Understanding The Fine Line Between Healthy Faith & Spiritual Abuse.*

39. Ibid, p. 31.

CHAPTER THREE

1. Mark G. Toulouse, "J. Frank Norris" in Charles H. Lippy, ed., *Twentieth Century Shapers of American Popular Religion* (New York: Greenwood Press, 1989), p. 315.

2. Alan Neely, "The History of the Alliance of Baptists," in Shurden, *The Struggle,* p. 103.

3. Baker, *The Southern Baptist Convention and Its People,* p. 218.

4. Ibid, p. 249.

5. Toulouse, "J. Frank Norris," p. 311.

6. Ibid, p. 315.

7. Ibid, p. 316.

8. Gustav Niebuhr, " 'Fundamentalist' Label Often Misunderstood, Baptists Say," *The Atlanta Journal and Constitution,* October 18, 1986.

9. Louis Moore, religion editor for the *Houston Chronicle,* used the term *fundamentalist* in his foreword to James C. Hefley's *The Truth in Crisis: The Controversy in the Southern Baptist Convention* (Dallas: Criterion Publications, 1986). Moore is now on the staff of the Southern Baptist Convention's Christian Life Commission in Nashville.

10. Robinson B. James, ed. *The Unfettered Word: Confronting the Authority-Inerrancy Question* (Macon: Smyth & Helwys Publishing, Inc., 1994), p. 13.

11. Turner, *Fundamentalism in the Southern Baptist Convention,* p. 462.

12. "Neo-Orthodoxy Is Problem, No Liberalism, Says Vines," *Baptist Standard,* June 22, 1988, p. 8. This is the position of Francis A. Schaeffer, founder of L'Abri Fellowship, who has been influential among Southern Baptist fundamentalists. See Schaeffer, *The Great Evangelical Disaster,* p. 51.

13. Dan Martin, "Smith Says 'New Peace' Is His Contribution," *Baptist Standard,* May 12, 1982, p. 4.

14. Dan Martin, "Rogers: Program Has Become 'Golden Calf'," *Baptist Standard,* May 19, 1992, p. 10.

15. Kenneth S. Kantzer, "Why I Still Believe the Bible Is True," *Christianity Today,* October 7, 1988, p. 22.

16. Ibid, pp. 23–24.

17. Kenneth S. Kantzer, "Problems Inerrancy Doesn't Solve," *Christianity Today,* February 20, 1987, p. 15.

18. Fisher Humphreys, "Biblical Inerrancy: A Guide for the Perplexed," quoting L. Russ Bush and Tom J. Nettles, *Baptists and the Bible* (Chicago: Moody Press, 1980), from p. 414 in *The Unfettered Word,* Robison B. James, ed., p. 51.

19. David S. Dockery, *The Doctrine of the Bible* (Nashville: Convention Press, 1991), p. 80.

20. Randy Frame, "Inerrancy Council Searches for Unity of Tough Issues," *Christianity Today,* February 6, 1987, p. 38.

21. "The Chicago Statement on Biblical Inerrancy," Appendix C., n.d., p. 34.

22. "Neo-Orthodoxy Is Problem, Not Liberalism, Says Vines," *Baptist Standard,* June 22, 1988, p. 8.

23. Turner, *Fundamentalism in the Southern Baptist Convention,* p. 426.

24. "Report of the Southern Baptist Convention Peace Committee (Nashville: The Sunday School Board of the Southern Baptist Convention, n.d.), p. 6.

25. Turner, *Fundamentalism and the Southern Baptist Convention,* p. 436.

26. Daniel Vestal, "The History of the Cooperative Baptist Fellowship," in Shurden, *The Struggle,* p. 253.

27. Personal interview with James Hefley in May 1985 and quoted in Hefley, *The Truth in Crisis: The Controversy in the Southern Baptist Convention,* p. 112.

28. Hefley, *Truth in Crisis: The Controversy in the Southern Baptist Convention,* p. 113.

29. Jim Galloway, "Baptist Presidency: A Battle of Biblical Proportions," *The Atlanta Journal and Constitution,* May 25, 1986.

30. Barnhart, *The Southern Baptist Holy War,* p. 104.

31. Hefley, *The Truth in Crisis: The Controversy in the Southern Baptist Convention,* p. 93.

32. Dan Martin, "Rogers: Program Has Become 'Golden Calf'," *Baptist Standard,* May 19, 1982, p. 10; Toby Druin, "Former Presidents Question Rogers's Plan," *Baptist Standard,* June 2, 1982, p. 4.; James C. Hefley, in *The Truth in Crisis: The Controversy in the Southern Baptist Convention,* p. 87, has Rogers say, "The Cooperative Program has become a sacred cow."

33. Tom Eblen, "Fundamentalists Critical of Louisville Institution," *The Atlanta Journal,* June 5, 1986.

34. Stephen Goode, "A Struggle for Earthly Power Bruises the Baptists," *Insight,* June 3, 1991, p. 22.

35. "Neo-Orthodoxy Is Problem, Not Liberalism, Says Vines," *Baptist Standard,* June 22, 1988, p. 8.

36. Ibid.

37. Toby Druin, "Bisagno, Chapman Plan Praised by Some, Criticized by Others," *The Baptist Standard,* March 21, 1990, p. 5.

38. Michael D'Antonio, "The Great Divide," *Los Angeles Times Magazine,* November 17, 1991, p. 36.

39. Barnhart, *The Southern Baptist Holy War,* p. 1.

40. Michael Hawn, "Southeastern Story Teaches Baptists Valuable Lessons," *SBC Today*, March 1989, p. 16.

41. Robert Dilday, "FMB Drops Funding for Swiss Seminary; European Baptist Leaders React Angrily," *Baptists Today,* October 31, 1991, p. 1.

42. Turner, *Fundamentalism in the Southern Baptist Convention,* p. 329.

43. Ibid, p. 330.

44. James L. Holly, "S.B.C. Resolution and Its Relationship to Freemasonry," p. 10 in *Freemasonry and The Southern Baptist Convention: A Partial Report for the Trustees of the Home Mission Board* (Beaumont, Texas: Mission & Ministry to Men, Inc., n.d.). Holly used the title *Freemasonry and The Southern Baptist Convention* or *The Southern Baptist Convention and Freemasonry* on more than one document or book.

45. Stan Hastey, "A History of the Associated Baptist Press," in Shurden, *The Struggle,* p. 176.

46. Stan Hastey has an excellent article on Pressler's charges and the resulting dismissal of the two journalist in "The History of the Associated Baptist Press" in Shurden, *The Struggle,* pp. 169–185.

47. Interested individuals may write to *Baptists Today* at 403 West Ponce de Leon, Decatur, Georgia 30030–2445.

48. John E. Brymer, "The Denominational Press: Imagemaker or Truth-seeker," *Florida Baptist Witness,* July 1, 1993.

49. James C. Hefley, *The Truth in Crisis: Bringing the Controversy Up-to-Date,* preface.

50. "BSSB Trustee Meeting Called Regarding Elder's Presidency," *Associated Baptist Press,* January 12, 1991.

51. Letter from James L. Holly to William E. Gordon, Jr., September 29, 1992.

52. J. B. Fowler, "Lloyd Elder's 'Retirement'," *Baptist New Mexican,* February 2, 1991, p. 2., and James A. Langley, "Forced Retirement of Lloyd Elder," *Capital Baptist,* February 28, 1991, pp. 4–5.

53. Toby Druin and Greg Warner, "Southwestern Seminary Trustees Fire Dilday; Students Left to Wonder 'Why'?" *Religious Herald*, March 17, 1994, p. 6.

54. Roddy Stinson, "Those Were Not Hyenas, but Southern Baptists," *San Antonio Express-News,* March 13, 1994, p. 3A.

55. Tom Teepen, "Baptist Moderates: Free at Last," *The Atlanta Constitution*, May 14, 1991, p. A8. Southern Baptists interested in receiving information about the Cooperative Baptist Fellowship should write to P.O. Box 450329, Atlanta, GA 31145–0329. Ask your church to place the *Cooperative Baptist Fellowship* in the church budget or designate your Cooperative Program offering to the Fellowship. The Fellowship will provide offering envelopes to individuals requesting them and will use money received to support their growing missionary force serving around the world.

56. Gayle White, "Moderate Baptists Search for East-West Bond," *The Atlanta Constitution,* April 25, 1992, p. E6.

57. Greg Warner and Jack U. Harwell, "Keith Parks Will Lead CBF Missions Program," *Baptists Today,* December 15, 1992, p. 1.

58. Cecil E. Sherman, "An Overview of the Moderate Movement," pp. 37–44, and Walter B. Shurden, "The Struggle for the Soul of the SBC: Reflections and Interpretations," pp. 280–86 in *The Struggle for the Soul of the SBC,* Walter B. Shurden, ed. (Macon: Mercer University Press, 1993).

59. Ron Taylor, "Baptist Art of Preaching Considered Major Factor in Convention politicking," *The Atlanta Journal,* May 22, 1986.

60. One moderate observed that after the pendulum swing to the far right, it fell off.

61. Sherman, "An Overview" in Shurden, *The Struggle,* p. 44.

62. "Conservative Strategists Meet in Louisville," *Religious Herald,* November 4, 1993.

63. Turner, *Fundamentalism in the Southern Baptist Convention,* p. 300.

64. Greg Warner, "Fundamentalist Leaders Gather for Damage-Control Session," *Baptists Today,* May 12, 1994, pp. 1, 5.

65. Ibid, p. 5.

66. Hefley, *The Truth in Crisis: The Controversy in the Southern Baptist Convention,* p. 42.

67. Baptist Press, June 22, 1981, quoted in Hefley, *The Truth in Crisis: The Controversy in the Southern Baptist Convention,* p. 83.

68. Jack U. Harwell, "SBC rejects further funds from Fellowship; elects Jim Henry president over Fred Wolfe," *Baptists Today*, July 14, 1994, p. 1.

69. Jim Burgin, "The Christian Reconstruction Movement," *Search,* May 1992, p. 14.

70. Rob Boston, "Thy Kingdom Come," *Church & State,* September 1988, p. 9.

71. Rodney Clapp, "Democracy as Heresy," *Christianity Today*, February 20, 1987, p. 19.

72. Jim Burgin, "The Christian Reconstruction Movement," p. 20.

73. Chad Brand, "Would Calvin Recognize It?" *Southern Baptist Public Affairs,* Fall/Winter 1991, p. 5.

74. Clapp, "Democracy as Heresy," p. 21.

75. William Hatfield, "Sinai Revisited: The Rise of Reconstructionism," *Southern Baptist Public Affairs,* Fall/Winter 1991, p. 3.

CHAPTER FOUR

1. Quoted in Turner, *Fundamentalism in the Southern Baptist Convention,* p. 304.

2. See Watson E. Mills, gen. ed. *Mercer Dictionary of the Bible* (Macon: Mercer University Press, 1990), pp. 36–38, for a fuller discussion and other resources on apocalyptic literature.

3. Hal Lindsey, *The Late Great Planet Earth* (Grand Rapids: Zondervan Publishing House, 1970), p. 161.

4. Ibid, p. 11.

5. Boyer, *When Time Shall Be No More,* p. 53

6. Jack T. Chick, "The Beast" (Chino, Calif.: Chick Publications, 1988), p. 9.

7. William W. Sweet, *The Story of Religion in America* (Grand Rapids: Baker Book House, 1973), p. 137.

8. Robert A. Baker, *A Summary of Christian History* (Nashville: Broadman Press, 1959), p. 351. Baker gives the figure of "less than 10 percent" in this book, but cited the figure of 7 percent in his class lectures.

9. Ahlstrom, *A Religious History of the American People,* p. 476

10. Ibid, p. 484.

11. The Book of Moses is Smith's addition to the Book of Genesis and is found in the Mormon scripture *Pearl of Great Price.*

12. Robin L. Carr, *Freemasonry and Nauvoo: 1839–1846* (Springfield, Ill.: The Masonic Book Club and The Illinois Lodge of Research, 1989), p. 16.

13. Ibid, p. 9.

14. Ibid, p. 64.

15. Ibid, p. 17.

16. Ibid, p. 14.

17. Quoted in Ahlstrom, *A Religious History of the American People,* p. 671.

18. Alphonse, Cerza, *Anti-Masonry: Light on the Past and Present Opponents of Freemasonry* (Columbia: Missouri Lodge of Research, 1962), p. 66.

19. Hal Lindsey, *The 1980s: Countdown to Armageddon* (King of Prussia: Westgate Press Inc., 1980), p. 117.

20. The New Revision Standard Version translates "prince of Rosh as "chief prince."

21. G. C. Huckaby, compiler, *The Louisiana Masonic Monitor* (New Orleans: Grand Lodge of the State of Louisiana, 1951), p. 61. This Masonic symbolism is also found in Albert Mackey, *An Encyclopaedia of Freemasonry and Its Kindred Sciences* (Chicago: The Masonic History Co., 1921), Vol. 2, p. 518, and Charles Bahnson, *North Carolina Lodge Manual* (Raleigh: Edwards & Broughton Co., 1929), p. 28.

22. A. Ralph Epperson, *The New World Order* (Tucson: Publius Press, 1990), pp. 51–52.

23. Cathy Burns, *Hidden Secrets of Freemasonry* (Mt. Carmel, Pennsylvania: Sharing, 1990), p. 12.

24. The Holy Bible (New York: The Douay Bible House, 1941), Isaias [Isaiah] 14:12 footnote.

25. Trent C. Butler, *Holman Bible Dictionary* (Nashville: Holman Bible Publishers, 1991), p. 1433.

26. Boyer, *When Time Shall Be No More,* p. 164.

27. Ibid, p. 138.

28. Ibid, p. 190.

29. "Jews Announce Plans To Rebuild 'Temple,' " *The Baptist Record,* July 18, 1974, p. 1.

30. Boyer, *When Time Shall Be No More,* p. 274.

31. Ibid, p. 275.

32. Averill, *Religious Right, Religious Wrong,* p. 135.

33. Boyer, *When Time Shall Be No More,* p. 275.

34. Ibid, p. 265.

35. Ibid, p. 178.

36. Ibid, p. 282.

37. Ibid, p. 283.

38. Undated advertisement received in March 1994 from "This Week in Bible Prophecy," Niagara Falls, New York.

39. Boyer, *When Time Shall Be No More,* p. 286.

40. Texe Marrs, "Rats Beheaded in Space," *Flashpoint,* March 1994, p. 3.

41. Francis A. Schaeffer, *The Great Evangelical Disaster* (Westchester: Crossway Books, 1984), p. 29.

42. Ahlstrom, *A Religious History of the American People,* p. 8.

43. Turner, *Fundamentalism in the Southern Baptist Convention,* p. 304.

44. Ibid, p. 328.

45. "VISN At a Glance," undated off-set from VISN.

46. "Religious Channel Changes Its Name," *Baptists Today*, January 6, 1994, p. 10.

47. "Networks Share Channel, Affiliates Worry About Mixed Signals," *Christianity Today,* September 14, 1992.

48. Ibid, p. 49.

CHAPTER FIVE

1. Bob E. Mathews, "Baseless Rumor On Religious Broadcasts Thrives," *The Christian Index,* December 3, 1992, p. 4.

2. Justo L. Gonzalez, *A History of Christian Thought,* Vol. I (Nashville: Abingdon Press, 1970), pp. 99–100.

3. Vedder, *A Short History of the Baptists,* p. 211.

4. Bob E. Mathews, "Baseless Rumor On Religious Broadcasts Thrives," *The Christian Index,* December 3, 1992, p. 4.

5. "Procter & Gamble Is Clean," *Newsweek,* April 7, 1980, p. 64; "Firm Has Devil of a Time Quelling Rumors," *The Atlanta Journal and Constitution,* January 23, 1982; Bob E. Mathews, "For Umpteenth Time: P&G Rumors Untrue," *The Baptist Messenger,* November 13, 1986, p. 6; "Procter & Gamble Threatens Suits Against Rumors," *Baptist and Reflector,* March 7, 1990; "P&G Sues Couple, Claiming They Spread Satanism Rumor," *The Atlanta Journal and Constitution,* August 1, 1990, p. D-6; "Procter & Gamble Wins Court Judgment," *The Christian Index,* April 18, 1991, p. 3; and "Rumors Resurface Linking P&G With Church of Satan," *Baptist New Mexican,* December 26, 1992.

6. John Broderick, "545 Days Left," *The Red Cloud Chief,* March 25, 1993, p. 10.

7. Turner, *Fundamentalism in the Southern Baptist Convention,* p. 265.

8. Hal Lindsey, *The 1980s: Countdown to Armageddon* (King of Prussia, Pa.: Westgate Press, Inc., 1980), pp. 134–138.

9. Ibid, pp. 140–141.

10. Texe Marrs, *Dark Majesty: The Secret Brotherhood and the Magic of A Thousand Points of Light,* p. 38. Italics in original text.

11. Ibid, pp. 122, 124.

12. Ibid, p. 115.

13. Ibid, p. 117.

14. Ibid, p. 70. Italics in original text.

15. Ibid, p. 135.

16. Undated flyer from Living Truth Ministries, Austin, Texas. Italics in original.

17. Advertisement for 60 minute audiotape, "The United Nations Plot," in *Flashpoint,* September 1993. Italics in original.

18. Undated advertisement for the audiotape "Bankruptcy U.S.A.: How You Can Escape the Coming Financial Nightmare."

19. "The Great Southern Baptist Cover-up," A Special Report from Texe

Marrs, Living Truth Ministries, Austin, Texas, no date. Italics are found in the original text.

20. J. R. Church, *Guardians of the Grail* (Oklahoma City: Prophecy Publications, 1989), pp. 239–46.

21. Ibid, p. 75.

22. Henry Wilson Coil, *Coil's Masonic Encyclopedia* (New York: Macoy Publishing & Masonic Supply Company, 1961), p. 600.

23. Church, *Guardians of the Grail,* p. 99.

24. Ibid, p. 196.

25. Kah, *En Route to Global Occupation,* p. 94.

26. Ibid, p. 107, quoting Mackey, I, p. 474.

27. Mackey, *Mackey's Revised Encyclopedia,* I, p. 474.

28. Ibid, pp. 51–56.

29. Ibid, p. 118.

30. Ibid, p. 119.

31. Ibid, p. 12.

32. Ibid, p. 19.

33. Salem Kirban, *Satan's Angels Exposed* (Huntingdon Valley, Pennsylvania: Salem Kirban, Inc., 1980), p. 161.

34. Ibid, pp. 162–63.

35. Pat Robertson, *The New World Order: It Will Change the Way You Live* (Dallas: Word Publishing, 1991), pp. 96–97.

36. Ibid, pp. 99–113.

37. Ibid, p. 103.

38. A. Ralph Epperson, *The New World Order* (Tucson: Publius Press, 1990), p. 295.

39. Ibid, p. 142.

40. William T. Still, *New World Order: The Ancient Plan of Secret Societies* (Lafayette, La.: Huntington House Publishers, 1990), p. 8. The reader will notice that a number of these sensational books are published by Huntington House Publishers.

41. Ibid, p. 10. The 1972 Republican National Convention was held in Miami, not San Diego, as originally planned.

42. James D. Shaw and Tom McKenney, *The Deadly Deception, p. 11.*

43. Letter from James D. Shaw to the Scottish Rite Temple, 371 N.W. 3rd Street, Miami, Florida, October 25, 1966.

44. James D. Shaw and Tom McKenney, *The Deadly Deception,* p. 90.

45. Letter from Roy L. Martin, 33°, to James D. Shaw, November 3, 1965.

46. Art deHoyos and S. Brent Morris, *Is It True What They Say About Freemasonry?* (Silver Spring: Masonic Service Association of the United States, 1994), p. 40.

47. Shaw and McKenney, *The Deadly Deception,* p. 63.

48. deHoyos and Morris, *Is It True What They Say About Freemasonry?,* pp. 46–47.

49. Ibid, pp. 48–49.

50. Michael White, "Campaign Against Mormonism Puts Dad, Son on

Opposing Sides," *The Salt Lake Tribune,* October 5, 1985, p. D-2.

51. Art Tolston, "Book Stores Deny Charge Of Censorship," *The Christian Index,* June 4, 1992, p. 6.

52. Decker, *The Questions of Freemasonry,* p. 37.

53. Ibid, pp. 39–40.

54. William Schnoebelen, *Masonry Beyond the Light* (Chino: Chick Publications, 1991), p. 38.

55. Ibid, p. 46.

56. Ibid, p. 70.

57. Ibid, p. 83.

58. Ibid, p. 203. The reader is referred to deHoyos and Morris, *Is it True What They Say About Freemasonry?*, p. 25, note 14, for another fanciful false claim by Schnoebelen.

59. *1985 Annual of the Southern Baptist Convention* (Nashville: Executive Committee, Southern Baptist Convention, 1985), p. 69.

60. Ankerberg and Weldon, *The Facts on The Masonic Lodge,* p. 34.

61. Pike, *Morals and Dogma*, p. 532.

62. A misspelled name on letters received from Holly also appeared on letters from Kunk and others, which indicated that Holly shared his mailing list with Kunk and others.

63. Larry Kunk, "What Is the Secret Doctrine of the Masonic Lodge and How Does It Relate to Their Plan of Salvation?" in Charles Burchett and James L. Holly, *Freemasonry and The Southern Baptist Convention: A Report for The Interfaith Witness Department of The Home Mission Board, Southern Baptist Convention,* September 17, 1992, Section 8, p. 12.

64. Letter with offset from Wayne Lela of Downers Grove, Illinois, June 23, 1992.

65. Letter from Eleanor Snyder, Bronson, Texas, February 14, 1994.

66. Letter to Gary Leazer from Kenneth Cornn, London, Kentucky, undated but received on November 19, 1992.

67. Herschel H. Hobbs, *Studying Adult Life and Work Lessons* (Nashville: Baptist Sunday School Board, Vol. 25, No. 4, [October-December 1992]:87).

68. *Study* (Unedited Manuscript), p. 64.

CHAPTER SIX

1. "Letter to the Editor" from Marvin Capehart, Home Mission Board trustee and pastor of the First Baptist Church, Alameda, New Mexico, *Baptist New Mexican,* May 8, 1993, p. 2.

2. Holly, I, p. 8.

3. "Proceedings," *1985 Annual of the Southern Baptist Convention* (Nashville: Executive Committee, 1985), p. 69. For a full copy of this resolution, see Holly, II, pp. 55–57.

4. Letter from Lynn E. May, Jr., August 14, 1992.

5. "Southern Baptists to Study Freemasonry," *Saints Alive in Jesus Newsletter,* July–August 1991, p. 5.

6. "Baptist VIEWpoll," Corporate Planning and Research Department,

Sunday School Board of the Southern Baptist Convention, November 1991.

7. Holly, II, p. 1.

8. David Winfrey, "Home Mission Board Declines Action on Freemasonry Issue," *Baptist Press,* March 12, 1992.

9. Art Tolston and David Winfrey, "Southern Baptists to Consider Stand on Freemasonry," *Indiana Baptist,* June 2, 1992, p. 29.

10. Art Tolston and David Winfrey, "Southern Baptists to Consider Stand on Freemasonry," *Indiana Baptist,* June 2, 1992, p. 29.

11. Holly, *The Southern Baptist Convention and Freemasonry,* pp. 53–54.

12. "Proceedings," *1992 Annual of the Southern Baptist Convention* (Nashville: Executive Committee, Southern Baptist Convention, 1992), pp. 60–61.

13. Ibid, p. 82. Only the messengers' home states are given in the SBC annuals.

14. Ibid, p. 86.

15. Holly, III, p. 14.

16. "Proceedings," *1992 Annual of the Southern Baptist Convention* (Nashville: Executive Committee, 1992), pp. 89–90.

17. Ankerberg and Weldon, *Bowing at Strange Altars,* p. 52.

18. "HMB's Interfaith Witness Director to Perform Freemasonry Study Commissioned by SBC," *Religious Herald,* July 23, 1992; "Interfaith witness Director to Perform Freemasonry Study," *Indiana Baptist,* July 28, 1992; "Freemasonry Study to Be Performed by Interfaith Witness Director," *Arkansas Baptist Newsmagazine,* July 30, 1992; and "HMB's Interfaith Witness Director Given Leave to Conduct Study of Freemasonry," August 1992.

19. J. Walter Carpenter, "The HMB Freemasonry Study – Good or Bad Idea?" *Southern Baptist Watchman,* 1993 Convention Edition, p. 10.

20. The "Freemasonry Report" to which I referred was later titled *A Study of Freemasonry.* It should not be confused with the seven-page "report" written later by the Home Mission Board administration and approved by the full board of trustees and the messengers to the Southern Baptist Convention in Houston the following June.

21. Bolded in the original memorandum to Lewis and Robinson.

22. Quoted in James C. Hefley, *The Truth in Crisis,* Vol. I, p. 10.

23. Reinhold Niebuhr, *Leaves from the Notebook of a Tamed Cynic* (San Francisco: Harper & Row, Publishers, 1929, 1957), p. 17.

24. Lavina Fielding Anderson, "The LDS Intellectual Community and Church Leadership: A Contemporary Chronology," *Dialogue: A Journal of Mormon Thought,* Vol. 26, No. 1 (Spring 1993): 26.

25. Minutes of meeting on file.

26. Ray Waddle and Greg Warner, "Study Easy on Masons; Holly Questions Objectivity," *Baptists Today,* March 18, 1993.

27. See Holly, III, pp. 45, 85–86.

CHAPTER SEVEN

1. Lavina Fielding Anderson, "The LDS Intellectual Community and Church Leadership: A Contemporary Chronology," *Dialogue: A Journal of Mormon Thought,* Vol. 26, No. 1 (Spring 1993): 16.

2. Turner, *Fundamentalism in the Southern Baptist Convention,* p. 301.

3. Ken Camp, "Criswell Says 'Shared Ministry' Disrupts Pastoral Authority, *The Baptist Witness,* February 27, 1986.

4. Roy Waddle and Greg Warner, "Study Easy on Masons; Holly Questions Objectivity," *Baptists Today,* March 18, 1993.

5. Anderson, "The LDS Intellectual Community and Church Leadership," p. 15.

6. Letter to Larry Lewis, all Home Mission Board directors, Baptist Press and Associated Baptist Press, November 3, 1993.

7. Holly, III, p. 311.

8. Holly, III, p. 25.

9. Holly, III, p. 25.

10. "Masons and Non-Masons React Favorably to Report," *Word & Way,* March 25, 1993, p. 3.

11. Martin King, "Lewis Disagrees with Masonic Critic's Charges," *Baptist and Reflector,* March 31, 1993.

12. I later learned that Branch forwarded a copy of the letter to James Walker, director of the Watchman Fellowship's Arlington, Texas, office, who forwarded the letter to Holly.

13. "Letter to the Editor," *Florida Baptist Witness,* June 10, 1993.

14. Copy in file.

15. John E. Roberts, "Review of the 136th Southern Baptist Convention," *Baptist Courier,* June 14, 1993, p. 3.

16. "A Brief Report Southern Baptist Convention Votes on Freemasonry," *Grand Lodge Bulletin,* Vol. 94, No. 3, September 1993, p. 58.

17. Craig Branch, "Freemasonry and Southern Baptists," *Mini-Expositor,* August 1993, p. 1.

18. Greg Warner, "HMB Finds Many Masonic Tenets Incompatible with Christianity," *Baptists Today,* April 1, 1993, pp. 1–2.

19. David Winfrey, "Holly Brings New Challenge to Freemasonry Report," *Baptist Press,* October 1, 1993.

20. Ibid.

21. Holly, III, p. 6.

22. "Baptist Loses Post over Masonic Talk," *The Arizona Republic,* November 6, 1993, p. F6.

23. Holly, III, p. 92.

24. "Dispute over Freemasonry Lands Baptist Church in Court," *Florida Baptist Witness,* December 23, 1993.

25. "Dispute over Freemasonry Lands Baptist Church in Court," *Religious Herald,* January 6, 1994, p. 9.

26. Holly, III, pp. 319–20.

27. Compare Baptist Press release, April 14, 1994, with "HMB Revisits Freemasonry, Clarifies Position," *The Christian Index,* April 21, 1994, pp. 1–2.

28. Ibid, p. 2.

29. Holly, III, pp. 11, 14.

30. Holly, III, p. 85.

31. Barnhart, *The Southern Baptist Holy War,* p. 30.

CHAPTER EIGHT

1. Each of these volumes are identified as volume I, II, or III in this book.

2. Holly, III, pp. 21–22.

3. Ibid, p. 337.

4. Ibid, p. 9.

5. Ibid, p. 31.

6. Ibid, p. 269.

7. Ibid, p. 160.

8. Ibid.

9. Ibid, p. 166.

10. *Study,* pp. 11 (twice), 16, 58, and 69.

11. Holly, III, p. 63.

12. Ibid, p. 88.

13. Ibid, p. 39.

14. Letter to Gary Leazer from James Holly, August 12, 1992, quoted in Holly, III, p. 48.

15. Holly, III, p. 57.

16. Holly, II, p. 43.

17. From a December 7, 1992, letter to Larry Lewis quoted in Holly, III, p. 78.

18. Holly, III, p. 9.

19. Ibid, p. 134.

20. Ibid, p. 77.

21. Ibid, p. iv.

22. Ibid, p. 79.

23. Ibid, p. 78.

24. *Holman Bible Dictionary,* p. 1143.

25. Holly, III, p. vi. Emphasis in original.

26. Ibid, p. 213.

27. Ibid, p. 3.

28. Ibid, p. 36.

29. Ibid.

30. Ibid, p. 35.

31. Ibid, pp. 35–36.

32. *Study,* p. 11.

33. Holly, III, p. 123.

34. Larry Kunk, "What Is the Secret Doctrine of the Masonic Lodge and How Does It Relate to Their Plan of Salvation?" (Unpublished manuscript, 1992), p. 1.

35. *Study* (Original manuscript), p. 51.

36. Ibid, p. 51.

37. Holly, II, p. 77.

38. Ibid, p. iii.

39. Holly, III, p. 50, citing *Study,* p. 13.

40. Decker, *The Question of Freemasonry,* p. 7.

41. Pike, *Morals and Dogma,* p. iv.

42. Kunk, "What Is the Secret Doctrine of the Masonic Lodge . . . ?" p. 15. Anti-Masons often refer to *Morals and Dogma* as the Masonic "bible." Wayne Lela, of Downers Grove, Illinois, who wrote and bragged, "Factually speaking, there are few if any people who know more about Masonry than yours truly," referred to *Morals and Dogma* as "a Masonic 'bible.' " His letter of July 22, 1992, is on file. Kenneth Cornn of London, Kentucky, in a undated letter on file, also referred to *Morals and Dogma* as "their Bible."

43. Burns, *Hidden Secrets of Masonry,* p. 27.

44. Holly, III, p. 209.

45. Pike, *Morals and Dogma,* pp. 82, 309, 524, 525, 539, 576, 643, 802.

46. See Hutchens, *A Glossary to* Morals and Dogma, p. 107, for references.

47. Pike, *Morals and Dogma,* p. 24.

48. Ibid, p. 81.

49. Ibid, p. 291.

50. Ibid, p. 309.

51. Ibid, p. 323.

52. Ibid, p. 547.

53. Ibid, p. 559.

54. Ibid.

55. Ibid, p. 301.

56. Ibid.

57. Ibid, p. 531.

58. Holly, III, p. 19.

59. Ibid, p. 18.

60. Ron Carlson, "Freemasonry and the Masonic Lodge," undated manuscript, p. 1.

61. Holly, III, pp. 118–19.

62. Ibid, p. 118.

63. Readers desiring to verify this may call any Shrine Temple, including the Kaaba Temple in Davenport, Iowa at telephone 319/323–1874; the Jerusalem Temple in New Orleans at 504/522–5512; and the Mount Sinai Temple in Montpelier, Vermont at 802/223–7661.

64. *Study,* p. 5.

65. Holly, III, p. 52. See also page 309.

66. Ibid, p. 101.

67. Ibid, p. 88.

68. Holly, II, pp. 34–36.

69. Hutchens, *A Bridge to Light,* p. 322.

70. Pike, *Morals and Dogma,* p. 859.

71. Ibid, pp. 859–61.

72. Ibid, p. 41.

73. Holly, III, p. 182, quoting *A Study of Freemasonry,* p. 34.

74. Ibid.

75. Holly, II, p. 35.

76. Pike, *Morals and Dogma,* p. 687.

77. Holly, III, p. 215.

78. Ibid, p. 190.

79. Pike, *Morals and Dogma,* p. 530.

CHAPTER NINE

1. John Leland, *The Rights of Conscience inalienable, and, therefore Religious Opinions not cognizable by Law: Or, The high-flying Churchman, stripped of his legal Robe, appears a Yaho* [New London, Connecticut, 1791], quoted in Baker, *A Baptist Source Book,* p. 41.

2. Holly, III, p. 94.

3. Ibid, p. iv.

4. Ibid, p. 104, quoting *Study,* pp. 5–6.

5. Ibid.

6. Tresner, *Perspectives, Responses & Reflections,* p. 7.

7. Holly, III, p. 179.

8. Ibid, p. 180.

9. Ibid, pp. 180–81 quoting *A Study of Freemasonry,* p. 33.

10. *Study,* p. 33.

11. Holly, III, p. 181.

12. Tresner, *Perspectives, Responses & Reflections,* p. 72.

13. Holly, III, p. 222.

14. *Study*, pp. 47–48.

15. Holly, III, p. 52.

16. *Study*, p. 13.

17. Holly, III, p. 51.

18. C. Fred Kleinknecht in Hutchens, *A Bridge to Light,* p. vii.

19. Holly, II, pp. v–vi.

20. Holly, I, p. 49.

21. Holly, II, p. 18.

22. Holly, III, p. 19.

23. Holly, II, p. 11–12, 76; III, p. 148, 158, 164 and so forth. See Index to volumes I, II, and III in volume III, p. 357.

24. Holly, III, p. 138.

25. Ibid, III, pp. 247–48, citing *Study,* pp. 53–54. The *Study* footnoted Ankerberg and Weldon, *The Secret Teachings of the Masonic Lodge,* p. 88, quoting *Coil's Masonic Encyclopedia,* p. 512. This entire quote is from *Coil's Masonic Encyclopedia* and was quoted verbatim by Ankerberg and Weldon.

26. *Study,* p. 55. Emphasis in original.

27. John J. Robinson, *A Pilgrim's Path* (New York: M. Evans and Company, Inc., 1993), pp. 36–37.

28. Holly, III, p. ii.

29. Ibid, p. 59.

30. Holly, II, p. 33.

31. Holly, I, p. 6.

32. Ibid, p. iv.

33. Ibid, p. 46.

34. James Holly, "Baptist Layman Responds to Evangelical/Catholic Agreement," *Florida Baptist Witness,* April 14, 1994, p. 7

35. Holly, III, p. 173.

36. *Study*, pp. 28–29.

37. Ibid, p. 32.

38. Ibid, p. 51.

39. Holly, III, p. 178.

40. Ibid, p. 307.

41. Holly, II, p. 10.

42. Toby Druin, "Armed Guards Ensure Closed-Door Privacy . . . Shackleford, Martin are Fired by Committee." *The Baptist Standard,* July 25, 1990, pp. 4–5.

43. "Baptist Panel Here Forced to Resign," *The Atlanta Constitution,* August 7, 1986, p. 15A.

44. "Dilday Fired by Trustees," *The Christian Index,* March 17, 1994, p. 2.

45. Greg Warner, "Fundamentalist Leaders Gather for Damage-Control Session," *Baptists Today,* May 12, 1994, pp. 1, 5.

46. Holly, II, p. 11.

47. Ibid. Bolded in Holly's text.

48. Mackey, *Encyclopedia of Freemasonry,* II, p. 561.

49. Holly, II, p. 10.

50. Ibid, p. 115.

51. *The Scottish Rite Journal,* June 1994, p. 64.

52. Holly, II, p. 35. This statement immediately follows a quote from Pike, *Morals and Dogma,* p. 861: "And this Equilibrium teaches us, above all, to reverence ourselves as immortal souls, and to have respect and charity for others, who are even such as we are, partakers with us of the Divine Nature." Holly borrowed and changed this statement to read "ever [*sic*] such as we are," and claims it refers to "Masons and their families." Pike used the statement to refer to all human beings, not just "Masons and their families," as Holly erroneously implies.

53. Ibid, p. 115.

54. Holly, III, pp. 183–84 citing *Study,* p. 15.

55. For a good discussion of the Masonic teaching concerning Hiram Abif, see deHoyos and Morris, *Is It True What They Say About Freemasonry?*, pp. 49–52.

56. Holly, III, p. 143, citing *Study,* p. 15. See Ankerberg and Weldon, *The Secret Teachings of the Masonic Lodge,* p. 131.

57. Ibid, p. 143.

58. Ibid, p. 18.

59. Holly, I, pp. 25–30.

60. *Study*, p. 15.

61. Holly, III, p. 286, quoting *Study,* p. 71.

62. Ibid.

63. Baker, *The Southern Baptist Convention and Its People,* p. 33.

64. Quoted in Holly, III, p. 47.

65. November 3, 1993, letter from Holly to Lewis quoted in Holly, III, p. 10.

66. Holly, III, p. 60.

67. Ibid, p. 61.

68. Ibid, p. 60.

69. Ibid, pp. 113, 206, 208.

70. Ibid, p. 221, citing *Study,* p. 49.

71. Ibid, p. 41.

72. Ibid, p. 50.

73. Ibid, iv.

74. Ibid, p. 297.

75. Ibid, p. 315.

76. Ibid, p. 313.

77. Ibid, p. 312.

78. Ibid, p. 318. The reference is to Revelation 3:14–20 where Laodicea, a city in southwest Asia Minor, is criticized for its apparent spiritual uselessness.

79. Ibid, iii.

80. Holly, II, p. 79.

81. Ibid, p. 281.

82. Ibid, p. 283. Emphasis in original.

83. Ibid, p. 284.

84. Ibid, p. 28.

85. Ibid.

86. Ibid, p. 42.

87. Letter to Home Mission Board directors, February 23, 1993.

88. Letter to Bill Gordon, September 29, 1992.

89. Holly, I, p. iv.

90. Holly, II, p. 107.

91. Holly, III, p. 75.

92. Frank S. Mead, *Handbook of Denominations* (Nashville: Abingdon, 1980), p. 165.

93. "National & International Religion Report," April 4, 1994 (Vol. 8, No. 8): 3.

94. Gordon, "A Critique," p. 2.

CHAPTER TEN

1. John Leland, *The Rights of Conscience inalienable, and, therefore Religious Opinions not cognizable by Law: Or, The highflying Churchman, stripped of his legal Robe, appears a Yaho* [New London, Connecticut, 1791], quoted in Baker, A Baptist Source Book, p. 40.

2. James L. Holly. *The Southern Baptist Convention and Freemasonry: Volume II Including the Complete Text of Volume I.* (Beaumont: Mission and Ministry to Men, Inc., 1993), p. 13. This book is the published edition, with revisions, of the manuscript mentioned in the next footnote.

3. Charles Burchett and James L. Holly. *Freemasonry and The Southern Baptist Convention: A Report for The Interfaith Witness Department of The Home Mission Board, Southern Baptist Convention* (Beaumont, Texas: Unpublished manuscript, 1992), p. 5.

4. My grandfather, Horace H. Leazer, who helped form the George Washington Masonic Lodge #618 in Donnellson, Iowa, in 1916, once told me that soon after he moved to a farm in Lee County, Iowa, in 1925, a Presbyterian elder stopped by to ask him to join the Klan. The elder was especially upset that my grandfather was friendly toward a Catholic family who lived a mile up the gravel road. My grandfather refused the invitation to join the Klan and the demand he ignore the Doyle family just because they were Catholic. Later, my grandfather was defeated by a Klansman in a school-board election. The Klan burned a cross near the school to celebrate the victory.

5. For insight on William J. Simmons, see his books, including *The Ku Klux Klan: Yesterday, Today and Forever* (Atlanta: Ku Klux Klan Press, 1916), *The Klan Unmasked* (Atlanta: William E. Thompson Publishing Co., 1923), and *American Menace, or the Enemy Within* (Atlanta: Bureau of Patriotic Books, 1926).

6. William W. Sweet, *The Story of Religion in America* (Grand Rapids: Baker Book House, 1950), p. 406.

7. "Fundamentalists Wrong About Bible, Vatican Says," *Atlanta Journal-Constitution,* March 19, 1994.

8. Joe W. Burton, *Road to Augusta* (Nashville: Broadman Press, 1976), p. 88.

9. Ibid, p. 87.

10. Burton, *Road to Augusta*, p. 90.

11. Ibid, p. 166.

12. Pat Cole, "King's Influence Still Felt Among Southern Baptists," *Religious Herald*, January 13, 1994, p. 14.

13. James Dotson, "First Black Mercer Student Recalls Difficult Years," *The Christian Index*, January 27, 1994, p. 12.

14. Dan Martin, *A Road to Reconciliation* (Atlanta: Home Mission Board, SBC, 1979), p. 8.

15. Quoted in Turner, *Fundamentalism in the Southern Baptist Convention*, p. 171.

16. Ibid, pp. 203–4.

17. "DOMs [Associational Directors of Missions] get document on SBC racism," *The Baptist Standard*, June 22, 1994, p. 18.

18. Unpublished manuscript on "Black Freemasonry" that will be included in an update of *Coil's Masonic Encyclopedia*.

19. Holly, III, p. 95.

20. "Race and Freemasonry," *The North Carolina Mason*, March/April 1994, p. 6.

21. *1990 List of Lodges* (Bloomington, Illinois: Pantagraph Printing & Stationery Co., 1990), p. 47.

22. Ibid, p. 69.

23. Unpublished manuscript for an updated entry on "Black Freemasonry" to be published in a revised edition of *Coil's Masonic Encycylopedia*.

24. "Race and Freemasonry," *The North Carolina Mason*, March/April 1994, p. 6.

25. Holly, II, p. 17.

26. "Race and Freemasonry," *The North Carolina Mason*, March/April 1994, p. 6.

27. Phone conversation with Thomas W. Jackson, Grand Secretary, Grand Lodge of Pennsylvania, F. & A. M., June 6, 1994.

28. Holly, III, pp. 99, 196.

29. Telephone interview with S. Brent Morris, April 8, 1994.

30. Letter from Joseph A. Walkes, Jr., 33°, to John W. Boettjer, 33, June 23, 1994. Letter on file.

31. Holly, III, p. 73. Highlighted in original.

32. Ibid, p. 73.

33. Gary Leazer, "Opportunities for the Future," *Masonic Messenger*, October 1993, pp. 18–19.

34. Leazer, "Opportunities for the Future," *Masonic Messenger*, p. 19.

35. Ibid, p. 19.

36. Ibid, p. 20.

37. Robert Ringer, *Million Dollar Habits* (New York: Wynwood Press, 1990), p. 216.

38. Ibid, p. 217.

39. Holly, III, p. 84, quoting "Opportunities for the Future," *Masonic Messenger*, p. 17. Highlighted sentence by Holly.

40. Ibid.

41. "Baptist Vote Vitalizes Masonry," *The Scottish Rite Journal,* August 1993, p. 36.

42. Ibid.

43. Leazer, "Opportunities for the Future," p. 19.

44. Holly, III, p. 90.

45. Ibid.

46. Leazer, "Opportunities for the Future," p. 19.

47. Holly, III, p. 90. Highlighted by Holly.

48. Ibid, p. 91. Highlighted by Holly.

49. Ibid, p. 29, quoting Leazer, "Opportunities for the Future," p. 18.

50. Leazer, "Opportunities for the Future," p. 18.

CHAPTER ELEVEN

1. J. Walter Carpenter, "The HMB Freemasonry Study – Good or Bad Idea," *Southern Baptist Watchman,* 1993 Convention Edition, p. 10.

2. John Ankerberg and John Weldon, *The Facts on The Masonic Lodge: Does Masonry Conflict With The Christian Faith?* (Eugene, Ore.: Harvest House Publishers, Inc., 1989), p. 14; John R. Rice, *Lodges Examined by The Bible* (Murfreesboro, Tenn.: Sword of the Lord Publishers, 1971), p. 32; Dale A. Byers, *I Left the Lodge* (Schaumburg, Ill.: Regular Baptist Press, 1988), p. 33; Cathy Burns, *Hidden Secrets of Masonry* (Mt. Carmel, Penn.: Sharing, 1990), p. 8.

3. Holly, III, p. 18. Emphasis added.

4. Ibid, p. 46.

5. Ibid, p. 32.

6. Ibid, p. 127.

7. Holly, I, p. 2.

8. Holly, III, p. 171.

9. Ankerberg and Weldon, *The Secret Teachings of the Masonic Lodge,* p. 43.

10. Schnoebelen, *Masonry: Beyond the Light,* p. 31.

11. Ibid, p. 36.

12. E. M. Storms, *Should a Christian Be a Mason?* (Fletcher, No. Car.: New Puritan Library, Inc., 1980), pp. 41–42.

13. Holly, III, p. 188.

14. *Study,* p. 23.

15. Holly, III, p. 165. Highlighted in original.

16. Carl J. Sanders, "A Mason Without Apology," *Freemasonry and Religion* (Washington, D.C.: Ancient and Accepted Scottish Rite of Freemasonry, Southern Jurisdiction, United States of America, 1990), n.p., quoted in *Study,* p. 23.

17. Albert G. Mackey, *Encyclopedia of Freemasonry,* Revised and Enlarged by Robert I. Clegg (Chicago: The Masonic History Company, 1946), Vol. II, p. 847.

18. Coil, *Coil's Masonic Encyclopedia,* p. 512.

19. Carpenter, "The HMB Freemasonry Study – Good or Bad Idea?" p. 10.

20. Pike, *Morals and Dogma,* p. 213. Also quoted in *Study,* p. 25.

21. Ibid, p. 25. Also quoted in *Study,* p. 25.

22. Holly, III, p. 169.

23. Pike, *Morals and Dogma,* p. 161.

24. Ibid, pp. 162–63.

25. Ibid, p. 161.

26. Holly, III, p. 169. Bolded in original.

27. Pike, *Morals and Dogma,* p. 212.

28. Ibid, p. 213.

29. Melvin Cammack, *John Wyclif and the English Bible* (New York: American Tract Society, 1938), p. 75.

30. "The Report on Freemasonry" refers to the six page summary offset prepared by the Home Mission Board for presentation to the Southern Baptist Convention, not *Study of Freemasonry*prepared by the Interfaith Witness Department.

31. *New World Dictionary of the American Language* (New York: Simon and Schuster, 1980), p. 1640.

32. Coil, *Coil's Masonic Encyclopedia,* p. 693.

33. Holy Bible (Wichita: Heirloom Bible Publishers, 1988), p. 30.

34. Cammack, *John Wyclif and the English Bible,* p. 75.

35. Mackey, *Encyclopedia of Freemasonry,* p. 1120.

36. *Study*, p. 28.

37. Holly, III, p. 190.

38. *Study,* p. 42, quoting John Calvin, *Commentary upon the Book of Psalms,* trans. James Anderson (Grand Rapids: Wm. B. Eerdmans Publishing Co., 1949), p. 309.

39. Ibid, quoting John Calvin, *Institutes of the Christian Religion,* trans. Henry Beveridge (Grand Rapids: Wm. B. Eerdmans Publishing Co., 1953), Book 1, p. 141.

40. Ibid, quoting Calvin, *Institutes of the Christian Religion,* Book 1, p. 157.

41. Ibid, pp. 42–43, quoting Wallace McLeod, *The Grand Design* (Des Moines: Iowa Research Lodge No. 2, 1991), p. 108.

42. Holly, III, p. 191.

43. Kit Haffner, "Freemasonry: Where Man an' Man Got Talkin'," *Aeropagus,* Pentecost 1992, p. 17.

44. John Ankerberg and John Weldon, *Bowing at Strange Altars: The Masonic Lodge and the Christian Conscience* (Chattanooga: Ankerberg Theological Research Institute, 1993), p. 30.

45. *Study,* p. 46, quoting *Masonic Code* (Montgomery: Grand Lodge of Alabama, 1963), p. 141.

46. Ankerberg and Weldon, *Bowing at Strange Altars,* p. 29. Emphasis added.

47. *Study*, p. 46.

48. Ankerberg and Weldon, *Bowing at Strange Altars,* p. 29.

49. Ibid, p. 27. See *Study,* p. 32.

50. Charles T. Murphy, Kevin Guinagh, and Whitney J. Oats, eds. "Apology," *Greek and Roman Classics in Translation* (New York: Longmans, Green and Co., 1947), p. 446.

51. M. H. Abrams, gen. ed., "Beowulf," *The Norton Anthology of English Literature (Revised),* Vol. I (New York. W. W. Norton & Company, 1968), p. 39.

52. Ibid, p. 83.

53. Holly, III, p. 181, quoting the *Study,* p. 33.

54. *Study* (Original Manuscript), p. 33.

55. Holly, III, p. 181.

56. *Holman Bible Dictionary,* p. 1164. Bold print added.

57. A. Berkeley Mickelsen, *Interpreting the Bible* (Grand Rapids: Wm. B. Eerdmans Publishing Company, 1963), p. 265.

58. Ibid, pp. 265–66.

59. Holly, III, p. 181.

60. Mickelsen, *Interpreting the Bible,* p. 278.

61. *Holman Bible Dictionary,* p. 461.

62. *Study*, pp. 11–12.

63. Holly, I, p. 18. Emphasis in original.

64. J. Edward Decker, *The Question of Freemasonry* (Issaquah, Wash.: Free the Masons Ministries, n.d.), pp. 12–14; Gary H. Kah, *En Route to Global Occupation* (Lafayette, La.: Huntington House Pub., 1992), p. 124; Jack Harris, *Freemasonry: The Invisible Cult in Our Midst* (Rowson, Md.: Jack Harris, 1983), pp. 24–25; William Schnoebelen, *Masonry Beyond the Light* (Chino, Calif.: Chick Publications, 1991), p. 191; Pat Robinson, *The New World Order* (Dallas: Word Publishing, 1991), p. 184; Cathy Burns, *Hidden Secrets of Masonry* (Mt. Carmel, Pa.: Sharing, 1990), p. 27; Muhammad Safwat al-Saqqa Amini and Sa'di Abu Habib, *Freemasonry* (New York: Muslim World League, 1982).

65. Letter on file, dated May 12, 1992.

66. Cult research specialist Bob Passantino in Doug Trouten, "HOAX! Why are Christians so eager to believe and spread unsubstantiated rumors?" *Word & Way*, May 30, 1991, p. 16.

67. *Study*, p. 12. See Wesley P. Walters, "A Curious Case of Fraud," *The Quarterly Journal,* vol. 9, no. 4 (Oct.–Dec. 1989), pp. 4, 7.

68. Holly, I, p. 19.

69. Holly, III, p. 130.

70. Holly, I, p. 19.

71. William E. Gordon, Jr. "A Critique of James L. Holly, *The Southern Baptist Convention and Freemasonry"* (unpublished manuscript, 1992), p. 8.

72. deHoyos and Brent, *Is It True What They Say About Freemasonry?*, pp. 9–12.

73. Holly, III, p. 130. Emphasis in original.

74. Ed Decker, *The Question of Freemasonry* (Lafayette: Huntington House Publishers, 1992), p. 16. Emphasis added.

75. Burns, *Hidden Secrets of Masonry,* p. 27.

76. Larry Eskridge of the Institute for the Study of American Evangelicals at Wheaton College, in Trouten, "HOAX!", *Word & Way,* p. 16.

77. *Study*, p. 12.

78. Holly, III, p. 131.

79. Ibid.

80. Holly, I, p. 19. See also *Study,* p. 44.

81. Ibid, p. 19; Gordon, "A Critique," p. 9. See also *Study,* p. 44.

82. Gordon, "A Critique," p. 9.

83. Ibid.

84. Holly, I, p. 19.

85. Gordon, "A Critique," p. 10.

86. Holly, III, p. 333.

87. Holly, II, p. 19.

88. "The Letter 'Humanum Genus' of The Pope, Leo XIII, Against Freemasonry and the Spirit of the Age," April 20, 1884, pp. 5–21. A discussion of this encyclical was removed from the original manuscript of the *Study* during the editing process.

89. "Fundamentalists Wrong About Bible, Vatican says," *Atlanta Journal-Constitution,* March 19, 1994.

90. Jose Maria Cardinal Caro y Rodriguez, *The Mystery of Freemasonry Unveiled* (Palmdale, California: Christian Book Club of America, 1957), p. 43. This edition is a revision of the original book published in 1928 after events surrounding the Chilean elections of 1924 and government laws concerning divorce and separation of the government from the Roman Catholic Church. These efforts, according to the Archbishop, were instigated by Masons.

91. Ibid, p. 94.

92. Ibid, p. 192.

CHAPTER TWELVE

1. Thought for a day from my desk calendar, January 27, 1994.

2. Ankerberg and Weldon, *The Secret Teachings of the Masonic Lodge,* p. 103.

3. Trent C. Butler, gen. ed., *Holman Bible Dictionary* (Nashville: Holman Bible Publishers, 1991), p. 561

4. Eric C. Rust, "Symbol," *Mercer Dictionary of the Bible,* p. 866.

5. Homer, *The Iliad,* trans. Samuel Butler, *Great Books of the Western World* (Chicago: Encyclopaedia Britannica, Inc., 1952), vol. 4, p. 8, 47, 50 and so forth.

6. Plato, "The Dialogues of Plato: Timaeus," trans. Benjamin Jowett, *Great Books of the Western World* (Chicago: Encyclopaedia Britannica, Inc., 1951), vol. 7, p. 447.

7. Brihad-Aranyaka Upanishad 1.5.1, Trans. Robert Ernest Hume, *The Thirteen Principal Upanishads* (Oxford: Oxford University Press, 1975), p. 86.

8. Emory Stevens Bruce, ed., "Names of God," *The Interpreter's Dictionary of the Bible* (Nashville: Abingdon Press, 1962), vol. 2, pp. 412–15.

9. Darrell W. Robinson, *The Doctrine of Salvation* (Nashville: Convention Press, 1992), p. 37, quoted in *Study,* p. 23.

10. Holly, III, p. 160.

11. Ibid, quoting Hutchens, *A Bridge to Light,* p. 220. Emphasis by Holly.

12. Ibid.

13. Pike, *Morals and Dogma,* pp. 487–88.

14. Holly, III, p. 438.

15. Ibid, pp. 182–83, quoting *Study,* p. 35.

16. *Study,* p. 36, quoting William Schnoebelen, *Masonry: Beyond the Light,* p. 149. Emphasis added.

17. Ibid, quoting Mackey, *Encyclopaedia of Freemasonry,* I, p. 332. Emphasis added.

18. Holly, III, p. 183, quoting *Study,* p. 36. The citation is taken from Ralph P. Lester, ed., *Look to the East: A Ritual of the First Three Degrees of Masonry* (Chicago: Ezra A. Cook Publications, Inc., 1975), pp. 184–90.

19. Coil, *Coil's Masonic Encyclopedia,* p. 309.

20. Holly, III, p. 183.

21. deHoyos and Morris, *Is It True What They Say About Freemasonry?,* pp. 51–52.

22. Pike, *Morals and Dogma*, p. 640.

23. Ibid, p. 641.

24. Holly, III, p. 182.

25. 2 Chron. 4:16 (New International Version and New Revised Standard Version).

26. 2 Chronicles 4:16; The Holy Scriptures According to the Masoretic Text (Philadelphia: Jewish Publication Society of America, 1917), p. 1097.

27. Robert L. Thomas, gen. ed. *New American Standard Exhaustive Concordance of the Bible* (Nashville: Holman, 1981), p. 1517.

28. Harry Carr, *The Freemason at Work* (London: Lewis Masonic, 1976), p. 214.

29. Holly, III, p. 212.

30. Pike, *Morals and Dogma,* pp. 576–77.

31. Holly, III, p. 212.

32. Pike, *Morals and Dogma,* p. 307.

33. Ibid, p. 17.

34. Ibid, p. 531.

35. See also Genesis 12:3, 28:14, and so forth.

36. Gonzalez, *A History of Christian Thought,* I: 228.

37. Ibid, p. 325.

38. From signed copy of "Clarification of Recommendation of 1993 HMB Freemasonry Report to SBC," n.d.

39. "HMB Revisits Freemasonry, Clarifies Position," *The Christian Index,* pp. 1–2.

40. "A Report on Freemasonry," p. 6.

41. Ankerberg and Weldon, *Bowing at Strange Altars,* p. 26. See *Study,* p. 54, and *Coil's Masonic Encyclopedia,* p. 512.

42. Ibid.

43. Ibid, quoting Coil, *Coil's Masonic Encyclopedia,* p. 512.

44. Pete Normand, "The Italian Dilemma," *American Masonic Review,* Spring 1994 (Vol. 3, No. 2): 10.

45. *Study,* p. 53.

46. Holly, III, p. 242.

47. *Study*, p. 53, quoting *Monitor of the Lodge* (Waco: The Grand Lodge of Texas, 1982), pp. 207, 211, 212.

48. Holly, III, p. 242.

49. Holly, II, p. 44.

50. Ibid. Highlighted by Holly.

51. Ibid.

52. Ibid, p. 78.

53. Ibid. Emphasis in original.

54. Ibid, pp. 302–303, quoting Pike, *Morals and Dogma*, pp. 286–87.

55. Pike, *Morals and Dogma*, pp. 278–87.

56. Ibid, p. 287.

57. Ibid, p. 76.

58. Coil, *Coil's Masonic Encyclopedia*, p. 375.

59. Holly, III, p. 261.

60. Pike, *Morals and Dogma*, p. 300.

61. Ibid, p. 301.

62. Ibid.

63. Ibid, p. 524.

64. Ibid, p. 525.

65. John Hick, *Evil and the God of Love* (Cambridge: Macmillan and Co., Ltd., 1966), p. 6.

66. Pike, *Morals and Dogma*, pp. 164, 542.

67. Ibid, pp. 542–68.

68. Ibid, p. 532.

69. Ibid, p. iv.

70. Ibid, p. 165.

71. Ibid, p. 166.

72. William Cooke Boone, *What We Believe* (Nashville: Convention Press, 1936), p. 39.

73. Ibid, p. 40.

74. A. H. Armstrong and R. A. Markus, *Christian Faith and Greek Philosophy* (New York: Sheed and Ward, 1960), p. 43.

75. Pike, *Morals and Dogma*, p. 527.

76. "The Bible," Holy Bible (Wichita: Heirloom Bible Publishers, 1988), p. 1. This Bible was given to me by Abe Hinson Lodge No. 472, Alexandria, La.

77. "Making a Success of the Christian Life Including Material for Personal Work," Holy Bible (Wichita: Heirloom Bible Publishers, 1988), p. 14.

78. "Biblical Index to Freemasonry: Eternal Life," Holy Bible (Wichita: Heirloom Bible Publishers, 1988), p. 41.

CONCLUSION

1. Jimmy Carter, speaking to the Cooperative Baptist Fellowship General Assembly in Birmingham, Alabama, May 13, 1993, quoted in *Baptists Today*, May 27, 1993, p. 3.

2. Holly, III, p. 4.

3. *Study* (Original Manuscript), p. 76. Bolded in original manuscript.

4. Ibid, p. 78. Bolded in original manuscript.

5. Ibid, p. 77, quoting Torbet, *A History of Baptists*, p. 276. See also *Study*, p. 71.

6. Holly, III, p. 4.

7. Ibid, p. 5.

8. Ibid, p. 6.

9. Holly, III, p. 14. Bolded by Holly.

10. Jack McGorman, Bible study on the Book of Galatians, Salt Lake City, December 5, 1992. This ditty was removed from the original manuscript of the *Study* before publication.

APPENDIX

1. *Freemasonry: A Report to Southern Baptists* [Unpublished] (Atlanta: Home Mission Board, 1993), pp. 2–3.

2. Ibid, p. 12.

3. Ibid, p. 16.

4. Letter from Richard S. Sagar, Atlanta, Georgia, July 23, 1992.

5. *Freemasonry: A Report to Southern Baptists*, p. 18. The quotation referring to Jesse Helms is from Morey, *The Origins and Teachings of Freemasonry*, p. 11.

6. Ibid, p. 34. See *Study*, pp. 34–35.

7. Ibid, p. 52.

8. Ibid, p. 51. The quote by E. Y. Mullins is from *The Christian Faith in Its Doctrinal Expression* (Philadelphia: The Judson Press, 1917), p. 373.

9. Ibid, p. 65. The Fisher quote was from *Behind the Lodge Door: Church, State and Freemasonry in America* (Bowie, Maryland: Shield Publishing, Inc., 1988), p. 76.

10. Ibid, p. 67.

11. Ibid, pp. 72–73. The quote by Holly is from *The Southern Baptist Convention and Freemasonry, Vol. I*, p. 1.

12. Ibid, p. 76.

13. Ibid, p. 77.

14. Ibid, p. 78.

15. Ibid, p. 5.

16. *Study*, p. 5.

17. *Freemasonry: A Report to Southern Baptists*, p. 28.

18. *Study*, pp. 28–29. Bolded in *Study*.

19. Still, *New World Order*, pp. 99–100.

20. *Freemasonry: A Report to Southern Baptists*, p. 31.

21. *Study*, p. 31.

22. *Freemasonry: A Report to Southern Baptists*, p. 32.

23. *Study*, p. 32. Bolded in *Study*.

24. *Freemasonry: A Report to Southern Baptists*, p. 32.

25. *Study*, p. 32. Bolded in *Study*.

26. *Freemasonry: A Report to Southern Baptists*, p. 33.

27. *Study*, p. 33.

28. *Freemasonry: A Report to Southern Baptists*, p. 33. Bold in the original.

29. *Study*, p. 33.

30. Compare *Freemasonry: A Report to Southern Baptists*, p. 39, with *Study*, p. 38.

31. *Interpreter's Dictionary of the Bible*, 1: 473.

32. Compare *Freemasonry: A Report to Southern Baptists*, p. 42, with *Study*, p. 44.

33. Holly, *The Southern Baptist Convention and Freemasonry*, I: 42.

34. Ibid, p. 26, quoting Mackey, *An Encyclopaedia of Freemasonry*, p. 375.

35. *Freemasonry: A Report to Southern Baptists*, p. 43, quoting Gordon, "A Critique," pp. 11–12.

36. Holly, *The Southern Baptist Convention and Freemasonry*, I: 27.

37. *Freemasonry: A Report to Southern Baptists*, p. 44, quoting Gordon, "A Critique," pp. 12–13.

38. Ibid, p. 45.

39. *Freemasonry: A Report to Southern Baptists*, p. 51. The quote by Ankerberg and Weldon is from *The Secret Teachings of the Masonic Lodge*, p. 78.

40. *Study*, p. 52.

41. *Freemasonry: A Report to Southern Baptists*, p. 76.

42. *Study*, p. 70.

43. Ibid, p. 29. Bolded in *Study*.

44. Ibid, p. 34.

45. Ibid, pp. 33, 37. Bolded in *Study*.

BIBLIOGRAPHY

BOOKS

1981 Annual of the Southern Baptist Convention. Nashville: Executive Committee of the Southern Baptist Convention, 1981.

1982 Annual of the Southern Baptist Convention. Nashville: Executive Committee of the Southern Baptist Convention, 1982.

1985 Annual of the Southern Baptist Convention. Nashville: Executive Committee, Southern Baptist Convention, 1985.

1992 Annual of the Southern Baptist Convention. Nashville: Executive Committee, Southern Baptist Convention, 1992.

1990 List of Lodges. Bloomington, Illinois: Pantagraph Printing & Stationery Co., 1990.

Abrams, M. H., gen. ed. *The Norton Anthology of English Literature (Revised).* 2 Vols. New York: W. W. Norton & Company, 1968.

Ahlstrom, Sydney E. *A Religious History of the American People.* New Haven: Yale University Press, 1972.

Amini, Muhammad Safwat al-Saqqa and Sa'di Abu Habib. *Freemasonry.* New York: Muslim World League, 1982.

Ammerman, Nancy. *Bible Believers: Fundamentalism in the Modern World.* New Brunswick: Rutgers University Press, 1987.

Ankerberg, John and John Weldon. *Bowing at Strange Altars: The Masonic Lodge and the Christian Conscience.* Chattanooga, Tenn.: Ankerberg Theological Research Institute, 1993.

——. *The Facts on the Masonic Lodge: Does Masonry Conflict with the Christian Faith?* Eugene, Oregon: Harvest House Publishers, Inc., 1989.

——. *The Secret Teachings of the Masonic Lodge.* Chicago: Moody Press, 1990.

Armstrong, A. H. and R. A. Markus. *Christian Faith and Greek Philosophy.* New York: Sheed and Ward, 1960.

Arterburn, Stephen and Jack Felton. *Toxic Faith: Understanding and Overcoming Religious Addiction.* Nashville: Thomas Nelson, Publishers, 1991.

Averill, Lloyd J. *Religious Right, Religious Wrong.* New York: The Pilgrim Press, 1989.

Baker, Robert A. *A Baptist Source Book With Particular Reference to Southern Baptists.* Nashville: Broadman Press, 1966.

——. *The Southern Baptist Convention and Its People: 1607–1972.* Nashville: Broadman Press, 1974.

Barnhart, Joe Edward. *The Southern Baptist Holy War.* Austin, Texas: Texas Monthly Press, Inc., 1986.

Boone, William Cooke. *What We Believe.* Nashville: Convention Press, 1936.

Boyer, Paul. *When Time Shall Be No More: Prophecy Belief in Modern American Culture.* Cambridge, Mass.: The Belknap Press of Harvard University Press, 1992.

Bruce, Emory Stevens, ed. *The Interpreter's Dictionary of the Bible.* 5 vols. Nashville: Abingdon Press, 1962.

Burns, Cathy. *Hidden Secrets of Masonry.* Mt. Carmel, Pa.: Sharing, 1990.

Burton, Joe W. *Road to Augusta: R. B. C. Howell and the Formation of the Southern Baptist Convention.* Nashville: Broadman Press, 1976.

Butler, Trent C., gen. ed. *Holman Bible Dictionary.* Nashville: Holman Bible Publishers, 1991.

Byers, Dale A. *I Left the Lodge.* Schaumburg, Ill.: Regular Baptist Press, 1988.

Calvin, John. *Commentary upon the Book of Psalms.* Translated by James Anderson. Grand Rapids: Wm. B. Eerdmans Publishing Co., 1949.

——. *Institutes of the Christian Religion.* Translated by Henry Beveridge. Grand Rapids: Wm. B. Eerdmans Publishing Co., 1953.

Cammack, Melvin Macye. *John Wyclif and the English Bible.* New York: American Tract Society, 1938.

Caro y Rodriguez, Jose Maria Cardinal. *The Mystery of Freemasonry Unveiled.* Palmdale, Calif.: Christian Book Club of America, 1957.

Carr, Harry. *The Freemason At Work.* London: Lewis Masonic, 1976.

Carroll, James M. *"The Trail of Blood". . . . Following the Christians Down Through the Centuries. . . . or The History of Baptist Churches From the Time of Christ, Their Founder, to the Present Day.* Lexington, Kentucky: Ashland Avenue Baptist Church, 1931.

Church, J. R. *Guardians of the Grail.* Oklahoma City: Prophecy Publications, 1989.

Cohen, Norman J., ed. *The Fundamentalist Phenomenon: A View from Within; A Response from Without.* Grand Rapids: William B. Eerdmans Publishing Company, 1990.

Coil, Henry Wilson. *Coil's Masonic Encyclopedia.* New York: Macoy Publishing & Masonic Supply Company, 1961.

Cothen, Grady C. *What Happened to the Southern Baptist Convention? A Memoir of the Controversy.* Macon, Georgia: Smyth & Helwys Publishing, 1993.

Draper, James T., Jr. *The Church Christ Approves.* Nashville: Broadman Press, 1974.

Decker, Ed. *The Question of Freemasonry.* Lafayette, Louisiana: Huntington House Publishers, 1992.

deHoyos, Art and S. Brent Morris. *Is It True What They Say About Freemasonry?* Silver Spring, Maryland: Masonic Service Association of the United States, 1994.

Dockery, David S. *The Doctrine of the Bible.* Nashville: Convention Press, 1991.
Easley, Kendell H. *Adult Bible Study, January–March 1994.* Nashville: Baptist Sunday School Board, 1993.
Epperson, A. Ralph. *The New World Order.* Tucson, Arizona: Publius Press, 1990.
Estep, William R., ed. *The Lord's Free People in a Free Land.* Fort Worth, Tex.: Faculty of the School of Theology, Southwestern Baptist Theological Seminary, 1976.
Freemasonry: A Report to Southern Baptists. Atlanta: Home Mission Board, 1993.
Gonzalez, Justo L. *A History of Christian Thought,* 2 volumes. Nashville: Abingdon Press, 1970, 1971.
Haggard, Forrest D. *The Clergy and The Craft.* N.C.: Missouri Lodge of Research, 1970.
Harris, Jack. *Freemasonry: The Invisible Cult in Our Midst.* Rowson, Maryland: Jack Harris, 1983.
Hefley, James C. *The Conservative Resurgence in the Southern Baptist Convention.* Hannibal, Missouri: Hannibal Books, 1991.
——. *The Truth in Crisis: The Controversy in the Southern Baptist Convention.* Dallas: Criterion Publications, 1986.
——. *The Truth in Crisis: Bringing the Controversy Up-to-Date.* Hannibal, Missouri: Hannibal Books, 1987.
Hick, John. *Evil and the God of Love.* Cambridge: Macmillan and Co., Ltd., 1966.
Higham, John. *Strangers in the Land: Patterns of American Nativism, 1860-1925.* New Brunswick, New Jersey: Rutgers University Press, 1955.
Hobbs, Herschel H. *Studying Adult Life and Work Lessons.* Nashville: Baptist Sunday School Board, Vol. 25, No. 4 (October-December 1992).
Holly, James L. *Freemasonry and The Southern Baptist Convention: A Report for The Interfaith Witness Department of The Home Mission Board, Southern Baptist Convention.* Beaumont, Tex.: Mission and Ministry to Men, Inc. (Unpublished), 1992.
——. *Freemasonry and The Southern Baptist Convention: A Partial Report for the Trustees of the Home Mission Board.* Beaumont: Mission and Ministry to Men, Inc. (Unpublished), n.d.
——. *The Southern Baptist Convention and Freemasonry.* Beaumont: Mission and Ministry to Men, Inc., 1992.
——. *The Southern Baptist Convention and Freemasonry, Volume II Including the Complete Text of Volume I.* Beaumont: Mission and Ministry to Men, Inc., 1993.
——. *The Southern Baptist Convention and Freemasonry: Volume III;* "A Critique of: A Study of Freemasonry" and "A Report on Freemasonry". Beaumont: Mission and Ministry to Men, Inc., 1994.
Holy Bible, King James Version. Wichita, Kan.: Heirloom Bible Publishers, 1988.
The Holy Bible, The Douay Version. New York: The Douay Bible House, 1941.
The Holy Bible, New Revised Standard Version. Nashville: Holman Bible Publishers, 1989.
The Holy Scriptures According to the Masoretic Text. Philadelphia: Jewish Publication Society of America, 1917.

Hume, Robert Ernest, trans. *The Thirteen Principal Upanishads.* Oxford: Oxford University Press, 1975.

Hutchens, Rex R. and Donald W. Monson. *The Bible in Albert Pike's* Morals and Dogma. Washington, D.C.: The Supreme Council, 33, Ancient and Accepted Scottish Rite of Freemasonry, Southern Jurisdiction, United States of America, 1992.

Hutchens, Rex R. *A Glossary To* Morals and Dogma. Washington, D.C.: The Supreme Council, 33, Ancient and Accepted Scottish Rite of Freemasonry, Southern Jurisdiction, United States of America, 1993.

Hutchins, Robert Maynard, ed. *Great Books of the Western World.* 54 vols. Chicago: Encyclopaedia Britannica, Inc., 1952.

James, Rob, ed. *The Takeover in the Southern Baptist Convention: A Brief History.* Decatur, Georgia: SBC Today, 1992.

James, Robison B., ed. *The Unfettered Word: Confronting the Authority-Inerrancy Question.* Macon, Georgia: Smyth & Helwys Publishing, Inc., 1994.

Kah, Gary H. *En Route to Global Occupation: A High Ranking Government Liaison Exposes the Secret Agenda for World Unification.* Lafayette, Louisiana: Huntington House Publishers, n.d.

Kirban, Salem, *Satan's Angels Exposed.* Huntingdon Valley, Pennsylvania: Salem Kirban, Inc., 1980.

Lester, Ralph P., ed. *Look to the East: A Ritual of the First Three Degrees of Masonry.* Chicago: Ezra A. Cook Publications, Inc., 1975.

Lindsey, Hal. *The 1980s: Countdown to Armageddon.* King of Prussia, Penn.: Westgate Press Inc., 1980.

Mackey, Albert G. *Encyclopedia of Freemasonry,* 3 vols. Revised and enlarged by Robert I. Clegg. Chicago: The Masonic History Company. 1946.

Markham, Don C. *Freemasonry and The Churches.* n.c.: Don C. Markham, 1982.

Martin, Dan. *A Road to Reconciliation: The Human Touch in Cooperative Ministries with National Baptists.* Atlanta: Home Mission Board, SBC, 1979.

McBeth, H. Leon. *The Baptist Heritage: Four Centries of Baptist Witness.* Nashville: Broadman Press, 1957.

McLeon, Wallace. *The Grand Design.* Des Moines: Iowa Research Lodge No. 2, 1991.

Mickelsen, A. Berkeley. *Interpreting the Bible: A Book of Basic Principles for Understanding the Scriptures.* Grand Rapids: Wm. B. Eerdmans Publishing Company, 1963.

Monitor of the Lodge. Waco: The Grand Lodge of Texas, 1982.

Morey, Robert A. *The Origins and Teachings of Freemasonry.* Southbridge, Massachusetts: Crowne Publications, Inc., 1990.

Mullins, E. Y. *The Christian Faith in Its Doctrinal Expression.* Philadelphia: The Judson Press, 1917.

Murphy, Charles T., Kevin Guinagh, and Whitney J. Oats. *Greek and Roman Classics in Translation.* New York: Longmans, Green and Co., 1947.

Naisbitt, John and Patricia Aburdene. *Megatrends 2000: Ten New Directions For the 1990's.* New York: William Morrow and Company, Inc., 1990.

New World Dictionary of the American Language. New York: Simon and Schuster, 1980.

Niebuhr, Reinhold. *Leaves From the Notebook of a Tamed Cynic.* San Francisco: Harper & Row, Publishers, 1929, 1957.

The Pearl of Great Price. Salt Lake City: The Church of Jesus Christ of Latter-day Saints, 1982.

Pike, Albert. *Morals and Dogma of the Ancient and Accepted Scottish Rite of Freemasonry.* Washington, D.C.: The Supreme Council of the Southern Jurisdiction, A.A.S.R., U.S.A., 1950.

——. *A Reply of Freemasonry in Behalf of Humanity to The Encyclical Letter* "Humanum Genus" *of the Pope Leo XIII.* Washington, D.C.: The Supreme Council of the Southern Jurisdiction of the Scottish Rite of Freemasonry, 1964.

Rice, John R. *Lodges Examined by The Bible.* Murfreesboro, Tenn.: Sword of the Lord Publishers, 1971.

Ringer, Robert. *Million Dollar Habits.* New York: Wynwood Press, 1990.

Robbins, Thomas and Dick Anthony, eds. *In Gods We Trust: New Patterns of Religious Pluralism in America.* New Brunswick, New Jersey: Transaction Publishers, 1990.

Robertson, Pat. *The New World Order: It Will Change The Way You Live.* Dallas: Word Publishing, 1991.

Robinson, Darrell W. *The Doctrine of Salvation.* Nashville: Convention Press, 1992.

Robinson, John J. *Born in Blood: The Lost Secrets of Freemasonry.* New York: M. Evans & Company, Inc., 1989.

——. *A Pilgrim's Path: One Man's Road to the Masonic Temple.* M. Evans & Company, Inc., 1993.

Schnoebelen, William. *Masonry: Beyond The Light.* Chino, Calif.: Chick Publications, 1991.

Shaeffer, Francis A. *The Great Evangelical Disaster.* Westchester, Ill.: Crossway Books, 1984.

Shaw, Jim and Tom McKenny. *The Deadly Deception: Freemasonry Exposed . . . By One of Its Top Leaders.* Lafayette, Louisiana: Huntington House, Inc., 1988.

Shurden, Walter B. *The Baptist Identity: Four Fragile Freedoms.* Macon: Smyth & Helwys Publishing, Inc., 1993.

——. *The Struggle for the Soul of the SBC: Moderate Responses to the Fundamentalist Movement.* Macon, Georgia: Mercer University Press, 1993.

Smith, H. Shelton, Robert T. Handy, and Lefferts A. Loetscher. *American Christianity,* 2 vols. New York: Charles Scribner's Sons, 1960.

Still, William T. *New World Order: The Ancient Plan of Secret Societies.* Lafayette, Louisiana: Huntington House Publishers, 1990.

Storms, E. M. *Should A Christian Be A Mason?* Fletcher, North Carolina: New Puritan Library, Inc., 1980.

A Study of Freemasonry. Atlanta: Home Mission Board, SBC, 1993.

Sweet, William W. *The Story of Religion in America.* Grand Rapids: Baker Book House, 1950.

Thomas, Robert L., gen. ed. *New American Standard Exhaustive Concordance of the Bible*. Nashville: Holman, 1981.

Thorn, Richard P. *The Boy Who Cried Wolf: The Book That Breaks Masonic Silence*. New York: M. Evans and Company, Inc., 1994.

Torbet, Robert G. *A History of the Baptists*. Valley Forge, Penn.: Judson Press, 1963.

Tresner, Jim, *Perspectives, Responses & Reflections*. Unpublished manscript.

——. *Questions and Answers on Freemasonry and Religion*. Jackson: Grand Lodge of Mississippi, n.d.

Van Deventer, Fred. *Parade to Glory: The Story of the Shriners and Their Caravan to Destiny*. Revised and updated by Orville Findley Rush. Tampa, Fla.: The Imperial Council, A.A.O.N.M.S., 1980.

Vedder, Henry C. *A Short History of the Baptists*. Valley Forge, Penn.: Judson Press, 1907.

DISSERTATIONS

Turner, Helen Lee. *Fundamentalism in the Southern Baptist Convention: The Crystallization of a Millennialist Vision*. Unpublished dissertation: University of Virginia, 1990.

ARTICLES

"1993 Facts & Figures, Shriners Hospitals for Crippled Children," *The Scottish Rite Journal*, June 1994.

Anderson, Lavina Fielding. "The LDS Intellectual Community and Church Leadership: A Contemporary Chronology" *Dialogue: A Journal of Mormon Thought*, Vol. 26, No. 1 (Spring 1993).

Allen, James B. "Nauvoo's Masonic Hall," *The John Whitmer Historical Association Journal* (Vol. 10, 1990): 39-49.

"Baptist Loses Post Over Masonic Talk," *The Arizona Republic*, November 6, 1993.

"Baptist VIEWpoll," Corporate Planning and Research Department, Sunday School Board of the Southern Baptist Convention, November 1991.

"Baptist Vote Vitalizes Masonry," *The Scottish Rite Journal*, August 1993.

Blaising, Craig A. "Contemporary Dispensationalism," *Southwestern Journal of Theology*, Vol. 36, No. 2 (Spring 1994).

Branch, Craig. "Freemasonry and Southern Baptists," *Mini-Expositor*, August 1993.

"A Brief Report: Southern Baptist Convention Votes on Freemasonry," *Iowa Grand Lodge Bulletin*, Vol. 94, No. 3 (September 1993).

Broderick, John. "545 Days Left," *The Red Cloud Chief*, March 25, 1993.

Camp, Ken. "Criswell Says 'Shared Ministry' Disrupts Pastoral Authority," *The Baptist Witness*, February 27, 1986.

Carpenter, J. Walter. "The HMB Freemasonry Study—Good or Bad Idea?" *Southern Baptist Watchman*, 1993 Convention Edition.

Clingenpeel, Michael J. "Don't Mess with the Annuity Board," *Religious Herald*, March 3, 1994.

Cole, Pat. "King's Influence Still Felt Among Southern Baptists," *Religious Herald*, January 13, 1994.

Cornell, George W. "At Issue: Christian and Mason," *Daily News-Sun* (Sun City, Arizona), April 23, 1993.

"Dilday Fired By Trustees," *The Christian Index*, March 17, 1994.

Dilday, Robert. "FMB Drops Funding for Swiss Seminary; European Baptist Leaders React Angrily," *Baptists Today*, October 31, 1994.

"Dispute over Freemasonry Lands Baptist Church in Court," *Florida Baptist Witness*, December 23, 1993.

"Diversity of Speakers, Subjects Marks Pastor's Conference, *Florida Baptist Witness*, June 23, 1994.

Dotson, James. "First Black Mercer Student Recalls Difficult Years," *The Christian Index*, January 27, 1994.

Druin, Toby. "Giving Panel Eyes Texas Cooperative Program," *The Baptist Standard*, April 27, 1994.

Druin, Toby and Greg Warner. "Southwestern Seminary Trustees Fire Dilday; Students Left to Wonder 'Why?'" *Religious Herald*, March 17, 1994.

Eblen, Tom. "Fundamentalists Critical of Louisville Institution," *The Atlanta Journal*, June 5, 1986.

"Firm Has Devil of a Time Quelling Rumors," *The Atlanta Journal and Constitution*, January 23, 1982.

"Freemasonry Study to Be Performed by Interfaith Witness Director," *Arkansas Baptist Newsletter*, July 30, 1992.

"Fundamentalists Wrong about Bible, Vatican Says," *The Atlanta Journal and Constitution*, March 19, 1994.

Galloway, Jim. "Baptist Presidency: A Battle of Biblical Proportions," *The Atlanta Journal and Constitution*, May 25, 1986.

Gordon, William E., Jr. "A Critique of James L. Holly, *The Southern Baptist Convention and Freemasonry*." Unpublished manuscript, 1992.

Grossman, Cathy Lynn. "Extremists' Actions Tarnish Fundamentalists' Image," *USA Today*, March 25, 1993.

Haffner, Kit. "Freemasonry: Where Man an' Man Got Talkin'." *Areopagus*. Pentecost 1992.

Harwell, Jack U. SBC Rejects Further Funds from Fellowship; Elects Jim Henry President over Fred Wolfe," *Baptists Today*, July 14, 1994.

Hawn, C. Michael. "Southeastern Story Teaches Baptists Valuable Lessons," *SBC Today*, March 1989.

"HMB Revists Freemasonry, Clarifies Position," *The Christian Index*, April 21, 1994.

"HMB's Interfaith Witness Director to Perform Freemasonry Study Commissioned by SBC," *Religious Herald*, July 23, 1992.

"Interfaith Witness Director to Perform Freemasonry Study," *Indiana Baptist*, July 28, 1992.

King, Martin. "Lewis Disagrees with Masonic Critic's Charges," *Baptist and Reflector*, March 31, 1993.

Leazer, Gary. "Opportunities for the Future," *Masonic Messenger*, October 1993.

Leonard, Bill J. "Lone Star Baptists: Fallout at Southwestern Seminary," *Christian Century*, April 20, 1994.

"The Letter *'Humanum Genus'* of The Pope, Leo XIII Against Freemasonry and the Spirit of the Age," April 20, 1884.

Marrs, Texe. "The Great Southern Baptist Cover-up," Austin: Living Truth Ministries, n.d.

Martin, Dan. "Smith Says 'New Peace' Is His Contribution," *Baptist Standard*, May 12, 1982.

"Masons and Non-Masons React Favorably to Report," *Word & Way*, March 25, 1993.

Matthews, Bob E. "Baseless Rumor on Religious Broadcasts Thrives," *The Christian Index*, December 3, 1992.

——. "For Umpteenth Time: P&G Rumors Untrue," *The Baptist Messenger*, November 13, 1986.

Metz, Gary. "Jack Chick's Anti-Catholic Alberto Comic Book Is Exposed as a Fraud," *Christianity Today*, March 13, 1981.

Nicholas, Tim. "W. A. Criswell Counsels Pastors in 2-hour Session," *Religious Herald*, January 13, 1994.

Niebhur, Gustav. "'Fundamentalists' Label Often Misunderstood, Baptists Say," *The Atlanta Journal and Constitution*, October 18, 1986.

Normand, Pete. "The Italian Dilemma," *American Masonic Review*. Spring 1994 (Vo. 3, No. 2).

"P&G Sues Couple, Claiming They Spread Satanism Rumor," *The Atlanta Journal and Constitution*, August 1, 1990.

"Procter & Gamble Is Clean," *Newsweek*, April 7, 1980.

"Procter & Gamble Threatens Suits Against Rumors," *Baptist and Reflector*, March 7, 1990.

"Procter and Gamble Wins Court Judgment," *The Christian Index*, April 18, 1991.

"Quayle Signs Books, Courts Votes," *Word & Way*, June 23, 1994.

"Race and Freemasonry," *The North Carolina Mason*, March/April 1994.

"Religious Identity: How Christians See Themselves," *USA Today*, March 25, 1993.

Roberts, John E. "Review of the 136th Southern Baptist Convention," *Baptist Courier*, June 14, 1993.

Robinson, John J. "Masons, Slavery and Coca-Cola," *The Scottish Rite Journal*, March 1993.

"Rumors Resurface Linking P&G with Church of Satan," *Baptist New Mexican*, December 1992.

Sanders, Carl J. "A Mason Without Apology," *Freemasonry and Religion.* Washington, D. C.: Ancient and Accepted Scottish Rite of Freemasonry, Southern Jurisdiction, United States of American, 1990.

"Snellville Conference Prompts Cancellation of BSSB Event," *The Christian Index*, January 13, 1994.

"Southern Baptists to Study Freemasonry," *Saints Alive in Jesus Newsletter*, July-August 1991.

Stephens, William H. "The Doctrine of the Bible: Inerrancy Term Holds Different Meanings," *Facts & Trends*, February 1992.

——. "The Inerrancy Issue: Inspiration and Interpretation," *Florida Baptist Witness*, February 13, 1992.

Taylor, Ron. "Baptist Art of Preaching Considered Major Factor in Convention Politicking," *The Atlanta Journal*, May 22, 1986.

——. "Modern Fundamentalists Have Roots in New South," *The Atlanta Journal*, May 19, 1986.

Teepen, Tom. "Southern Baptists Embrace Civil Religion," *The Atlanta Constitution*, June 7, 1991.

Toalston, Art. "Book Stores Deny Charge of Censorship," *The Christian Index*, June 4, 1992.

Toalson, Art and David Winfrey. "Southern Baptist to Consider Stand on Freemasonry," *Indiana Baptist*, June 2, 1992.

Tresner, Jim. "The Word from Houston," *The Oklahoma Mason*, August-September 1993 (Vol. 61, No. 4).

Trouten, Doug. "HOAX! Why Are Christians So Eager to Believe and Spread Unsubstantiated Rumors?" *Word & Way*, May 30, 1991.

Waddle, Ray and Greg Warner. " Study Easy on Masons; Holly Questions Objectivity," *Baptists Today*, March 18, 1993.

Walters, Wesley P. "A Curious Case of Fraud," *The Quarterly Journal*, Vol. 9, No. 4 (October-December 1989).

Warner, Greg. "HMB Finds Many Masonic Tenets Incompatible with Christianity," *Baptists Today*, April 1, 1993.

Warner, Greg and Jack U. Harwell. "Keith Parks Will Lead CBF Missions Program," *Baptists Today*, December 15, 1992.

Weldon, John. "The Masonic Lodge and The Christian Conscience," *Christian Research Journal*, Winter 1994 (Vol. 16, No. 3).

White, Michael. "Campaign Against Mormonism Puts Dad, Son on Opposing Sides," *The Salt Lake Tribune*, October 5, 1985.

Winfrey, David. "Holly Brings New Challenge to Freemasonry Report," *Baptist Press*, October 1, 1993.

——. "Home Mission Board Declines Action on Freemasonry Issue," *Baptist Press*, March 12, 1992.

Wood, Presnall H. "The White House and SBC Resolutions?" *Baptist Standard*. July 21, 1982.

Acknowledgments

I want to express appreciation to my father, Herbert H. Leazer of Argyle, Iowa, who taught me to always do the right thing, even when pressured to compromise my convictions.

I want to thank my father-in-law, the Reverend Jack L. Bilbo of Milton, Florida, who taught me about God's love for me and encouraged me to never forget that He always watches over me.

Many other people influenced me in different ways to lead me to this point in this pilgrimage called life. Some were authors, both living and deceased, whose books challenged my preconceived ideas and taught me that the burden of truth is often heavy. I have tried to give due credit to the appropriate sources in this book. Every writer, however, recalls ideas from his or her past reading for which the exact source cannot be recalled. I apologize to those writers who find I have borrowed ideas without proper acknowledgment.

Others who were important influences on me are college and seminary professors; laypersons; and men, women, and children. Friends and loved ones listened when I was hurting. Each taught me valuable lessons that have made me what I am today. I thank them all.

I thank the staffs of the Pitts Theology Library, Chandler School of Theology, Emory University, Atlanta, Georgia; the Roberts Library, Southwestern Baptist Theological Seminary, Fort Worth, Texas; and the Atlanta Masonic Temple Library, Atlanta, Georgia, for their wonderful assistance.

I thank Masons who opened their libraties to me while anti-Masons called for my removal as head of the study and threatened to have me fired.

I thank the readers of this manuscript: Dr. Walter B. Shurden, Callaway Professor of Christianity and the chair of the Department of Christianity at Mercer University, Macon, Georgia; Richard E. Fletcher, PGM, 33°, executive secretary, The Masonic Service Association of the United States,

Washington, D.C.; Thomas W. Jackson, 33°, grand secretary, Grand Lodge of Pennsylvania, F. & A. M., Philadelphia, Pa.; Dr. John W. Boettjer, 33°, editor of *The Scottish Rite Journal*, Washington, D.C.; Dr. S. Brent Morris, 33°, book review editor for *The Scottish Rite Journal*; and Dr. James T. Tresner, 33°, director of the Masonic Leadership Institute of the Masonic Charity Foundation of Oklahoma and editor of *The Oklahoma Mason*. Each of these men gave of themselves and offered many suggestions to improve both the accuracy and style of the manuscript. I admit I did not use all of their suggestions, and so perhaps this book is not as good as it could have been. I accept full responsibility for any and all errors that anyone might find. As much as is humanly possible, I tried to be fair and accurate in discussing what was a most difficult period in my life.

I want to thank the many members of the Smoke Rise Baptist Church in Stone Mountain, Georgia, who supported my family and me with their prayers and words of encouragement.

And finally, I especially want to express my deepest appreciation to Ruth, my best friend and partner for twenty-five years. She would not let me quit when I was ready to give up. Our children, David and Sonya, are always a joy to their parents. I would ask Ruth, David, and Sonya's forgiveness for reneging on my primary role as husband and father during the many hours I spent in research and writing.

Gary Leazer
Stone Mountain, Georgia

INDEX